Spock: Up and Running

Writing Expressive Tests in Java and Groovy

Rob Fletcher

Beijing · Boston · Farnham · Sebastopol · Tokyo

Spock: Up and Running

by Rob Fletcher

Copyright © 2017 Rob Fletcher. All rights reserved.

Printed in the United States of America.

Published by O'Reilly Media, Inc., 1005 Gravenstein Highway North, Sebastopol, CA 95472.

O'Reilly books may be purchased for educational, business, or sales promotional use. Online editions are also available for most titles (*http://oreilly.com/safari*). For more information, contact our corporate/institutional sales department: 800-998-9938 or *corporate@oreilly.com*.

Editors: Nan Barber and Brian Foster	**Indexer:** Judith McConville
Production Editor: Kristen Brown	**Interior Designer:** David Futato
Copyeditor: Bob Russell, Octal Publishing, Inc.	**Cover Designer:** Karen Montgomery
Proofreader: Christina Edwards	**Illustrator:** Rebecca Demarest

May 2017:   First Edition

Revision History for the First Edition

2017-05-05:   First Release

See *http://oreilly.com/catalog/errata.csp?isbn=9781491923290* for release details.

978-1-491-92329-0

[LSI]

Table of Contents

Part I.   Spock 101

Part II. Advanced Spock

Part III.   Integrating Spock

Introduction

Welcome to *Spock: Up and Running*. I'm excited and privileged to be your guide as you learn about the most innovative thing to happen to testing on the Java Virtual Machine (JVM) since the first release of JUnit.

From the time I first began writing unit tests (badly), I've always been interested in making my tests as well-structured, readable, and straightforward as possible. I embraced the move from JUnit 3 to JUnit 4 with Hamcrest and have experimented with everything from FitNesse to Cucumber, TestNG to Jasmine, and ScalaTest to Spek. I don't think anything has made the impact on my testing style that Spock has.

For me, Spock is absolutely the "killer app" of the Groovy ecosystem. Sure, GPars made concurrency easy, Gradle saved builds from XML hell, and Grails made throwing together the basics of a web app the work of minutes rather than hours. But nothing exploits Groovy's dynamic style to build something that genuinely makes things easier and better as successfully as Spock.

And Spock makes things better not just for the 80 percent of cases, but across the board. I have every respect in the world for JUnit—it's without doubt one of the most important innovations in the history of the JVM—but I can't think of any case I can tackle better with JUnit than I can with Spock.

I hope you find Spock as logical, fascinating, and useful as I do.

Meet Spock

Spock is a test framework—some would even say language—built on top of Groovy. It was developed by Peter Niederwieser, first released in 2009, and, after a long genesis, version 1.0 was released in 2015. Version 1.1 followed in 2017, and that's the version we'll be using in this book.

Although Spock builds on top of JUnit's test runner it's quite different syntactically. Spock enforces a behavior-driven development (BDD)-style structure. Instead of using methods to apply assertions, Spock infers that simple Boolean expressions in particular contexts behave as assertions. Instead of integrating external libraries like JMock or Mockito, Spock has its own test doubles with dedicated syntax for defining expectations and behavior (although you can use something else if you want). Spock also has syntax for defining parameterized tests that goes far beyond the capabilities of JUnit's @RunWith(Parameterized.class).

Above all, Spock specifications are very readable and expressive. Groovy's brevity and lack of ceremony is harnessed to a syntax that makes tests read very well as executable documentation.

A Short Background on Groovy

Groovy is a dynamic, optionally typed language for the JVM that was released in 2007; as of this writing, it is currently up to version 2.4.7. Unlike some alternate JVM languages, Groovy uses very Java-like syntax. In fact, until the release of Java 8, almost all Java code was also valid Groovy code (only one obscure loop formation wasn't supported). However, Groovy adds the ability to optionally type declarations, and supports duck typing, higher-order functions, metaprogramming capabilities, runtime method dispatch, and a number of other features.

Originally envisaged as a scripting language for the JVM, Groovy grew beyond that into a full-fledged alternate language with its own ecosystem of libraries, web frameworks, and so on. In 2012, Groovy added optional static compilation capabilities and can now target the Android platform.

Groovy's profile was boosted by two major developments: Grails, a Rails-like web framework that used Groovy code on top of an opinionated Spring and Hibernate stack; and Gradle, a build tool that combined the opinionated declarative style of Maven with the scripting capabilities of Make. When Google made Gradle the official build tool for the Android platform, an entire new community of developers was suddenly exposed to the Groovy ecosystem.

Spock is built on top of Groovy, and Spock specifications are implemented as .groovy files. However, Spock specifications aren't just JUnit tests written in Groovy. There's a whole lot more to Spock than that.

Syntax that would make no sense in Groovy might be valid in Spock. Spock is a domain-specific language (DSL) in the truest sense that happens to be built on top of Groovy.

I've deliberately avoided as much advanced Groovy as possible in the examples. We're not here to do incredible things with metaprogramming or to debate whether that's a good idea. The Groovy code used in the example specifications is, wherever possible, simple, concise, idiomatic, and unsurprising.

Who Is This Book For?

In the past decade, automated testing has gone from a frequently derided fringe practice to the mainstream. Resistance is futile. I think it's fair to say that the majority of developers at least acknowledge the benefits of writing tests, even if they only pay lip service to the discipline of testing their own software.

But to many developers, testing is a tough discipline to master. It feels to many people like it shouldn't be something that they should dedicate a lot of time to, but writing tests is unlike writing production software. It's an orthogonal, albeit related, skill. Beyond just the tests themselves, designing software that is amenable to testing often requires a shift in approach that can be difficult to overcome.

Hopefully, coming to this book, you are at least convinced that automated testing sounds like a good idea.

If you'd like to begin writing tests, and Spock looks like an interesting tool for doing so, this book is for you.

If you have tried writing tests and found it difficult to grasp how to proceed, this book is for you.

If you write tests but find it difficult to test some aspects of your code, this book is for you.

If you just want to write tests that are less prone to breaking as the system changes, this book is for you.

You don't need to be a Groovy developer—in fact, this book assumes that you have no knowledge of the Groovy language. There's a Groovy primer in Appendix A should you need it. All the nontest code used in the examples in this book is written in Java.

(Well okay, there's a tiny bit of JavaScript, too.)

The point is, you don't need to be a Groovy expert to get the best out of this book. In fact, you don't even need to have any intention of ever writing production code in Groovy. One of the things I'm keenest to convey here is that Spock is *great* for testing Java code.

If you do know some Groovy, great. You can skip the appendix!

About This Book

My first unit test was written for a coding exercise given to me as part of an interview with ThoughtWorks (I didn't get the job). I'm sure it was pretty terrible. I wrote a single test method for each public API method in the class under test. I tested multiple aspects of the behavior in each test method and missed numerous edge cases. I wasn't focused on behavior or using the tests to guide the design of the code so that it was easier to understand or write more tests for.

I'd have loved a book on the practice of writing tests. But it was the early 2000s. JUnit was pretty new. Test-driven development (TDD) was a radical practice considered ridiculously utopian by most "serious" developers. The material that was available was mostly focused on the details of JUnit or a high-level view of the TDD approach. There wasn't much out there that would just help me write *better* tests.

These days, that's no longer the case. I hope this book is a good addition to the library of excellent material available to today's software developer.

Developers today are spoiled for choice. Every language I can think of has one or more frameworks for composing and running automated tests.

But writing *good*, well-structured tests is still an elusive skill. Writing tests that clearly separate dummy data from test logic is tricky. Learning to use mocks and stubs appropriately is a mountain to climb—so much so that some will tell you mocks and stubs are a bad thing altogether. Certainly, when used badly, they result in tests that are difficult to read and more difficult still to maintain. Used well, they are powerful tools for designing and testing for a "separation of concerns."

In this book, I don't want to just show you how to use Spock. I want to show you how to use it well; how to write tests that don't require constant maintenance as the project progresses; how to write tests that communicate to the reader what the behavior of the system and its components is; and how to write tests that help you identify problems when they fail rather than feeling like just another meaningless bit of bureaucracy you have to get past on the way to deploying your code.

It's even possible to test drive a book now.

The examples in this book are all working code. The entire book is a Gradle project; the code listings are included from actual specifications that execute as the book "builds."

Hopefully that means there are minimal errors!

Navigating This Book

Through the course of this book, we'll build up a simple web application—*Squawker* —that allows users to post short messages. Squawker users can follow one another, mention one another in messages, view a timeline of messages from the users they follow, or just squawk out into the void!

Hopefully, this concept sounds pretty familiar; that's certainly the idea. I'd rather you were able to attach the testing concepts in the book to a recognizable, practical idea than have to spend several chapters describing what the application does in exhaustive detail.

Some chapters will divert from the Squawker example where it makes more sense. I'd rather switch to a standalone example than try to bash the square peg of Squawker into the round hole of the topic at hand.

The book is organized into three parts. In Part I, we dive into Spock 101, learning the basics of Spock, its syntax, and everything you need to get from zero to writing simple unit tests.

Chapter 2 and Chapter 3 discuss how to structure specifications and how to write assertions. Chapter 4 discusses the lifecycle of Spock specifications and feature methods. Chapter 5 introduces interaction testing with mocks and stubs, and the intuitive syntax Spock employs for dealing with them. Chapter 6 deals with parameterized tests—writing feature methods that run for multiple sets of data.

Part II takes you beyond the basics into some advanced topics such as how to write idiomatic Spock code (Chapter 7), driving parameterized tests with file or database input (Chapter 8), and Spock's support for asynchronous testing (Chapter 9). We'll also look in Chapter 10 at how to extend Spock using JUnit rules and other test libraries and how to write custom Spock extensions. Finally we'll bring everything together in Chapter 11 with a standalone fully worked TDD example.

Part III is all about integrating Spock and going beyond unit tests. We'll look at integration testing (Chapter 12) and testing REST APIs (Chapter 13) and web applications via the browser (Chapter 14). We'll finish up with a quick look at using Spock to test code written in other languages on the JVM including JavaScript (Chapter 15). To round out the section, there's another standalone example dealing with testing reactive code (Chapter 16).

At the back of the book is a Groovy primer, Appendix A. One of things I'm keen to get across in this book is that Spock is not just for testing applications written in Groovy. I use Spock for testing Java applications every day. Although this book assumes you are familiar with Java, no knowledge of Groovy is necessary. All the application code in the examples is written in Java. Groovy is used only for Spock specifications.

The Groovy primer is not—nor is it intended to be—a comprehensive language resource, but it should be enough to help you through any Groovy code used in the examples throughout the rest of the book.

If you're completely unfamiliar with Groovy it might be wise to skip ahead to the Groovy primer and start there. If you're somewhat familiar with Groovy, it should serve as a good memory aid or reference. If you're all up to speed on Groovy, great, feel free to skip the primer altogether.

Conventions Used in This Book

The following typographical conventions are used in this book:

Italic

> Indicates new terms, URLs, email addresses, filenames, and file extensions.

`Constant width`

> Used for program listings, as well as within paragraphs to refer to program elements such as variable or function names, databases, data types, environment variables, statements, and keywords.

`Constant width bold`

> Shows commands or other text that should be typed literally by the user.

`Constant width italic`

> Shows text that should be replaced with user-supplied values or by values determined by context.

 This icon signifies additional information beyond the example at hand.

 This icon signifies a tip, suggestion, or general note.

 This icon indicates a warning or caution.

Using Code Examples

Supplemental material (code examples, exercises, etc.) is available for download at *https://github.com/robfletcher/spock-up-and-running*.

This book is here to help you get your job done. In general, if example code is offered with this book, you may use it in your programs and documentation. You do not need to contact us for permission unless you're reproducing a significant portion of the code. For example, writing a program that uses several chunks of code from this book does not require permission. Selling or distributing a CD-ROM of examples from O'Reilly books does require permission. Answering a question by citing this book and quoting example code does not require permission. Incorporating a significant amount of example code from this book into your product's documentation does require permission.

We appreciate, but do not require, attribution. An attribution usually includes the title, author, publisher, and ISBN. For example: "*Spock: Up and Running* by Rob Fletcher (O'Reilly). Copyright 2017 Rob Fletcher, 978-1-491-92329-0."

If you feel your use of code examples falls outside fair use or the permission given above, feel free to contact us at *permissions@oreilly.com*.

O'Reilly Safari

 *Safari* (formerly Safari Books Online) is a membership-based training and reference platform for enterprise, government, educators, and individuals.

Members have access to thousands of books, training videos, Learning Paths, interactive tutorials, and curated playlists from over 250 publishers, including O'Reilly Media, Harvard Business Review, Prentice Hall Professional, Addison-Wesley Professional, Microsoft Press, Sams, Que, Peachpit Press, Adobe, Focal Press, Cisco Press, John Wiley & Sons, Syngress, Morgan Kaufmann, IBM Redbooks, Packt, Adobe Press, FT Press, Apress, Manning, New Riders, McGraw-Hill, Jones & Bartlett, and Course Technology, among others.

For more information, please visit *http://oreilly.com/safari*.

How to Contact Us

Please address comments and questions concerning this book to the publisher:

O'Reilly Media, Inc.
1005 Gravenstein Highway North
Sebastopol, CA 95472
800-998-9938 (in the United States or Canada)
707-829-0515 (international or local)
707-829-0104 (fax)

We have a web page for this book, where we list errata, examples, and any additional information. You can access this page at *http://bit.ly/spock_UR*.

To comment or ask technical questions about this book, send email to *bookquestions@oreilly.com*.

For more information about our books, courses, conferences, and news, see our website at *http://www.oreilly.com*.

Find us on Facebook: *http://facebook.com/oreilly*

Follow us on Twitter: *http://twitter.com/oreillymedia*

Watch us on YouTube: *http://www.youtube.com/oreillymedia*

Acknowledgments

This book has been a long-gestating project.

I first began with the intention of self-publishing, but although I had drafted a few chapters, I realized that I needed the encouragement and editorial support of a publisher or I was never realistically going to get the thing finished. So, thanks are definitely due to Brian Foster and Nan Barber at O'Reilly who encouraged me and helped me get the shape of the book right.

Thanks also to the technical reviewers, Leonard Brünings, Marcin Erdmann, and Colin Vipurs, who picked up on problems and provided invaluable feedback.

The decision to write the book was made in a conversation with Luke Daley in my back garden in London. Luke's work on Geb, Gradle, and particularly Ratpack has been inspirational. He is genuinely one of the most ridiculously smart and productive people I've ever met.

Obviously I'm very grateful to Peter Niederwieser, the creator of Spock, for his work and for contributing the project to the community.

Over the course of writing this book, I've changed jobs and changed continents. I've met and worked with many people who have inspired and encouraged me. Thanks are due to the many fantastic colleagues I've had over the years in London:

- Dave Townsend at Logica who first introduced me to JUnit many, many years ago.
- Simon Baker, Gus Power, Tom Dunstan, Kris Lander, Jerome Pimmel, Kevin Richards, Shin Tai, Dora and Zsolt Varszegi, and the rest of the crew at Energized Work, where I really learned whatever craft I can lay claim to.
- Jim Newbery, Sarah O'Callaghan, Glenn Saqui, and Joffrey Tourret at Sky.

…and in California:

- Chris Berry, Diptanu Choudhury, Cameron Fieber, Andy Glover, Adam Jordens, Ben Malley, Dianne Marsh, Clay McCoy, Mike McGarr, Chris Sanden, John Schneider, Jeremy Tatelman, Danny Thomas, and Zan Thrash at Netflix.

…and those who seemed to stalk me from one continent to the next:

- Nathan Fisher, Tomás Lin, and John Tregoning.

The many people in the automated testing and Groovy communities and beyond who I've met at conferences, meetups, or over GitHub and Twitter: Andres Almiray, Jeff Beck, Burt Beckwith, Kyle Boon, Craig Burke, Michael Casek, Cédric Champeau, John Engelman, Danny Hyun, Shaun Jurgemeyer, Guillaume Laforge, Stephané Maldini, J.B. Rainsberger, Graeme Rocher, Marco Vermeulen, Aaron Zirbes, and many more.

Even Dan Woods, who started and finished his own book for O'Reilly (*Learning Ratpack*) in the time it took me to write this one and never hesitated to remind me of that fact. If you appreciate this book, don't forget to *#unfollowdanveloper*.

Above all, I want to thank my kids, Alex and Nicholas, for putting up with a sleep-deprived dad who was already hunched over a laptop when they woke in the morning.

PART I

Spock 101

In this section of the book, you'll learn about the mechanics of writing specifications with Spock. We'll go from the basics of how to construct a specification through how assertions work in Spock, how a specification's lifecycle behaves, on to interaction testing using mocks and stubs, and data-driven testing using parameters to apply the same tests to different data. By the end of the section, you should have a good idea of how to work with Spock and enough knowledge to go ahead and use it. Some of the topics in this section will be revisited later and explored in greater depth or from another angle.

CHAPTER 1

The "Up and Running" Part

Installation

Spock is available from the Maven Central and JCenter repositories. As of this writing, the current version is 1.1.

There are different versions for compatibility with Groovy 2.0+, 2.3+, and 2.4+. If you're not using Groovy in the production code of your project there's no reason to use anything other than the newest version of Groovy. Groovy need only be a test dependency of your project.

Running with the JUnit Runner

Spock is compatible with JUnit's test runner. It should be possible to run Spock specifications anywhere you can run JUnit tests; that means with IDEs like IntelliJ Idea and Eclipse and command-line build tools such as Gradle and Maven.

Running with Gradle

To include Spock in a project built with Gradle, you simply need to include the spock-core library, as follows:

```
apply plugin: "groovy" ❶

repositories {
  jcenter() ❷
}

dependencies {
  testCompile "org.spockframework:spock-core:1.1-groovy-2.4" ❸
}
```

❶ Include the Groovy Gradle plugin

❷ Include the JCenter repository (or `mavenCentral`)

❸ Include Spock on the `testCompile` classpath

With this setup, neither Spock nor Groovy will be included in the production artifacts built by Gradle.

When Groovy Is Used in the Project

If your project *does* use Groovy in its production code, you can simply add Groovy to the main classpath and Spock to the test classpath, as demonstrated here:

```
apply plugin: "groovy"

repositories {
  jcenter()
}

dependencies {
  compile "org.codehaus.groovy:groovy-all:2.4.8"
  testCompile "org.spockframework:spock-core:1.1-groovy-2.4"
}
```

Spock will transitively include Groovy, but the version will be synchronized with whatever version you include in the main classpath.

Synchronizing Groovy Versions Between Main and Test Classpaths

If, and only if, your main project includes the `groovy` dependency rather than the `groovy-all` dependency, you should explicitly synchronize the version of Spock's transitive dependency, like so:

```
dependencies {
  compile "org.codehaus.groovy:groovy:2.4.8"      ❶
  testCompile "org.spockframework:spock-core:1.1-groovy-2.4"
}

configurations.all {
  resolutionStrategy {
    force "org.codehaus.groovy:groovy-all:2.4.8"    ❷
  }
}
```

❶ The `compile` classpath includes Groovy but not using the `groovy-all` artifact on which Spock depends.

---

❷ We use a `resolutionStrategy` to ensure Spock pulls in a compatible version of `groovy-all`.

Running with Maven

Maven setup is a little more complex than Gradle because Maven does not natively know how to compile Groovy code. It's still fairly straightforward, though:

```
<build>
  <plugins>

    <plugin>
      <groupId>org.codehaus.gmavenplus</groupId>
      <artifactId>gmavenplus-plugin</artifactId>
      <version>1.5</version>
      <executions>
        <execution>
          <goals>
            <goal>testCompile</goal>
          </goals>
        </execution>
      </executions>
    </plugin>

    <plugin>
      <artifactId>maven-surefire-plugin</artifactId>
      <version>2.18.1</version>
      <configuration>
        <useFile>false</useFile>
        <includes>
          <include>**/*Spec.java</include>
        </includes>
      </configuration>
    </plugin>

  </plugins>
</build>

<dependencies>

  <dependency>
    <groupId>org.spockframework</groupId>
    <artifactId>spock-core</artifactId>
    <version>1.1-groovy-2.4</version>
    <scope>test</scope>
  </dependency>

</dependencies>
<!--tag::maven[]-->
</project>
```

The gmavenplus plugin enables Maven to compile Groovy code. In the example, I've included it only for the testCompile goal.

The Surefire plugin is only required to ensure Maven's test runner executes files ending in *Spec.

CHAPTER 2

Specification Basics

Spock is a straightforward and expressive language for writing automated tests for software. It is based on the Groovy programming language but can be used to test code written in any language that runs on the Java Virtual Machine (JVM)—Java, Scala, Kotlin, even JavaScript. In this first chapter, we look at how to create *specifications* in Spock; how individual tests, or *feature methods*, are structured; how to make assertions; and how the lifecycle of a specification works.

If you've used JUnit or another unit testing framework before, some of the ideas might seem familiar. However, don't worry if you haven't. Although Spock is built on top of JUnit's test runner, that's really just to make the Spock specifications easy to run anywhere JUnit tests can run. The syntax used to express test code in Spock is pretty different.

Anatomy of a Specification

Spock test classes—known as *specifications*—are written in Groovy.

Here is a simple Spock specification:

```
import spock.lang.*

class IntegerSpec extends Specification {

  def "an integer can be incremented"() {
    given:
    int i = 1

    when:
    i++

    then:
```

```
        i == 2
    }
}
```

This is an extremely straightforward test that just ensures the integer increment operator 0 works as expected. If you know Java, there are probably some familiar things (the `import` statement, class and variable declarations, increment operator, and Boolean expression) and some less familiar things (the `def` keyword; weird-looking method names, `given:`, `when:`, and `then:`; *block labels*; and of course the lack of any semicolons or scope keywords).

Award yourself extra points for observation if you wondered where the assertion is, given that there's no `assert` keyword or JUnit-like method call.

 If you know Java but haven't used Groovy before, it might be worth skipping ahead to Appendix A before continuing. It's up to you; Groovy concepts are used sparingly and introduced slowly in the course of the book.

Each specification is a single class that extends from `spock.lang.Specification`. In more complex scenarios, you can create inheritance hierarchies, abstract subclasses of `Specification`, and so on. We'll see some uses for that type of inheritance hierarchy later in the book. Most simple unit test specifications extend directly from `Specification`, though.

By convention, the specification class name ends with `"Spec"` but can be anything at all. The class contains one or more *feature methods* that implement individual tests. It can contain any other methods you might need, as well.

Each feature method is equivalent to a JUnit method annotated with `@Test` in that it can pass or fail depending on the result of assertions made by the method. Any failing assertion (or any uncaught exception) causes the feature method as a whole to fail. If all assertions pass and there are no uncaught exceptions, the feature method passes.

Feature methods are `public` (i.e., the default visibility for a method in Groovy, so there is no need to specify it) and have no parameters. Feature method names in Spock can be—and by convention are—quote delimited strings rather than the camel-case standard in JUnit and Java generally.

 Actually it's not quite true to say that feature methods do not accept parameters. Later in the book, we'll look at a circumstance in which that is possible. It's a fairly infrequent usage, though.

Feature methods are split into *blocks* preceded by a label. Block labels are the keywords of the Spock language, and blocks have different semantics and behavior according to their label.

---

void versus def

`def` is Groovy's dynamic type reference. When used with a variable or field declaration, it means that the type should be inferred from the righthand side of the expression. In addition, it's possible to assign a value of a different type to that variable. When used as a method return type it means that the type being returned can be anything.

You can type feature methods can as either `void` or `def`. The Spock documentation and most examples you might encounter in the wild use `def`, but the use of `void` has caught on to some extent with people who reason that `def` implies that a feature method returns something when in fact it doesn't.

The examples in this book use `def`. Feel free to use whatever you prefer in your own specifications.

Why Use Quoted Strings for Feature Method Names?

Spock places great emphasis on optimizing the reports generated when specifications are run. Take a look at the reports in Tables 2-1 and 2-2 and consider which you find easier to read.

Table 2-1. Typical JUnit-style test names

Test	Duration	Result
aMessageThatIsTooLongIsNotWrittenToTheDatabase	0.002s	passed
anExceptionIsThrownIfTheDatabaseConnectionIsStale	0.007s	passed
followingAnotherUserIsPersisted	0.086s	passed
followingListIsReadFromDatabaseAndCached	0.003s	passed
postingAMessageInsertsItToTheDatabase	0.013s	passed
timelineIsFetchedFromDatabase	0.001s	passed
usersCannotFollowThemselves	0.001s	passed

Table 2-2. Spock feature method names

Test	Duration	Result
a message that is too long is not written to the database	0.002s	passed
an exception is thrown if the database connection is stale	0.007s	passed
following another user is persisted	0.086s	passed

Test	Duration	Result
following list is read from database and cached	0.003s	passed
posting a message inserts it to the database	0.013s	passed
timeline is fetched from database	0.001s	passed
users cannot follow themselves	0.001s	passed

An Introduction to Spock's Blocks

A JUnit test is essentially a straightforward Java method. Along the way, it should make one or more assertions using one of the `assert…` methods. JUnit does not enforce any structure in the test method. Nevertheless, a certain typical structure has emerged. This is commonly known as *arrange, act, assert* or *given, when, then*. Essentially:

- *Given…* some preconditions are in effect
- *When…* an action is taken
- *Then…* the outcome is x

A JUnit test for the Squawker `User` class might look something like this:

```
@Test
public void aUserCanFollowAnotherUser() {
  User user = new User("kirk");
  User other = new User("spock");

  user.follow(other);

  assertThat(user.getFollowing().size(), equalTo(1));
  assertThat(user.getFollowing(), hasItems(other));
}
```

The construction of the two `User` objects is the *given* step, in which the test sets up the context it needs. The call to the `follow` method is the *when* step, in which the action being tested occurs. The assertions are the *then* steps, in which the outcome of the action is validated.

Behavior-driven development (BDD) codified the *given, when, then* structure and tools such as Cucumber are built around it.

Cucumber and Gherkin

Cucumber's *Gherkin* syntax treats Given, When, and Then as keywords. Text following the keyword is used to look up a *step definition*, which is a code implementation of the description. A Cucumber scenario for the preceding JUnit test might look something like this:

```
Given a user called @kirk
And a user called @spock
When @kirk follows @spock
Then @kirk is following 1 user
And @kirk is following @spock
```

A step definition would look like this:

```
private Map<String, User> users;

@When("@(.+) follows @(.+)")
public void followUser(String userName, String otherName) {
  User user = users.get(userName);
  User other = users.get(otherName);
  user.follow(other);
}
```

Typical Spock specifications are also built around the *given, when, then* structure. Spock uses keywords to define *blocks*, which are sections of a feature method with particular semantics and where certain special behavior might apply. Three of the block keywords are *given*, *when*, and *then*.

Block labels must appear directly in the body of the feature method itself. Although the block labels share the *given, when, then* structure with other test frameworks such as Cucumber and can even have descriptive text associated with them (as we'll see later), there is no separation of description and implementation in a Spock feature method. The block labels are not method calls that dispatch to an implementation that exists elsewhere, as with the similar keywords in Cucumber. Instead, you can think of Spock's block labels as headers.

Labels are just followed by regular Groovy code. For example, a *given* label is directly followed by code that establishes the preconditions of the test. A *when* label is followed by the code that performs the action being tested. A *then* label is followed by assertions about the state that exists following the action. Identical labels in different feature methods do not share an implementation, although you are certainly free to create your own helper methods that can be shared.

To implement a Spock version of the previous JUnit test, we could do the following:

```
def "a user can follow another user"() {
  given:
  def user = new User("kirk")
  def other = new User("spock")

  when:
  user.follow(other)

  then:
  user.following.size() == 1
  user.following.contains(other)
}
```

The content of the method is not terribly different than the JUnit test. There are syntactic differences now that we're using Groovy rather than Java—the use of `def` and the ability to simplify `user.getFollowing()` to `user.following`. Beyond that, the first thing that you'll probably notice is that the test is explicitly broken up into labeled blocks. Also, instead of an `assertThat` call, the final line of the method is a simple Boolean expression. Why is this? Special semantics apply in each block and modify the behavior. In the context of a `then:` block, any Boolean expression is automatically treated as an assertion without the need for the `assert` keyword or any special assertion methods.

Groovy Assertions

One of the reasons JUnit offers various `assert…` methods rather than using Java's `assert` keyword is so that you can output detailed, high-quality diagnostics in the event of an assertion failure.

When using Groovy, the error thrown when an `assert` statement fails contains a breakdown of the individual values in the Boolean expression. Often, this provides excellent diagnostics of the failure and results in more concise, readable test code than the rather verbose nested method calls required by JUnit.

Of course, it's worth pointing out that this is a feature originally implemented by Spock and later adopted by the Groovy language!

Block Taxonomy

Now that you know that feature methods are divided into labeled blocks, let's take a look at each of the block types and briefly discuss their semantics. The blocks available in Spock are as follows:

given:

> Used for establishing the context of the test. Things like creating objects, setting up specific data, navigating to a page on a website, or logging in before testing

---

access controlled functionality would all be appropriate things to put in this block.

setup:

Simply an alias for given:. The examples in this book use given:, and that is the form that you'll most commonly encounter.

when:

Contains the behavior being tested. Certain Spock features such as mocks depend on the *action* part of the test occurring in the when: block. A when: block *must* be followed by a then: block.

then:

Makes assertions about the outcome of the when: block. Any Boolean statement in a then: block is automatically treated as an assertion, so there is no need to use the assert keyword. A then: block *must* be preceded by a when: block.

expect:

Makes assertions in the same way as a then: block but without requiring a preceding when: block. This is useful either alone for simpler tests such as verifying the initial state of an object or for verifying preconditions before when: and then: blocks.

cleanup:

Allows the safe tear-down of resources that will occur regardless of the outcome of any assertions in preceding blocks. You can think of this as analogous to the finally keyword.

where:

This is used for parameterized feature methods.

and:

This is used to extend any preceding block. This is useful purely to break up the blocks to make them easier to read.

The where: block is covered extensively in Chapter 6. For now, let's examine how you use the basic blocks.

Basic Block Usage

The blocks in a feature method must appear in the appropriate order. All blocks are optional, although, as previously pointed out, when: and then: must appear together if they appear at all. Obviously, a feature method without a then: or expect: block is useless because it's not asserting anything. However, a feature method can be as simple as a single `expect:` block. For example, let's test to make sure a brand new `User` object is not following anyone:

```
def "a new user is not following anyone"() {
  expect:
  new User("kirk").following.isEmpty()
}
```

Let's extend the feature method we saw earlier to verify the precondition that the `User` is not following anyone initially:

```
def "a user can follow another user"() {
  given:
  def user = new User("kirk")
  def other = new User("spock")

  expect:
  user.following.isEmpty()

  when:
  user.follow(other)

  then:
  user.following.size() == 1
  user.following.contains(other)
}
```

We now use an `expect:` block to verify the initial state of the user before any action is taken. The `when:` and `then:` blocks are unchanged.

Label Syntax

If you are familiar with some of the lesser-used features of Java, you might recognize the syntax of Spock's block labels; they are in fact labels used with the Java `break` keyword.

```
loop:
  while (true) {
    System.out.println(i);
    if (--i == 0) {
      break loop;
    }
  }
```

The use of `break` in this way is generally frowned upon (it's not a million miles from a *goto* statement after all), and so the label syntax has become fairly obscure.

Spock repurposes labels to define the start of blocks in a feature method. Because the labels are stored in the bytecode generated when the `Specification` class is compiled, Spock is able to use them when transforming the class to apply its behavior.

The Specification Lifecycle

So far, we've looked at a very simple, completely self-contained feature method. However, most specification classes will contain multiple feature methods, and they might well all share some concerns. They likely deal with the same test subject and could also use some of the same collaborators and fixtures.

Specification classes can—and all but the simplest usually do—contain fields that might represent the test subject, fixtures, and so on. Like with JUnit tests, fields are initialized before *each feature method* is run (actually each iteration of a feature method, but don't worry about that until we discuss the `where:` block).

Revisiting the previous example, we can do away with the simple `given:` block and instead use a field for the test subject and other objects, which allows us to share them with other feature methods:

```
def user = new User("kirk") ❶
def other = new User("spock")

def "a user can follow another user"() {
  when:
  user.follow(other)

  then:
  user.following.size() == 1
  user.following.contains(other)
}

def "a user reports if they are following someone"() {
  expect:
  !user.follows(other)

  when:
  user.follow(other)

  then:
  user.follows(other)
}
```

❶ Note that each of the two feature methods uses a different actual instance of `user` and `other` because the fields are reinitialized before each feature is run.

Fixture methods: setup and cleanup

In the section on block taxonomy, we saw the `given:` and `cleanup:` blocks that can appear in an individual feature method. However, now we're using fields shared between features, and we don't want to have to repeat common setup and cleanup code.

In a JUnit test, we'd use methods annotated with `@Before` and `@After`. Spock provides something similar via methods named `setup` and `cleanup`. The `setup` and `cleanup` methods are rather like `given:` and `cleanup:` blocks that apply to *every* feature method in the specification class. The `setup` method is executed once before *each* feature method is run and after any fields are initialized. The `cleanup` method is run after each feature method regardless of whether it passes or fails.

 When dealing with parameterized feature methods that use the `where:` block, the `setup` and `cleanup` fixture methods are applied around *each iteration*. We cover the `where:` block in much more detail in Chapter 6.

Both methods should be typed `def` or `void` and should not have any parameters.

Spock also supports `setupSpec` and `cleanupSpec` methods that execute before the first and after the last feature method, respectively. They are analogous to methods annotated with `@BeforeClass` and `@AfterClass` in JUnit. However, unlike JUnit's methods, `setupSpec` and `cleanupSpec` should *not* be declared as `static`.

To see an example of the order in which lifecycle methods are executed, here's a simple specification that prints something to standard output when each method is executed:

```
def setupSpec() {
   println "> setupSpec"
}

def cleanupSpec() {
   println "> cleanupSpec"
}

def setup() {
   println "-> setup"
}

def cleanup() {
   println "-> cleanup"
}

def "feature method 1"() {
   println "--> feature method 1"
   expect:
   2 * 2 == 4
}

def "feature method 2"() {
   println "--> feature method 2"
   expect:
```

```
    3 * 2 == 6
}
```

Here's the output when you run the specification:

```
> setupSpec
-> setup
--> feature method 1
-> cleanup
-> setup
--> feature method 2
-> cleanup
> cleanupSpec
```

Later in the book, we'll see more about how to use `setupSpec` and `cleanupSpec` to manage shared fields that are not reinitialized before each feature method.

Block Descriptions

Spock blocks can include a description string. A useful technique when practicing test-driven development is to "plan out" the specification method using described blocks before filling in the code.

Revisiting the earlier example, we could start with an empty feature method:

```
def "a user can follow another user"() {
  given: "two users"
  when: "the first user follows the second"
  then: "the first user is now following the second and no-one else"
}
```

Subsequently, we can add in the implementations of each block.

A well-written block description can make the test easier to understand. Like comments, though, there's a danger of the description getting stale if the test changes later.

Again, like comments, overly obvious block descriptions just add noise. You should try to make a block description describe the general case being tested rather than the specifics of any fixtures in use.

Why Not Just Use Comments Instead of Block Descriptions?

The block description is similar to a comment but with the important distinction that it is retained in the compiled bytecode. Later, you will see how you can create a Spock extension that extracts block descriptions from the compiled code to output a Gherkin-like scenario file.

and: blocks

Look at the block descriptions in the previous example again. Notice that the `then:` block's description essentially describes *two* assertions: the first user is following the second *and* is not following anyone else. To make the test read better, we can split this up into two blocks using another Spock block, `and:`, as demonstrated here:

```
def "a user can follow another user"() {
  given: "two users"
  when: "the first user follows the second"
  then: "the first user is now following one user"
  and: "the first user is following the second user"
}
```

The `and:` block can follow *any* of the standard Spock blocks. All it does is split the block into multiple sections so as to enhance readability. The semantics associated with the preceding block continue through the `and:` block. For example, all Boolean expressions in an `and:` block that follows a `then:` or `expect:` block are treated as assertions, just as they would be in the preceding block.

Each primary block can be followed by any number of `and:` blocks.

Common uses for `and:` are for establishing multiple unrelated preconditions in the `given:` block, and the verification of secondary conditions or side effects in the `then:` block. Using `and:` blocks with appropriate descriptions to split up the primary block can make the method much more comprehensible.

A Note on Comprehensibility

We cannot emphasize enough that after correctness, comprehensibility is *the most important feature* of test code. When you are dealing with regressions in tests that someone else has written, you'll be thanking that person if the feature methods are nicely structured in logical blocks with good descriptions; conversely, you'll be cursing the poor soul if everything is lumped together into plain `when:` and `then:` blocks, tens of lines long.

As a rule of thumb, a block label with five or more lines of code following each block label is crying out for a higher level of abstraction. It's always worth remembering that Spock specifications are classes like any other: they can contain private methods for breaking up long or reused pieces of code. Going further, it's possible to implement advanced abstractions such as the page model pattern commonly used in browser-based end-to-end tests for web applications.

It's absolutely possible to do horrible things like writing all your setup code in among the actions in a `when:` block or scattering the `assert` keyword around outside `then:` and `expect:` blocks rather than taking care to structure a feature method properly. Please don't. Use `given:` blocks and the `setup` method appropriately. Split up primary blocks by using and: so that each block adheres to the single responsibility principle (*http://en.wikipedia.org/wiki/Single_responsibility_principle*). Use good feature method names. Use block descriptions judiciously and, where you do use them, *keep them up to date*. Think about whether an expect: block would make more sense than when: and then: blocks.

Time invested upfront in crafting a readable test will almost certainly be recovered later when debugging regressions or adapting the specifications to new requirements.

Summary

In this chapter, you learned the following:

- How to define a Spock specification class
- How to define a feature method
- The various block types used in feature methods and how they relate to one another
- Something about the special behavior that applies in each block, such as automatic assertions in then: and expect: blocks
- How to use fields in a specification class and the lifecycle that governs them
- How to use the setup and cleanup methods

Comparison with JUnit

If you're a JUnit user, you might find the following comparison of some of the terminology and concepts in JUnit with their equivalents in Spock useful:

JUnit	Spock
Test class	Specification class
Test method	Feature method
@Before	def setup()
@After	def cleanup()
@BeforeClass	def setupSpec()
@AfterClass	def cleanupSpec()

CHAPTER 3

Spock Assertions

In Chapter 2, you learned that any Boolean expression in a `then:` block or `expect:` block is treated as an assertion. In this chapter, we examine assertions in depth. You will learn about various techniques for writing concise and expressive assertions using Groovy's enhancements to the core Java APIs. We also discuss the importance of good diagnostics in your Spock specifications and how to structure assertions to provide the most information in case of a failure.

I have three goals when writing assertions in tests. Listed most important first, they are:

Good diagnostics
> If the assertion fails I should be able to see very easily in the test report what exactly is wrong. I don't want a generic exception or a poorly worded message that doesn't really tell me anything beyond "something is wrong."

Expressiveness
> When I look at the test, I want to be able to see right away what is being asserted without having to scratch my head over convoluted code. When I introduce a regression, I want to be able to determine whether the test I have broken is still valid or is now obsolete due to the change I am implementing.

Conciseness
> This is related to expressiveness in that the shorter a piece of code is, the easier it is to read. However, there's a point beyond which brevity comes at the cost of comprehensibility. Short is good but not when it begins to resemble an obfuscated code contest entry!

The Importance of Good Diagnostics

If you've practiced or read about TDD, you're almost certainly familiar with the mantra "Red...Green...Refactor."

The cycle for implementing a feature (at any scale) in TDD is *red*: write a failing test; *green*: write the simplest code that makes the test pass; *refactor*: eliminate duplication and introduce appropriate abstractions while keeping the test passing.

Steve Freeman and Nat Pryce point out in *Growing Object-Oriented Software Guided by Tests* [goos] that a vital part of the "red" step is ensuring that the test fails for the right reason and produces a good diagnostic description of the failure.

You should write tests defensively with the assumption that you *will* need to revisit them to debug regressions at some point in the future. Six months down the line when you can't remember what you were thinking when you wrote the test, good diagnostic output can save you a headache.

Never Trust a Test That You Haven't Seen Fail

One of the advantages of the *test first* approach is that you can ensure the test is correctly detecting a failure. If you write a test after implementing the code, it's easy to mistakenly write a test that doesn't correctly exercise the desired behavior and would pass even if the code didn't do what it is supposed to.

Make sure also that the test doesn't just fail but that it fails for the right reason: because the assertion fails in the way you intended rather than because there's an error in the test itself that causes an exception.

The Power Assert

Spock introduced a feature that has subsequently been adopted into the core Groovy language called the *power assert*. Java's `assert` keyword was really designed for enforcing invariants in production code rather than for implementing unit tests. In Java when an assertion fails, an `AssertionError` is thrown, but not a great deal of information about what caused the failure is discernible from the error object itself. Although it's possible to add a message to the assertion like this:

```
assert a == b : String.format("expected %d to equal %d", a, b);
```

Doing so for every assertion in a suite of tests would soon grow pretty tiresome. For more complex assertions, the construction of the message would probably require considerably more code than the assertion itself!

JUnit introduced various methods such as `assertEquals` so that good diagnostics would be output in the test report. JUnit 4+ introduced the `assertThat` method with the use of Hamcrest matchers to provide a framework for defining composable assertions that produce good-quality diagnostic messages in the event of a failure.

Hamcrest matchers are powerful, extremely flexible, and produce excellent diagnostics (when implemented well). However, Hamcrest matchers are fairly complex to implement, and there are some curious omissions from the `CoreMatchers` class such as a way to assert that a string matches a regular expression.

Spock's power assert takes a different approach to the problem. Because of the flexibility afforded by Groovy, Spock's power assert is able to use simple Boolean expressions while retaining high-quality diagnostics. The same assertion made in Spock provides much more useful output than a standard Java `assert` without requiring a custom assertion message:

```
given:
int a = 1
int b = 2

expect:
a == b
```

If you look in the test report, you will find this:

```
Condition not satisfied:

a == b
| | |
1 | 2
  false
```

The message contains the assertion statement broken down into its constituent parts and showing the values of the variables, methods, and operators that make up the expression.

More complex Boolean expressions are broken down. Let's look again at the failure generated by the test for a user following another user in our application before the `User.follow` method is implemented:

```
user.following.contains(other)
|    |         |       |
|    []        false   squawker.User@689259a
squawker.User@323c17
```

You can clearly see the value of both variables `user` and `other`, the value of the `user.following` property (an empty collection), and the result of the `contains` method.

Improving Assertion Failures by Using toString

The values displayed for the two User objects are not particularly helpful, because they are the result of calling the default Object.toString method. To improve the diagnostic you can implement a User.toString method:

```
@Override
public String toString() {
  return "@" + username;
}
```

With that in place, the assertion failure becomes:

```
user.following.contains(other)
|    |         |        |
|    []        false    @spock
@kirk
```

Power assert output makes it incredibly easy to implement really good diagnostics of assertion failures using nothing more than simple Boolean expressions and standard operators and methods.

Type Information in Power Asserts

The fact that the power assert relies on the toString value of the various components of the assertion expression is a double-edged sword. Although it's very easy to provide some good output, what happens when the toString value of an instance of one class is the same as that of another? For example, it might be difficult to spot the problem if comparing an int with a numeric String.

Fortunately, Spock helps us out here. Let's assume that we've made a naïve mistake in the specification and tried to compare a User instance with a toString value:

```
when:
user.follow(other)

then:
user.following[0] == other.toString()
```

Spock detects that the toString values on either side of the expression are the same but the types are different, so it adds that information to the assertion message. The report now contains this:

```
user.following[0] == other.toString()
|    |          |  |  |  |
|    [@spock]   |  |  |  |  @spock (java.lang.String)
@kirk          |  |  @spock
               |  |  @spock
               |  false
               @spock (squawker.User)
```

Using Groovy for Effective Assertions

The Groovy language includes many capabilities not present in Java. In addition, it extends many of the standard Java types with additional methods. It's a good idea to become familiar with these because many are useful in composing concise, highly readable assertions in Spock specifications.

To demonstrate some of these capabilities, we're going to implement a new feature in Squawker allowing a user to post messages. We're adding two methods to the User class:

```
public Message post(String text, Instant postedAt) ❶
public List<Message> getPosts() ❷
```

❶ Creates and returns a new message containing the specified text

❷ Returns a list of the Message objects the user has posted

We could begin with a test like this:

```
def "a user can post a message"() {
  when:
  user.post("@kirk that is illogical, Captain!", now())

  then:
  user.posts.size() == 1
  def message = user.posts[0]
  message.text == "@kirk that is illogical, Captain!"
}
```

We're asserting that after the user has posted a message, the getPosts method returns a list with a single Message whose text is correct.

Using List Comprehensions and List Literals

We can simplify the assertion, though. Groovy implements a functional-programming style *map* operation on collections and arrays. If you use the *spread* operator 0. followed by a property name belonging to the collection *element* type, the result is a List of the values of that property on each element. For example:

```
def kirk = new User("kirk")
def spock = new User("spock")
def scotty = new User("scotty")
def users = [kirk, spock, scotty]
assert users*.username == ["kirk", "spock", "scotty"]
```

The spread operator works in exactly the same way when calling a method on each member of the collection:

```
assert users*.toString() == ["@kirk", "@spock", "@scotty"]
```

Using the spread operator, our assertion could instead be implemented like this:

```
def "a user can post a message"() {
  when:
  user.post("@kirk that is illogical, Captain!", now())

  then:
  user.posts*.text == ["@kirk that is illogical, Captain!"]
}
```

The feature method now compares a List<String> of the text property of every message returned by getPosts() with another List<String> containing the expected text. The righthand side of the assertion expression is a Groovy List literal.

The assertion for the size of the list of posts is now redundant because we're no longer only asserting the text of the *first* message, so the test would fail anyway if the list was the wrong size.

The equivalent Java code for the assertion would be something like this:

```
List<String> messageTexts = new ArrayList<>();
for (Message message : user.getPosts()) {
  messageTexts.add(message.getText());
}
List<String> expected = Collections.singletonList(messageText);
assertThat(messageTexts, equalTo(expected));
```

Although there are more concise ways to express the assertion using the stream API in Java 8 or a Hamcrest matcher, this gives you a good idea of what the Groovy code is doing.

If you want to add a feature method to ensure that posts are returned most recent first, you can use this same technique:

```
def "a user's posts are listed most recent first"() {
  when:
  user.post("It's life, Jim", now())
  user.post("but not as we know it", now())

  then:
  user.posts*.text == ["but not as we know it", "It's life, Jim"]
}
```

In fact, when accessing properties on members of a collection, the 0 in the spread operator is redundant. Groovy will evaluate any unknown property reference on a collection against each member of the collection. The example earlier could be written as follows:

```
def kirk = new User("kirk")
def spock = new User("spock")
def scotty = new User("scotty")
def users = [kirk, spock, scotty]
assert users.username == ["kirk", "spock", "scotty"]
```

In this book, I've tended to prefer using the spread operator because I think the implicit form can be a little confusing for people who are less familiar with Groovy. It also makes it easier for me to change my mind between using a property and a method. You should use whichever you are comfortable with in your own code.

Asserting Something About Every Item in a Collection

The Message class also records which user posted the message. You should ensure that when a user posts a message that the correct value is stored in the postedBy property of the message.

You could implement such a test like this:

```
def "the posting user is recorded in the message"() {
  when:
  user.post("Fascinating!", now())
  user.post("@bones I was merely stating a fact, Doctor.", now())

  then:
  user.posts[0].postedBy == user
  user.posts[1].postedBy == user
}
```

Warning: Assertions in Loops

The automatic assertion behavior of a then: or expect: block *does not* apply in the scope of any block expressions such as for loops or if statements.

It might occur to you to test the previous example like this:

```
then:
for (post in user.posts) {
  post.postedBy == user
}
```

However, this will not work. Worse, it will *appear to* work because the test will pass regardless. The expression in the loop *is* evaluated but because it is in the nested scope of the loop, it is *not* converted into an assertion. This kind of thing is exactly why, as we've stated before, you should never trust a test you haven't seen fail.

Consider that the following assertion appears to pass:

```
expect:
for (int i = 1; i <= 10; i++) {
  i == -i
}
```

If you're really interested in *why* this happens, read on.

Spock applies a compile-time AST (abstract syntax tree) transformation to the code inside a then: or expect: block. It looks for Boolean expressions or expressions that can be coerced to Boolean (which in Groovy covers just about any expression with a value) and transforms them into assertions. A loop like the for loops in the preceding examples looks like a single expression, and in Groovy—unlike some languages— loop expressions and conditionals do not have a value. Spock sees the for loop as a void expression and does not convert it into an assertion.

Theoretically, it would be possible to enhance Spock's AST transformation to traverse the block inside a loop and find Boolean-like expressions there but the idea is fraught with edge cases and unintended side effects. How deep should the parser go? What should be done with intermediate lines of code in more complex expressions? Should only the last line be assumed to be an assertion or all lines?

A better way to handle this assertion is by using the every method that Groovy attaches to collections. This method takes a closure parameter and returns true if that closure returns true when called with every member of the collection in turn. If the closure returns false for any of the collection's members, the every method itself returns false.

 In fact, Groovy makes the every(Closure) method and others like it available on *all* objects, not just collections and arrays. On other types of objects, the closure is invoked only once, with the object itself as a parameter.

Here is the feature method reworked to use every:

```
def "the posting user is recorded in the message"() {
  when:
  user.post("Fascinating!", now())
  user.post("@bones I was merely stating a fact, Doctor.", now())

  then:
  user.posts.every {
    it.postedBy == user
  }
}
```

This avoids some unnecessary duplication. There is a problem, however. The assertion failure doesn't create a very good message if the test fails. For example, if the post method fails to set the posting user on the message at all, this is what is output to the test report:

```
user.posts.every { it.postedBy == user }
   |     |       |
   |     |       false
   |     [squawker.Message@154b0848, squawker.Message@17b645b0]
   @spock
```

Not terribly useful. Because we can't see what the postedBy value of the individual messages actually *is*, we can't determine what's wrong with it.

The solution is to combine the use of every with the list comprehension you learned previously:

```
def "the posting user is recorded in the message"() {
  when:
  user.post("Fascinating!", now())
  user.post("@bones I was merely stating a fact, Doctor.", now())

  then:
  user.posts.postedBy.every {
    it == user
  }
}
```

Now, every is called on the list of postedBy values mapped from the list of messages. The report shows us exactly what is wrong; we haven't actually set the postedBy field:

```
user.posts.postedBy.every { it == user }
   |     |      |          |
   |     |      |          false
   |     |      [null, null]
   |     [squawker.Message@154b0848, squawker.Message@17b645b0]
   @spock
```

Expressive Assertions with Groovy Operators

Groovy, unlike Java, supports operator overriding. In fact, the various operators are implemented by methods. For example, operators such as <, >, <=, and >= use the compareTo implementation of the object on the lefthand side of the expression if it implements java.util.Comparable.

Using operators such as == with anything other than primitives looks "wrong" to programmers accustomed to Java, where it would likely be incorrect. However, it is correct and idiomatic in Groovy because Groovy operators are aliases for underlying methods that classes can override. Although there's no reason why you can't use methods such as compareTo and equals as you would in Java, after you become used to Groovy, the operator form is more legible and concise.

Squawker messages should be ordered most recent first by default. We'll need to store a timestamp when a message is created and make the Message class implement Compa rable<Message>. To test the behavior we can simply use the < and > operators:

```
def user = new User("spock")

def "messages are ordered most recent first"() {
  given:
  def clock = Clock.fixed(now(), UTC)
  def olderMessage = new Message(user, "Fascinating.", clock.instant())

  and:
  clock = Clock.offset(clock, Duration.of(1, MINUTES))
  def newerMessage = new Message(user, "Live long and prosper.", clock.instant())

  expect:
  newerMessage < olderMessage

  and:
  olderMessage > newerMessage
}
```

We could implement the test by checking the return value of the compareTo method directly, but using an operator is more concise and more clearly communicates the desired behavior—ordering messages correctly—rather than exposing the implementation detail.

In an earlier test, we asserted that the collection returned by getFollowing() included a particular user by using the Collection.contains(Object) method. We could reimplement this by using Groovy's in operator:

```
def "a user can follow another user"() {
  when:
  user.follow(other)

  then:
  user.following.size() == 1
  other in user.following
}
```

Expecting Exceptions

It's an important consideration when writing tests to not test only the *happy path*. That is, don't just test what happens when everything goes right; the user enters correct data, external dependencies are available and working correctly, and so on. It's just as important, if not more so, to test that your program correctly handles error conditions, incorrect input, unreliable external services, and network failures.

Frequently, the right way for a unit to handle an error is to throw an exception. With Spock, it's possible to expect a `when:` step to throw an exception.

For a very simple example, let's look at the `User` class again. The `getPosts()` method returns a list of messages posted by the user. Of course, it shouldn't be possible for the caller to violate the encapsulation of the `User` class by modifying that list.

Here, we'll use another Groovy operator 0 implemented by the `leftShift` method. Groovy enhances the collection API to allow elements to be appended using 1.

```
def "the list of posts is not modifiable"() {
  when:
  user.posts << new Message(user, "Fascinating!", now())

  then:
  thrown(UnsupportedOperationException)
}
```

Spock's `thrown(Class<E extends Throwable>)` method must appear in a `then:` block and asserts that the preceding `when:` block threw an exception of the specified type.

If the `getPosts()` method returns a modifiable list, the test will fail and report the following message:

```
Expected exception java.lang.UnsupportedOperationException,
but no exception was thrown
```

 The `thrown` method will pass only if the exception was thrown from within the `when:` block. This is another instance of the special behavior of different block types discussed in Chapter 1. The `thrown` method will fail if an exception is thrown from any other block in the feature method, even if it is an exception of the expected type.

Interrogating the Exception

Occasionally, it's necessary to assert something about the exception itself, and to that end the `thrown` method also returns the exception instance.

Let's turn to another example where this can be useful. Squawker allows only messages of up to 140 characters, so if a user attempts to post a longer message, an exception should be thrown:

```
def "a posted message may not be longer than 140 characters"() {
  given:
  def messageText = """"Lieutenant, I am half Vulcanian. Vulcanians do not
    speculate. I speak from pure logic. If I let go of a hammer on a planet
    that has a positive gravity, I need not see it fall to know that it has in
    fact fallen."""

  expect:
  messageText.length() > Message.MAX_TEXT_LENGTH

  when:
  user.post(messageText, now())

  then:
  def e = thrown(IllegalArgumentException)
  e.message == "Message text cannot be longer than 140 characters"
}
```

Type Inference and the Thrown Method

It's possible to omit the parameter passed to `thrown` if you are assigning the returned exception to an explicitly typed variable. For example:

```
IllegalArgumentException e = thrown()
```

Idiomatic Groovy code tends not to explicitly type local variables because the type can be inferred from the righthand side of the expression that initialized the variable. However, this can be useful if you're using an IDE that doesn't recognize Groovy's type inference rules.

Grouping Assertions on the Same Object

When writing multiple assertions against the same object, Spock allows you to group them together by using the `with(Object, Closure)` method. All property and method names inside the closure are resolved against the object, and the semantics of the current block apply. Therefore, when `with` is used in a `then:` or `expect:` block, all Boolean expressions are treated as assertions.

This means that instead of writing repetitive code like this:

```
def "initial state of a user is correct"() {
  given: def user = new User("kirk")

  expect:
```

```
    user.username == "kirk"
    user.following.isEmpty()
    user.posts.isEmpty()
    user.registered instanceof Instant
}
```

The assertions can be grouped like this:

```
def "initial state of a user is correct"() {
  given:
  def user = new User("kirk")

  expect:
  with(user) {
    username == "kirk"
    following.isEmpty()
    posts.isEmpty()
    registered instanceof Instant
  }
}
```

Spock's with and Groovy's with

Be aware that Spock's with(Object, Closure) method is not the same as Groovy's Object.with(Closure). Accidentally using the Groovy form in a then: or expect: block will result in the assertions not working. The following code will compile but not assert anything.

```
expect:
user.with {
  username == "kirk"
  following.isEmpty()
  posts.isEmpty()
  registered instanceof Instant
}
```

Groovy's with method can be useful in reducing repetition in given blocks, just be careful not to use it in then: or expect: blocks.

Summary

Bringing some of these techniques together, we'll now create a full specification for retrieving a *timeline* of posts from Squawker. A user's timeline contains their posts and the posts of any users they are following, ordered most recent first.

We'll introduce a new annotation—@spock.lang.Subject—which simply documents the variable or field that represents the unit-under-test (we'll see more about documentation annotations later):

```
package squawker

import java.time.*
import spock.lang.*
import static java.time.Instant.*
import static java.time.ZoneOffset.*
import static java.time.temporal.ChronoUnit.*

class TimelineSpec extends Specification {

    ❶
    @Subject user = new User("khan")
    def followedUser = new User("kirk")
    def otherUser = new User("spock")

    ❷
    def setup() {
        user.follow(followedUser)   ❸

        def now = Instant.now()
        ❹
        postMessage(otherUser, now.minus(6, MINUTES),
            "His pattern indicates two-dimensional thinking.")
        postMessage(user, now.minus(5, MINUTES),
            "@kirk You're still alive, my old friend?")
        postMessage(followedUser, now.minus(4, MINUTES),
            "@khan KHAAANNNN!")
        postMessage(followedUser, now.minus(3, MINUTES),
            "@scotty I need warp speed in three minutes or we're all dead!")
        postMessage(otherUser, now.minus(2, MINUTES),
            "@bones I'm sorry, Doctor, I have no time to explain this logically.")
        postMessage(user, now.minus(1, MINUTES),
            "It is very cold in space!")
    }

    def "a user's timeline contains posts from themselves and followed users"() {
        expect:
        with(user.timeline()) {
            size() == 4

            ❺
            it*.postedBy.every {
                it in [user, followedUser]
            }

            ❻
            !it*.postedBy.any {
                it == otherUser
            }
        }
    }
}
```

```
def "a user's timeline is ordered most recent first"() {
  expect:
  with(user.timeline()) {
    postedAt == postedAt.sort().reverse() ❼
  }
}

def "a timeline cannot be modified directly"() {
  when:
  user.timeline() << new Message(
    user,
    "@kirk You're still alive, my old friend?",
    now()
  )

  then:
  thrown(UnsupportedOperationException)
}

private void postMessage(User poster, Instant at, String text) {
  def clock = Clock.fixed(at, UTC)
  poster.post(text, clock.instant())
}
}
```

❶ We create three users, one of which is the *subject* of the test whose timeline will be tested.

❷ We use a setup method to establish the same data fixtures for each feature method.

❸ The subject user follows only *one* of the other users.

❹ We then post several messages from each user using a private fixture method.

❺ We combine the every method with a list comprehension inside a with closure! We're asserting that all messages in the timeline were posted by the user they follow or by the user themselves.

❻ We use a similar Groovy method (any) to ensure that none of the messages in the timeline are from the user our subject user *does not* follow. The any method, as you can probably guess, returns true if the closure returns true for one or more elements in a collection. Strictly speaking, this assertion is redundant because there's no way it could fail if the previous assertion passed.

❼ We ensure that the messages are sorted correctly by comparing the list comprehension of their timestamps with a reverse-sorted version of the same list of timestamps. We could compare the timeline list itself with a sorted version because the Message class' compareTo method orders by timestamp. But if the assertion failed, the message would show us a list of Message.toString values, which wouldn't tell us anything about what is wrong with the ordering.

Testing Dates and Timestamps

Date and timestamp values are notoriously difficult to deal with correctly in tests. Ideally, the Message class would not expose a way to set the message timestamp, because it would just be assigned in the constructor using Instant.now(). However, that makes testing very tricky—how could we set up fixtures for messages that were posted earlier?

One way would be to use a package-protected constructor or something similar to allow tests to set the timestamp to a desired value. The Guava library provides a @VisibleForTesting (*http://docs.guava-libraries.googlecode.com/git/javadoc/com/google/common/annotations/VisibleForTesting.html*) annotation to document these kinds of elements.

I prefer not to include production code that only the tests are supposed to use. There's too much danger that either other production code will end up using it inappropriately or the code will behave differently so that the test is actually invalid.

Another approach would be to use the *extract and override* technique, as described by Roy Osherove in *The Art of Unit Testing* [osherove]. This involves using a protected method to create the timestamp and then overriding that method in the instance under test:

```
public class Message {
  private final Instant postedAt = currentTime();

  protected Instant currentTime() {
    Instant.now()
  }
}

def fixedInstant = // create a fixed timestamp somehow ❶
def message = new Message() { ❷
  @Override protected Instant currentTime() { ❸
    fixedInstant
  }
}
```

❶ A field in the test holds the value of the fixed instant used in place of the real current timestamp.

❷ Instead of using an instance of the Message class directly, the specification creates an anonymous inner class that extends Message.

---

❸ The anonymous inner class overrides the currentTime method and simply returns the fixed instant.

I have mixed feelings about this technique because it feels like opening backdoors in production code. It also won't work with immutable classes that are declared final or those using Groovy's @Immutable annotation.

If we were using Joda time, we'd have a simpler alternative because the library provides a way to override the global clock.

Instead, I've chosen to require the message timestamp to be passed in to the constructor. That way we can easily set a value for test purposes. The production system can use its own Clock instance to generate timestamps.

CHAPTER 4

Managing Resources

So far, the User and Message classes in the Squawker application have existed only in memory. We've specified some of the behavior, but ultimately, the data itself is going to need to be persisted somehow.

How (Not) to Approach Persistence Testing

Testing persistence is one of the most frequently encountered types of integration test. If done incorrectly it can mean death to a suite of tests because they will run slowly and be incredibly brittle.

One of the most common antipatterns encountered is to test everything by reference to a single monolithic fixture containing an ever-growing volume of data that attempts to cater to every corner-case. The fixture will soon become the victim of combinatorial explosion—there are so many combinations of entities in various states required that the sheer amount of data becomes overwhelming and impossible to monitor. Tests based on monolithic fixtures tend to be replete with *false moniker* testing—*"I know the pantoffler widget is the one set up with three variants, one of which has a negative price modifier and is zero-rated for tax."*

If any kind of write-testing is done, it's almost certainly going to mean restoring the database between each test. Given the complexity of all the foreign-key constraints in that huge fixture, it's going to be a practical impossibility to do that in any other way than by truncating all of the tables and setting everything up again. Before you know it, the test suite takes hours to run and no one has any idea whether it works anymore.

This might sound like an exaggeration, but I once worked on a project that did exactly this. A gargantuan XML file would populate an entire database *before each and every test*. Each of the test classes extended `AbstractTransactionalSpringCon textTests` and thus would also initialize the entire Spring application context before each test. Teams had to coordinate data changes because adding new fixtures or modifying existing ones could break unrelated tests. The "integration suite" job on the continuous integration server took more than three-and-a-half hours to run, and I don't recall it ever passing.

Don't do that.

You should always try to set up the *minimum* amount of data required for the specific test. That doesn't mean not sharing fixtures between tests for which there are commonalities but only where appropriate.

As far as possible you should try to keep everything in-memory, as well. When testing the peculiarities of a particular database's SQL syntax, that's obviously not going to work, but a lightweight in-memory database such as H2 (*http://www.h2data base.com/*) is an excellent option for the majority of persistence tests.

Testing a Persistence Layer

The first thing we need to test is persisting `User` instances to a database. We'll create a data access object (DAO) (*http://en.wikipedia.org/wiki/Data_access_object*) class `Data Store` with methods for writing to and reading from the database.

We'll begin with a feature method that tests storing a user object. Don't worry about how the `handle` and `dataStore` fields are initialized right now: we're coming to that. All you need to know at the moment is that `handle` is the direct connection to the database, and `dataStore` is the DAO we're testing.

```
Handle handle
@Subject DataStore dataStore

def "can insert a user object"() {
  given:
  def clock = Clock.fixed(now(), UTC) ❶

  and:
  def user = new User("spock", clock.instant()) ❷

  when:
  dataStore.insert(user) ❸

  then:
  def iterator = handle.createQuery("select username, registered from user")
                       .iterator() ❹
  iterator.hasNext() ❺
```

```
with(iterator.next()) {
  username == user.username
  registered.time == clock.instant().toEpochMilli()
} ❻

and:
!iterator.hasNext() ❼
}
```

❶ Because the test needs to ensure the registered timestamp is inserted to the database correctly, we'll use a fixed clock to generate the timestamps.

❷ Create a user object.

❸ Invoke the `insert` method of our DAO passing the user.

❹ Query the database directly.

❺ Assert that we get a first row back.

❻ Assert that the `username` and `registered` values on the first row correspond to the values on the user object.

❼ Assert that no further rows were found.

The feature method is reasonably straightforward; however, one thing merits discussion. The test queries the database directly to verify the insert operation has worked. It would likely result in more concise code if the test used another DAO method to read the database back again. This feels wrong, though. The DAO class is the subject of the test so if any of the assertions failed, it would not be possible to determine whether the problem lies in inserting the data or reading it back. The least ambiguity in any potential failure arises if the test reads the database directly.

That's not to say that reading the database is always the right thing to do. The question, as always, is *what behavior am I trying to test here?* In this case, the question we're interested in is *does the persistence layer work? Is the correct data being written to the database?* Given that, it's appropriate to directly read the database. A browser-based end-to-end test that fills in a form should almost certainly *not* then look directly in the database to see if the data was persisted correctly. Even a test for a different aspect of the DAO might use the insertion and query methods if their behavior is adequately covered elsewhere.

Similarly, we will want to test that data is read from the database correctly. In that case, it's appropriate to insert data directly to the database because we're interested in the translation between database rows and objects.

Let's add that feature method to the specification:

```
def "can retrieve a list of user objects"() {
  given:
  def timestamp = LocalDateTime.of(1966, 9, 8, 20, 0).toInstant(UTC)
  ["kirk", "spock"].each {
    handle.createStatement("""insert into user (username, registered)
                                    values (?, ?)""")
            .bind(0, it)
            .bind(1, timestamp)
            .execute()
  }

  when:
  def users = dataStore.findAllUsers()

  then:
  with(users.toList()) {
    username == ["kirk", "spock"]
    registered.every {
      it == timestamp
    }
  }
}
```

Managing Resources with the Spock Lifecycle

The feature method in the previous example uses a dataStore object, which is a DAO wrapping a database connection. A database connection is a classic example of a managed resource that needs to be acquired and disposed of correctly. We saw setup and cleanup methods in Chapter 2; now we'll take a look at lifecycle management in a little more depth.

JDBI

For the persistence in the Squawker application we're using JDBI (*http://jdbi.org/*), which is a lightweight library for mapping a relational database to a strongly typed Java API. The underlying database is an H2 in-memory database.

For the purposes of this chapter, it's not essential that you know JDBI. The concepts are general enough that they could apply to almost any persistence solution.

JDBI allows for simple working examples with a minimum of configuration and a concise API for doing direct database access.

Before the feature method can run, there are some things that you need to do:

- Acquire a connection to the database
- Configure the object-relational mapping (ORM)

- Create the DAO we are testing
- Ensure that the tables needed to store our data in fact exist

Afterward, to clean up, the specification must do the following:

- Clean up any data that was created
- Dispose of the database connection properly

Test Leakage

A very important feature of any unit test is that it should be idempotent. That is to say, the test should produce the same result regardless of whether it is run alone or with other tests in a suite and regardless of the order in which the tests in that suite are run. When side effects from a test affect subsequent tests in the suite, we can describe that test as *leaking*.

Test leakage is caused by badly managed resources. Typical causes of leakage include data in a persistent store that is not removed, changes to a class' metaclass that are unexpectedly still in place later, mocks injected into objects reused between tests, and uncontrolled changes to global state such as the system clock.

Test leakage can be very difficult to track down. Simply identifying *which* test is leaking can be time consuming. For example, the leaking test might not affect the one running *directly* after it, or continuous integration servers might run test suites in a different order from that of the developer's computers, leading to protests of *but, it works on my machine!*

As a starting point, we'll use a `setup` and `cleanup` method, as we saw in "Block Taxonomy" on page 12:

```
@Subject DataStore dataStore

def dbi = new DBI("jdbc:h2:mem:test")
Handle handle

def setup() {
  dbi.registerArgumentFactory(new TimeTypesArgumentFactory())
  dbi.registerMapper(new TimeTypesMapperFactory())

  handle = dbi.open()
  dataStore = handle.attach(DataStore)

  dataStore.createUserTable()
}
```

```
def cleanup() {
  handle.execute("drop table user if exists")
  handle.close()
}
```

This means that the database connection is acquired and disposed of before and after *each* feature method. Given that we're using a lightweight in-memory database, this is probably not much overhead. Still, there's no reason why we can't reuse the same database connection for every feature method.

In JUnit, we could accomplish this by using a static field managed via methods annotated with @BeforeClass and @AfterClass. Spock specifications *can* contain static fields but can better accomplish the same thing using the @spock.lang.Shared annotation.

Notice that when the cleanup method drops the tables, it does so by using drop table user if exists. It's a good idea to try to avoid potential errors in cleanup methods because they can muddy the waters of debugging problems.

Here, if anything fundamental went wrong with initializing the DataStore class the specification might not get as far as creating the table, so when cleanup tries to drop it, a SQLException would be thrown.

Fields annotated with @Shared have a different lifecycle to regular fields. Instead of being reinitialized before each feature method is run they are initialized only once—when the specification is created, before the *first* feature method is run. @Shared fields are *not* declared static. They are regular instance fields, but the annotation causes Spock to manage their lifecycle differently. As we'll see later, they are also useful when parameterizing feature methods using the where: block.

It doesn't make sense to manage @Shared fields with the setup and cleanup method. Instead, Spock provides setupSpec and cleanupSpec methods. As you'd expect, these are run, respectively, before the first and after the last feature method. Again, they are *not* static, unlike methods that use JUnit's @BeforeClass and @AfterClass annotations. Just like setup and cleanup, setupSpec and cleanupSpec are typed def or void and do not have parameters.

We can make the dbi field in the specification @Shared and then only perform the ORM configuration once in a setupSpec method.

```
@Subject DataStore dataStore

@Shared dbi = new DBI("jdbc:h2:mem:test") ❶
Handle handle
```

```
def setupSpec() {  ❷
  dbi.registerArgumentFactory(new TimeTypesArgumentFactory())
  dbi.registerMapper(new TimeTypesMapperFactory())
}

def setup() {
  handle = dbi.open()
  dataStore = handle.attach(DataStore)

  dataStore.createUserTable()
}

def cleanup() {
  handle.execute("drop table user if exists")
  handle.close()
}
```

❶ The dbi field is now annotated @Shared.

❷ A setupSpec method now handles class-wide setup.

At this stage, we're still opening a connection and creating tables before each test and then dropping the tables and releasing the connection after. Even though each feature method will need its own data, it seems like the table itself could persist between features.

```
@Subject @Shared DataStore dataStore  ❶

@Shared dbi = new DBI("jdbc:h2:mem:test")
@Shared Handle handle  ❷

def setupSpec() {
  dbi.registerArgumentFactory(new TimeTypesArgumentFactory())
  dbi.registerMapper(new TimeTypesMapperFactory())

  handle = dbi.open()  ❸
  dataStore = handle.attach(DataStore)
  dataStore.createUserTable()
}

def cleanupSpec() {  ❹
  handle.execute("drop table user if exists")
  handle.close()
}

def cleanup() {
  handle.execute("delete from user")  ❺
}
```

❶ Now, the DAO instance is @Shared so that we can use it to create the tables it requires in setupSpec.

❷ The database handle we need to create the DAO also needs to be @Shared.

❸ We now create the handle and the DAO in setupSpec rather than setup.

❹ Instead of dropping the tables in cleanup we do so in cleanupSpec.

❺ In cleanup, we'll ensure that all data is removed from the *user* table so that each feature method is running in a clean environment.

Using @Shared in this way results in some tradeoffs. It's important to manage shared fields very carefully to ensure state does not leak between feature methods. In the preceding example, we had to add a cleanup step to ensure that any data persisted by the feature methods is deleted.

 In this specification, we've made the test subject @Shared, meaning that it is not reinitialized before each feature method. Although generally this is not a good idea, it's reasonable if—like in this case—the test subject is stateless.

Yes, the *database* is stateful, but we need to manage that anyway, regardless of the lifecycle of the DAO instance.

It's not always obvious that state is leaking between feature methods until you restructure the specification or run things in a different order. As we saw in "Basic Block Usage" on page 13, an expect: block can appear *before* a when: block as a way of verifying preconditions before the action of the test starts. If there's any danger of state leakage, using an expect: block at the start of the feature method to verify the initial state is a good option. Let's add that to the feature method we saw earlier:

```
def "can insert a user object"() {
  given:
  def clock = Clock.fixed(now(), UTC)

  and:
  def user = new User("spock", clock.instant())

  expect:
  rowCount("user") == 0 ❶

  when:
  dataStore.insert(user)

  then:
  def iterator = handle.createQuery("select username, registered from user")
                    .iterator()
  iterator.hasNext()
  with(iterator.next()) {
```

```
    username == user.username
    registered.time == clock.instant().toEpochMilli()
  }

  and:
  !iterator.hasNext()
}

private int rowCount(String table) {
  handle.createQuery("select count(*) from $table")
        .map(IntegerColumnMapper.PRIMITIVE)
        .first()
} ❷
```

❶ The feature method now ensures that the database is in the expected state before performing the tested action.

❷ A helper method allows for a concise assertion in the expect: block.

Specifications and Inheritance

The lifecycle management that the specification is doing is probably not just applicable to tests for persisting users, but for similar tests that also need to integrate with the database. So far we've made the User class persistent, but we need to do the same for the Message class. We'll add some methods to the DataStore DAO with a specification that tests reading from and writing to the database:

```
class MessagePersistenceSpec extends Specification {

  @Subject @Shared DataStore dataStore
  User kirk, spock

  @Shared dbi = new DBI("jdbc:h2:mem:test")
  @Shared Handle handle

  def setupSpec() {
    dbi.registerArgumentFactory(new TimeTypesArgumentFactory())
    dbi.registerMapper(new TimeTypesMapperFactory())

    handle = dbi.open()

    dataStore = handle.attach(DataStore)

    dataStore.createUserTable()
    dataStore.createMessageTable()
  }

  def cleanupSpec() {
    handle.execute("drop table message if exists")
    handle.execute("drop table user if exists")
```

```groovy
    handle.close()
}

def setup() {
  kirk = new User("kirk")
  spock = new User("spock")
  [kirk, spock].each { dataStore.insert(it) }
}

def cleanup() {
  handle.execute("delete from message")
  handle.execute("delete from user")
}

def "can retrieve a list of messages posted by a user"() {
  given:
  insertMessage(kirk, "@khan KHAAANNN!")
  insertMessage(spock, "Fascinating!")
  insertMessage(spock, "@kirk That is illogical, Captain.")

  when:
  def posts = dataStore.postsBy(spock)

  then:
  with(posts) {
    size() == 2
    postedBy.every { it == spock }
  }
}

def "can insert a message"() {
  given:
  def clock = Clock.fixed(now(), UTC)
  def message = spock.post(
    "@bones I was merely stating a fact, Doctor.",
    clock.instant()
  )

  when:
  dataStore.insert(message)

  then:
  def iterator = handle.createQuery("""select u.username, m.text, m.posted_at
                                       from message m, user u
                                       where m.posted_by_id = u.id""")
                     .iterator()
  iterator.hasNext()
  with(iterator.next()) {
    text == message.text
    username == message.postedBy.username
    posted_at.time == clock.instant().toEpochMilli()
  }
```

```
    and:
    !iterator.hasNext()
  }

  private void insertMessage(User postedBy, String text) {
    handle.createStatement("""insert into message
                            (posted_by_id, text, posted_at)
                            select id, ?, ? from user where username = ?""")
        .bind(0, text)
        .bind(1, now())
        .bind(2, postedBy.username)
        .execute()
  }
}
```

This code is doing an awful lot of the same work as the test for user persistence. It
would make sense to extract a common superclass that can do some of the lifecycle
management and provide some utility methods, such as the rowCount method we
used earlier.

One of the advantages of the fact that @Shared fields and the setupSpec and cleanup
Spec methods are nonstatic is that they can participate in inheritance hierarchies.
Let's refactor and extract a superclass:

```
abstract class BasePersistenceSpec extends Specification {

  @Shared DataStore dataStore

  @Shared dbi = new DBI("jdbc:h2:mem:test")
  @Shared Handle handle

  def setupSpec() {
    dbi.registerArgumentFactory(new TimeTypesArgumentFactory())
    dbi.registerMapper(new TimeTypesMapperFactory())

    handle = dbi.open()
    dataStore = handle.attach(DataStore)
    dataStore.createUserTable()
  }

  def cleanupSpec() {
    handle.execute("drop table user if exists")
    handle.close()
  }

  def cleanup() {
    handle.execute("delete from user")
  }

  protected int rowCount(String table) {
    handle.createQuery("select count(*) from $table")
```

```
                .map(IntegerColumnMapper.PRIMITIVE)
                .first()
        }
    }
```

Here, we've simply moved all the lifecycle methods and fields up from `MessagePersis` `tenceSpec`. The `@Subject` annotation is gone from the `dataStore` field because it's no longer appropriate, and the `rowCount` method is now `protected` rather than `private`. Otherwise, the code is unchanged.

We don't need anything else for the `UserPersistenceSpec` class, but `MessagePersis` `tenceSpec` has to manage the `message` table as well as the `user` table.

The feature methods remain unchanged but we can now remove the common parts of the lifecycle management code that are currently handled by the superclass:

```
class MessagePersistenceSpec extends BasePersistenceSpec {
    User kirk, spock

    def setupSpec() {
        dataStore.createMessageTable()
    }

    def cleanupSpec() {
        handle.execute("drop table message if exists")
    }

    def setup() {
        kirk = new User("kirk")
        spock = new User("spock")
        [kirk, spock].each { dataStore.insert(it) }
    }

    def cleanup() {
        handle.execute("delete from message")
    }
```

If you're paying attention, you might notice something missing from the lifecycle methods in this derived class. None of them are invoking the superclass method they override! Because forgetting to do so will likely cause problems that can be difficult to debug and could be prone to copy-and-paste errors, Spock helps you by doing the right thing automatically.

If a specification's superclass has any of the lifecycle management methods, they are *automatically* executed along with those of the specification itself. It is *not* necessary to call `super.setup()` from a specification's `setup` method, for example.

Execution Order of Lifecycle Methods in an Inheritance Hierarchy

Thinking about the order in which the lifecycle methods execute, you might also notice a couple of interesting things:

- The base class' setupSpec method initializes the dataStore DAO field, and the subclass setupSpec method uses it to create the message table.

- The base class' cleanupSpec method calls handle.close() (which is JDBI's way of closing the database connection), but the subclass cleanupSpec method uses the handle field to drop the message table.

Spock treats the lifecycle methods like an onion skin. Execution of the setupSpec and setup methods proceeds *down* the inheritance tree, whereas the cleanupSpec and cleanup methods execute in the opposite order *up* the inheritance tree.

Let's look at a simple example of an inheritance hierarchy that prints something to standard output in each lifecycle method:

```
abstract class SuperSpec extends Specification {
  def setupSpec() {
    println "> super setupSpec"
  }

  def cleanupSpec() {
    println "> super cleanupSpec"
  }

  def setup() {
    println "--> super setup"
  }

  def cleanup() {
    println "--> super cleanup"
  }
}

class SubSpec extends SuperSpec {
  def setupSpec() {
    println "-> sub setupSpec"
  }

  def cleanupSpec() {
    println "-> sub cleanupSpec"
  }

  def setup() {
    println "---> sub setup"
  }
```

```
    def cleanup() {
      println "---> sub cleanup"
    }

    def "feature method 1"() {
      println "----> feature method 1"
      expect:
      2 * 2 == 4
    }

    def "feature method 2"() {
      println "----> feature method 2"
      expect:
      3 * 2 == 6
    }
  }
```

The output generated is as follows:

```
> super setupSpec
-> sub setupSpec
--> super setup
---> sub setup
----> feature method 1
---> sub cleanup
--> super cleanup
--> super setup
---> sub setup
----> feature method 2
---> sub cleanup
--> super cleanup
-> sub cleanupSpec
> super cleanupSpec
```

This means that the setupSpec method in BasePersistenceSpec executes *before* the setupSpec method in MessageStoreSpec. Therefore, dataStore has been acquired before it's used to create the message table. Conversely, the cleanupSpec method of BasePersistenceSpec is executed *after* the one in MessageStoreSpec, so handle has not been closed when we try to use it to drop the message table.

Of course, if you have more complex requirements for execution order, there's nothing to prevent you from defining abstract methods in the base class that are referenced from the lifecycle methods and implemented in different ways in the subclasses.

Summary

In this chapter, we covered how to manage resources and fixtures with Spock's lifecycle hooks. You learned about the following:

- The four lifecycle methods setupSpec, setup, cleanup and cleanupSpec
- Using @Shared fields for objects that are not reinitialized between each feature method
- Structuring specifications in inheritance hierarchies and what that means for the execution order of the lifecycle methods

---

Exercise: Handling Time Zones

Write a feature method that ensures the postedAt timestamp on a message is correct if stored in the database in one time zone and retrieved in another.

CHAPTER 5

Interaction Testing

Testing how the code-under-test deals with collaborators by using mock and stub test doubles is called *interaction testing*. This is one of the most misunderstood and abused techniques in automated testing. Inappropriate use of mocks and stubs can tightly couple your test code to the implementation details, causing brittle tests and making refactoring difficult because changes in *how* a unit works can break tests, even though the behavior is still correct. At the same time, mocks and stubs can enable a modular design that uses Inversion of Control (IoC) to define the relationships between units resulting in loosely coupled code that cooperates through well-defined interfaces.

Mocks and Stubs

The terms "mock" and "stub" are used inconsistently in discussions of testing. They are both forms of *test double*—a stand-in for a real code unit that is a collaborator of the unit under test. "Collaborator" simply means some other object whose methods are invoked by the unit under test. In Spock, and in this book, the terms are used as follows:

Mock

> A test double that tracks when its methods are called and the parameters that are passed to them. Tests can then verify that calls were made as expected.

Stub

> A test double whose methods will return a predetermined response or take a predetermined action such as throwing an exception. Stubs do not track the calls made to them but can use sequences of predetermined responses or actions to behave differently when their methods are called multiple times.

In this chapter, we look at Spock's support for mocks and stubs along with how, and crucially, *when* to use each type. We look at the differences between mocks and stubs, how they are defined, and how we can attach behavior to them. Most important, we discuss how to prevent the kind of tight coupling that can make overuse of mocks so painful.

We can now persist the User and Message classes of the Squawker application, but methods on User such as follow(User), getFollowing(), getPosts(), and time line() are not yet reading from the database. The DataStore DAO will act like a factory for user instances, so we'll extend the User class with a PersistentUser that is accessible only to the factory methods. Internally, PersistentUser has an instance of the DataStore DAO that it can use to perform further queries or updates.

When testing PersistentUser, we don't want to use the real DAO; its methods have already been tested against the database independently. We don't want the overhead of managing database connections, tidying up tables, and so on. What we're interested in is "does the PersistentUser method use the DAO correctly?" We need to *isolate* the PersistentUser and test its interactions with its collaborators. To do that, we can *mock* the DAO.

Asserting that a Method Is Called

Let's begin with a simple case: testing that when a user follows another user, the relationship is persisted via the DAO. In practical terms, we want to ensure that the fol low method of the DataStore is called and is passed the correct parameters:

```
def dataStore = Mock(DataStore) ❶
@Subject user = new PersistentUser(dataStore, "spock", now()) ❷

def "following another user is persisted"() {
  given:
  def other = new User("kirk")

  when:
  user.follow(other) ❸

  then:
  1 * dataStore.follow(user, other) ❹
}
```

In this example, several interesting things are happening, and a couple of new bits of syntax are introduced:

❶ We create a *mock* DataStore by using Spock's Mock(Class) factory method.

❷ We create a PersistentUser instance that is the test subject.

❸ The when: block calls the `follow` method of the test subject.

❹ The then: block asserts that the `follow` method of `DataStore` is called once with the two users as parameters.

Mock and Stub Type Inference

You can omit the parameter to the `Mock` or `Stub` factory methods if Spock can infer the type from the lefthand side of the declaration.

In this example, we could equally declare the mock by using:

```
DataStore dataStore = Mock()
```

Most often, this comes down to a matter of preference, although IDEs that do not understand Spock's type inference might cope better when the type is declared on the lefthand side.

The then: block contains what at first sight looks like a curious expression—a method call result multiplied by 1! In fact, this is an example of Spock's highly expressive syntax for asserting the cardinality of calls to a mocked method.

Reading the statement from left to right, it states "assert that exactly 1 call is made to the `dataStore.follow` method, passing `user` and `other` as parameters."

Before the behavior is implemented, the feature method fails and we get the following report when the specification runs:

```
Too few invocations for:

1 * dataStore.follow(user, other)   (0 invocations)
```

The Position of Mock Verifications

One of the strengths of Spock's mock syntax is that the verification of method invocations appears in the then: block *after* the action occurs. The resulting specifications read very well as the *result* of the action—the mocked method being invoked—appears in the same place as any other assertion would.

Most Java-based mock libraries require that the *expected* method invocations are set up beforehand and then a verification method of some kind is called after the action. For example, our specification rewritten using JMock would look like this:

```
@Test
public void followingAnotherUserIsPersisted() {
    final User other = new User("kirk");

    context.checking(new Expectations() {
        {
```

```
        oneOf(dataStore).follow(user, other);
      }
    });

    user.follow(other);

    context.assertIsSatisfied();
  }
```

Specifying Invocation Cardinality

Now you know how to expect a single call to a mocked method, but what happens if a method is called too many times? In the preceding example, the expectation was that a *single* call is made to the mocked method. We saw the report generated when the mocked method was *not* called at all. Let's look at another example in which we want to ensure that the mocked method is not called too many times.

The User.getFollowing() method fetches a list of other users whom a user follows. Now that we're persisting following status to the database, this method needs to perform a query to get the list we want. However, if the method is called multiple times, it makes sense that it doesn't *keep on* querying the database. The base User class already maintains a list of followed users so PersistentUser can simply override the method and use the superclass implementation as a result cache. We can test it like this:

```
def "the following list is read from the database and cached"() {
  given:
  def otherUsers = ["kirk", "bones", "scotty"].collect {
    new User(it, now())
  }

  when: "the list of followed users is requested multiple times"
  def result1 = user.following
  def result2 = user.following

  then: "the database is queried only once"
  1 * dataStore.findFollowing(user) >> otherUsers

  and: "both calls return consistent results"
  result1 == otherUsers as Set
  result2 == result1
}
```

Here, we're asserting that although User.getFollowing() is called twice, the database is queried only once. The feature method also checks that both calls return the same results. If we implement PersistentUser.getFollowing() in a naïve way so that it simply queries the database on every call, the specification will fail and we'll get this report:

```
Too many invocations for:

1 * dataStore.findFollowing(user) >> otherUsers   (2 invocations)

Matching invocations (ordered by last occurrence):

2 * dataStore.findFollowing(@spock)   <-- this triggered the error
```

Declaring the Return Value from a Mocked Method

Notice that the feature method in this example uses the right-shift operator >> to configure the return value of the `dataStore.findFollowing(user)` call. In this case,
regardless of how many times the mocked method is called, it will always return the
same value. Later, we'll see how to define more complex behavior for returning data
from mocks.

If no return value is specified in this way and the method is not void, a default *"zero
value"* is returned. The exact value is determined by the return type—`false` for
Boolean methods, *zero* for numeric primitives, and `null` for object types.

Parameter Predicates

So far, we've seen literal parameters used on mock method calls. When Spock
matches a call to the `dataStore.follow(user, other)` in our first example, it will
use the `equals` implementation of the actual parameter with the expected parameter
to determine if the call matches the expectation. Sometimes, you don't have access to
the expected parameter object (if it's constructed within the code being tested, for
example) or want to be less strict about the parameters. There are a couple of ways to
do this. The first is to use a closure that makes an assertion about the parameter.

Let's now implement a persistent version of `User.post(String)`. Internally, this constructs a `Message` object and stores it via `DataStore.insert(Message)`. Because the
message is constructed inside the `post` method, the specification does not have access
to it.

We can use the `dataStore` mock to test that the message is inserted:

```
def "posting a message inserts it to the database"() {
  given:
  def messageText = "Fascinating!"

  when:
  user.post(messageText, now())

  then:
  1 * dataStore.insert({ it.text == messageText })
}
```

The closure parameter predicate used in the then: block asserts that the actual value passed has a property called text with a value equal to the expected message text.

If the implementation of the post method sets the text incorrectly, we'll get a report like this:

```
Too few invocations for:

1 * dataStore.insert({ it.text == messageText })   (0 invocations)

Unmatched invocations (ordered by similarity):

1 * dataStore.insert(squawker.Message@237e142b)
```

The insert method of the mock *was* called but with an argument that did not pass the closure test.

Note that we're just seeing the toString output of the Message object in the "unmatched invocations" section of the report there. A better toString implementation would improve the quality of the error message, but there is no detailed breakdown of the argument mismatch the way there is with a Boolean expression.

Disallowing Unexpected Calls or "Strict Mocking"

Spock mocks are *lenient*, meaning that they allow calls that were not explicitly expected. As mentioned in the previous section, unexpected calls to nonvoid methods return a *"zero value."* Lenient mocking has the important advantage that it allows you to concentrate on the interactions that are the subject of the test while ignoring any that might be incidental. However, sometimes you need to ensure that a call is *not* made, and Spock allows you to do that by simply declaring the cardinality as *zero*.

Recall that messages in Squawker may not be longer than 140 characters. If a user attempts to post a longer message it should throw an exception *and* no attempt should be made to write the value to the database.

```
def "a message that is too long is not written to the database"() {
    given: "some message text that exceeds the maximum allowed length"
    def messageText = """On my planet, 'to rest' is to rest, to cease using
                        energy. To me it is quite illogical to run up and down
                        on green grass using energy instead of saving it."""

    expect:
    messageText.length() > Message.MAX_TEXT_LENGTH

    when: "a user attempts to post the message"
    user.post(messageText, now())

    then: "an exception is thrown"
    thrown(IllegalArgumentException)
```

```
      and: "no attempt is made to write the message to the database"
      0 * dataStore.insert(_)
    }
```

If the length of the message is ignored and the database insert is attempted anyway, the feature method will fail and issue the following report:

```
Too many invocations for:

0 * dataStore.insert(_)   (1 invocation)

Matching invocations (ordered by last occurrence):

1 * dataStore.insert(squawker.Message@1dd64fb5)   <-- this triggered the error
```

Looser Matching with Wildcard Parameters

Notice the underscore character used as the parameter predicate to the mock method. 0 is Spock's wildcard variable, which you can use in a number of ways. When you use it as a parameter predicate like this, it means *"any single value."*

You can mix the use of wildcards with other parameter predicates in the same call. You can also cast the wildcard using _ as <class> to enforce the type of the parameter without enforcing the particular value.

A special syntax is available for matching *any number of* parameters. As an example, let's create a feature method that ensures a user cannot attempt to follow himself:

```
    def "users cannot follow themselves"() {
      when:
      user.follow(user)

      then:
      thrown(IllegalArgumentException)

      and:
      0 * dataStore.follow(*_)
    }
```

The 0 parameter predicate means zero or more parameters of any type with any value.

Wildcard Shortcuts

0 is an example of a wildcard shortcut. In the previous examples, we asserted that particular methods, DataStore.post and DataStore.follow, were not called. We could go further and decide we want to ensure that *no methods at all* are called on the mock. We can use the wildcard as a method name constraint as well as a parameter predicate:

```
0 * dataStore._(_)
```

There's a problem there, though. We're only asserting that no methods *that accept a single parameter* are invoked. We could use the 0 construct again, but there's no need, because Spock gives you the option of omitting the parameters altogether when using a wildcard method name constraint:

```
0 * dataStore._
```

This means "assert there are no calls to any method on the dataStore mock."

When there are potential interactions with multiple mocked collaborators, we can use the wildcard in place of the target constraint, as well:

```
0 * _._
```

This means "assert there are no calls to any method on any mock." In fact, there's an even shorter way of writing that:

```
0 * _
```

Defining Behavior for Mocked Methods

There's an important consideration that needs to be covered with the Persisten tUser class. Instances are acquired from the DAO and are intended to be used only while the DAO is still connected to the database. After the DAO's close() method is called, the database connection will go stale and start throwing exceptions if anything tries to use it.

There's not a lot the PersistentUser class can do about such an exception, but it's a violation of how the class should be used. We can trap the exception and wrap it with an IllegalStateException to convey this.

We've seen how to return a value from a mocked method, but how can we instruct the dataStore mock to throw an exception? As well as simply using a return value with the right-shift operator, Spock allows a closure to define the behavior of the method:

```
def "an exception is thrown if the database connection is stale"() {
  when:
  user.posts

  then:
  1 * dataStore.postsBy(user) >> {
    throw new UnableToCreateStatementException(null)
  } ❶

  and:
  def e = thrown(IllegalStateException) ❷
```

```
    e.cause instanceof UnableToCreateStatementException
  }
```

❶ Here, instead of a simple return value, we're using a closure that throws an exception. Spock invokes the closure if a call is made to the mock that matches the target, method, and parameter predicates.

❷ We're asserting that if the DAO throws a particular type of exception, our method wraps it with an `IllegalStateException` and throws that.

Removing Invocation Constraints with Stubs

A stub is like a mock in that it emulates the behavior of a real object. It differs from a mock in that we don't want to verify that the stub is invoked; we want only to declare that if and when it *is* invoked, it behaves in a certain way.

Look again at the previous example. The behavior we're interested in is that the `Per sistentUser.getPosts()` method throws an `IllegalStateException`, and yet we're still asserting that precisely one call is made to the DAO. This doesn't feel right. We have other tests that prove the DAO is invoked correctly by the `getPosts()` method, so why make the assertion again? After all, if the interaction doesn't happen, the exception will never be thrown and the feature method will fail anyway.

One option is that we can replace the cardinality constraint of the mock expression with a wildcard:

```
def "an exception is thrown if the database connection is stale"() {
  when:
  user.posts

  then:
  _ * dataStore.postsBy(user) >> {
    throw new UnableToCreateStatementException(null)
  }

  and:
  def e = thrown(IllegalStateException)
  e.cause instanceof UnableToCreateStatementException
}
```

That's still not really sufficient. Really, we want to treat the `dataStore` object as a *stub*. To do that we simply need to move the behavior declaration to the `given:` block and remove the cardinality constraint:

```
def "an exception is thrown if the database connection is stale"() {
  given:
  dataStore.postsBy(user) >> {
    throw new UnableToCreateStatementException(null)
  }
```

```
when:
user.posts

then:
def e = thrown(IllegalStateException)
e.cause instanceof UnableToCreateStatementException
}
```

This reads much better. Going from top to bottom through the spec we can read the following:

- "Given any call to `dataStore.postsBy(user)` will throw an `UnableToCreateSta tementException`"
- "When we fetch a list of posts from a user"
- "An `IllegalArgumentException` is thrown that wraps the original exception"

We probably want to go slightly further here, though. We don't particularly care precisely which method is invoked or with what parameters. Wildcard parameters work exactly the same way with stubs as they do with mocks:

```
def "an exception is thrown if the database connection is stale"() {
  given:
  dataStore._ >> {
    throw new UnableToCreateStatementException(null)
  }

  when:
  user.posts

  then:
  def e = thrown(IllegalStateException)
  e.cause instanceof UnableToCreateStatementException
}
```

When Should I Use a Mock and When Should I Use a Stub?

This is a question that comes up a lot when discussing testing. The distinction between mocks and stubs as different types of test doubles seems to confuse some developers. Many seem to think that an argument can be made for always using mocks and never using stubs, or vice versa. In fact, mocks and stubs have different purposes, and which to use depends on what your test needs.

Many developers use mocks as a general-purpose test double. I frequently see tests that I would consider overly strict because they are asserting that mock interactions occur. What they are really trying to test is the way the system responds when a collaborator behaves in a certain way.

Ask yourself: what is the test attempting to prove? If the test is concerned with proving that the test subject interacts with a collaborator in a particular way, use a mock. If the fact that a collaborator behaves in a certain way exposes particular behavior in the test subject and the outcome of *that* behavior is what you are testing, use a stub.

Think of the behavior you're testing in terms of indirect inputs and outputs. If the collaborator is an *input*—that is, the fact that it returns a particular value or throws a particular exception *causes* the behavior you're testing—you probably want to use a stub. If the interaction with the collaborator is an *output*—something you need to prove occurs in order for the behavior of your code to be correct—you want a mock.

A good rule of thumb is that if you need to define the behavior of the test double— have it return a value or throw an exception—you probably want a stub. If you're defining the behavior of the test double, it seems likely that you're testing *how your code reacts to that behavior*. In other words, the test double is an *input* to your system. In turn, that probably means that you don't really need to verify that the interaction occurred, because without it, the code under test would behave differently and the test would fail. If you have other assertions that are indirectly dependent on the behavior of the test double, verifying the interaction using a mock is probably not adding anything and might just be making your test brittle.

This is just a heuristic, though. There are absolutely times when you need to assert that an interaction occurred *and* specify the behavior of that interaction.

Thinking about how the test reads can also be a good way to clarify if you should use a mock or a stub.

Spock's syntax is particularly helpful in that regard because stubbed behavior is declared as a *precondition* in the `given:` block, and mocked behavior as an *assertion* in the `then:` block. Try writing block descriptions before the test code and see if that helps.

Adding block descriptions to the example here, we might get something like the following:

```
given: "the database connection is stale"
when:  "we try to get a list of the user's posts"
then:  "an IllegalStateException is thrown"
```

Try to rearrange this so that the *"database connection is stale"* part occurs in the `then:` block. It's pretty difficult to make it read sensibly.

Mixing Mocks and Stubs

Spock's stubs and mocks are interchangeable. In fact, the same object can simultaneously behave as a stub and a mock.

Perhaps we're testing a background process that invalidates the login credentials of any user who has not updated her password in the past six months. We might want to *stub* the method in the DAO that finds users with an out-of-date password, and *mock* the method that updates their status.

Summary

In this chapter we looked at the fundamentals of how to use Spock's mocks and stubs for interaction testing. We also discussed some of the pitfalls of overly strict mock usage that can cause tests to be too tightly coupled to the details of the implementation and therefore brittle.

We'll return to some more advanced and specialized mock and stub usage later in the book, but armed with the information in this chapter, you have all you need to use Spock's mocks and stubs effectively.

CHAPTER 6

Parameterized Specifications

In "Block Taxonomy" on page 12, we briefly mentioned the `where:` block with the promise that it would be explained more fully in a later chapter. This is that chapter, and we will dive deep into the primary use of the `where:` block: parameterized testing.

Parameterized testing is executing common test logic against different data. "Data" typically means inputs or expected outputs. In Spock, the common test logic is represented as a feature method, like those we've seen already, and the data is represented by parameters defined in a `where:` block. For each set of parameters, the feature method is executed once. Thus, you can apply the same test to a variety of values, boundary conditions, or edge cases.

JUnit has a couple of mechanisms for doing parameterized testing, which we'll look at briefly and hopefully see that Spock's `where:` block offers a much simpler and more flexible way to achieve the same result.

To begin, we'll look at a simple feature method that checks a range of invalid values and ensures that they are all rejected.

We included some simple validation in the `User` class we created in Chapter 2, but if we're going to allow people to register for Squawker accounts, we should really ensure that their registration details are correct. We'll add a new `RegistrationService` class that handles the creation of new user accounts. For the moment, the only thing we need in order to create a `User` is a *username* string. We can worry about passwords and other data later. For now, we'll add a method `public User register(String username)` to the new service.

We'll disallow any of the following as a username:

- `null`
- An empty string
- Any characters other than simple alphanumerics or underscores
- An existing username (regardless of case; for example, if there's already a *"spock"* we won't allow a *"Spock"*)

Naïvely, we'll begin with the following feature methods:

```
def "a new user cannot register with a null username"() {
  when:
  service.register(null) ❶

  then:
  thrown(RegistrationException) ❷

  and:
  0 * dataStore.insert(_ as User) ❸
}

def "a new user cannot register with a blank username"() {
  when:
  service.register("")

  then:
  thrown(RegistrationException)

  and:
  0 * dataStore.insert(_ as User)
}

def "a new user cannot register with an empty username"() {
  when:
  service.register("     ")

  then:
  thrown(RegistrationException)

  and:
  0 * dataStore.insert(_ as User)
}

def "a new user cannot register with a username containing illegal characters"() {
  when:
  service.register("@&%\$+[")

  then:
  thrown(RegistrationException)
```

```
  and:
  0 * dataStore.insert(_ as User)
}

def "a new user cannot register with the same username as an existing user"() {
  given:
  dataStore.usernameInUse("spock") >> true ❹

  when:
  service.register("spock")

  then:
  thrown(RegistrationException)

  and:
  0 * dataStore.insert(_ as User)
}
```

There's an awful lot of duplication in these feature methods.

❶ Each method is attempting to register a user with a different type of invalid username, but each is making exactly the same assertions…

❷ that a RegistrationException is thrown and…

❸ that no attempt is made to insert a new user to the database via the DataStore.

❹ The only variation is when one feature method simulates a username clash using a stub of the dataStore.usernameInUse method.

With a structure like this, it's needlessly expensive to add additional cases for similar conditions. Also, if requirements change, it's necessary to make similar changes to numerous tests. Viewing the specification class as a description of behavior, it seems clear that all of these feature methods correspond to the same behavior: *"a user cannot register with an invalid username."*

The word *"invalid"* covers a variety of meanings, but the essential behavior remains the same. We need to prove that any representative example of an invalid username is rejected. It would also be nice if it were easy to add further cases as we define them or as we discover inadequacies in the current username policy and want to fix them.

Antipattern: Testing Variants by Using Loops

A bad way to solve this would be to iterate over some invalid usernames and test that each of them is rejected, as follows:

```
given:
dataStore.usernameInUse("spock") >> true

and:
def invalidUsernames = [null, "", "    ", "@&%\$+[", "spock"]

when:
invalidUsernames.each {
  try {
    service.register(it)
    assert false, "expected RegistrationException to be thrown"
  } catch (RegistrationException e) {
    // expected
  }
}

then:
0 * dataStore.insert(_ as User)
```

There are several problems here:

- The test will *fail fast* as soon as one of the values in invalidUsernames is incorrectly accepted. If we have a number of problems affecting individual cases, we'd fix one only to find the next failed, fix that, find another failure, and so on. It's not a good specification of behavior, because you can't see all of the failures (the places where our code fails to meet that specification) at once.

- We're using the mock DataStore at the end of the test to ensure that nothing has been inserted but that assertion is not tied to a specific rule—it's applied at the end after we've tried all of them. With a more complex scenario, it might not be possible to define a condition that applies across all cases like that.

- We're confusing action and assertion in our test. The primary thing being asserted is that a RegistrationException is thrown, but the validation of that happening is part of the where: block. There's no way for us to use Spock's thrown method to validate multiple exceptions thrown from the where: block, so we have no choice but to do an ugly *try/catch* with a hard failure if execution is allowed to continue past the service.register call.

Paramaterization in JUnit

JUnit provides a couple of ways of doing parameterized testing. The most commonly encountered is the `org.junit.runners.Parameterized` test runner. Let's see how our `RegistrationSpec` class would look implemented as a parameterized JUnit test:

```
@RunWith(Parameterized.class)
public class RegistrationParameterizedTest {

  @Parameters
  public static Collection<Object[]> invalidUsernames() { ❶
    Object[][] data = new Object[][] {
      {null}, {""}, {"   "}, {"@&%$+["}, {"spock"}
    };
    return Arrays.asList(data);
  }

  @Rule public final JUnitRuleMockery context = new JUnitRuleMockery() {
    {
      setImposteriser(ClassImposteriser.INSTANCE);
    }
  };

  private DataStore dataStore = context.mock(DataStore.class);
  private RegistrationService service = new RegistrationService(dataStore);
  private String username; ❷

  public RegistrationParameterizedTest(String username) { ❸
    this.username = username;
  }

  @Test(expected = RegistrationException.class)
  public void cannotRegisterWithAnInvalidUsername() {
    context.checking(new Expectations() {
      {
        allowing(dataStore).usernameInUse("spock"); will(returnValue(true));
        never(dataStore).insert(with(any(User.class)));
      }
    });

    service.register(username); ❹
  }
}
```

❶ A *public static* method annotated with `@Parameterized` provides parameters for the test. The method must return a `Collection` of object arrays. Each element in the collection represents a single set of parameters and is used to reflectively call the test's constructor. Even when there is only a single parameter for each iteration, as in this case, it must be wrapped in an array.

❷ Each parameter value is defined as a field in the test itself.

❸ The test must have a public constructor with a parameter corresponding to each element in the data returned by the @Parameters method.

❹ The parameter values are referenced from the test method.

Although it's better than writing a slew of almost identical test methods there are a number of problems with this solution:

- The test method itself and its parameters are not defined in a very cohesive way. The parameters are not bound to parameters on the test method, but on the class.

- The return type of the @Parameters method is complex. It's easy for you to make a mistake in the definition of the data returned by the @Parameters method that will cause initialization to fail. With more complex parameter sets, that kind of error can be difficult to spot.

- The parameters are at class level, not method level. This means that each test method must share the same set of parameters. If we want other tests that are logically part of this specification but require different sets of parameters, they need to be defined in a separate test class.

- When the test executes, it will output a separate entry in the test report for each iteration—which is good. However, there's no way to tie a failing iteration back to the individual set of parameters used.

Another option with JUnit is to use the @Theories runner, as shown here:

```
@RunWith(Theories.class)
public class RegistrationTheory {

    @DataPoints
    public static String[] invalidUsernames = {
        null, "", " ", "@&%$+[", "spock"
    }; ❶

    @Rule public final JUnitRuleMockery context = new JUnitRuleMockery() {
        {
            setImposteriser(ClassImposteriser.INSTANCE);
        }
    };

    private DataStore dataStore = context.mock(DataStore.class);
    private RegistrationService service = new RegistrationService(dataStore);

    @Theory
    public void cannotRegisterWithAnInvalidUsername(String username) { ❷
```

```
    context.checking(new Expectations() {
      {
        allowing(dataStore).usernameInUse("spock"); will(returnValue(true));
        never(dataStore).insert(with(any(User.class)));
      }
    });

    try {
      service.register(username);
      fail("Should have thrown RegistrationException"); ❸
    } catch (RegistrationException e) {
      // expected
    }
  }
}
```

❶ The data points for this example are in a simple array. It's possible to have multiple methods and fields annotated with @DataPoints @DataPoint, in which case the @Theories runner will execute the test for every possible combination.

❷ The test method is annotated with @Theory instead of @Test and accepts parameters that match the data points.

❸ Unfortunately the @Theory annotation does not allow for expected exceptions the way @Test does, so it's necessary to use a *try/catch* block that directly causes the test to fail if the expected exception is not thrown.

Although the @Theories runner provides a more flexible way to define data points and passes the data points directly to the test method rather than the class constructor, it has some drawbacks of its own. The biggest downside is that the test report it generates does not contain separate entries for each iteration of the test. If one iteration fails the test simply reports a failure, and it's up to the developer to determine which particular combination of data points caused the problem.

Spock's where: block

Spock provides a fantastic method for reducing duplication by running a feature method several times with a different set of parameters each time. Instead of separate methods for each similar case, you can use the where: block to define an iterable set of data points. The feature method will then execute once for every data point, as demonstrated here:

```
def "a new user cannot register with an invalid username"() {
  given:
  dataStore.usernameInUse("spock") >> true

  when:
```

```
    service.register(username) ❷

    then:
    thrown(RegistrationException)

    and:
    0 * dataStore.insert(_ as User)

    where:
    username << [null, "", "        ", "@&%\$+[", "spock"] ❶
}
```

❶ In the where: block, we use the << *left shift* operator to define a set of data points known as a *data pipe* for the username variable. Note that the variable is not defined anywhere else, it's just a name in the where: block.

❷ Parameters defined in the where: block are available in the body of the test. Here we're using the username to attempt an invalid registration.

This means that we can collapse all the previous feature methods into a single method that is executed once for every data point we provide in the where: block. A failure with one data point will not prevent the subsequent iterations from running, so all results are available after every test run.

You can use anything that implements java.lang.Iterable as a data pipe for a where: block parameter, and the feature method will run once for every element. The example here uses a simple *List* literal but @Shared or static fields work the same as methods returning *Iterable* data. Later in the book, we'll see a couple of examples of dynamically building data pipes. For this chapter, we'll stick with literals, though.

In this case, the definition of the stub behavior of dataStore done in the given: block is only necessary for one of the iterations. There's a good argument that rather than collapsing everything down to a single feature method, you should use two because the behavior is a little different and the presence of the stub could confuse someone trying to understand what the test is telling them about how the production code works.

Every iteration of the feature method is isolated from the others as well as from any other feature methods in the specification class. This means that the setup and cleanup lifecycle methods are executed before and after *each iteration*.

Spock's where: block has one huge advantage over JUnit parameterized tests in that the parameters are confined to a single feature method. Specification classes can contain multiple parameterized feature methods, each with their own unique set of parameters. You can include nonparameterized feature methods in the same class, and it will run normally. Spock makes it incredibly easy to add iteration to an existing feature method by simply adding a `where:` block and replacing regular variables or hardcoded values with the `where:` block parameters.

Separating Iteration Reporting by Using @Unroll

If one or more iterations of the previous parameterized feature method fails, we'll see a single failure in the test report. This isn't ideal, because it means that we need to use a debugger, some *println* statements, or some other mechanism to determine which iteration of the method and therefore which element in the data pipe caused the problem.

Spock has a really nice solution for this, as well. Meet the `@spock.lang.Unroll` annotation.

Annotating the feature method with `@Unroll` will cause a separate test report entry to be generated for each iteration rather than a single report entry for the entire feature method. The report output will look something like this:

Test	Duration	Result
a new user cannot register with an invalid username[0]	0.001s	passed
a new user cannot register with an invalid username[1]	0s	passed
a new user cannot register with an invalid username[2]	0.001s	passed
a new user cannot register with an invalid username[3]	0s	passed
a new user cannot register with an invalid username[4]	0.001s	passed

Adding @Unroll Descriptions

Although this is helpful, it doesn't really assist much in finding which particular set of data points caused the failure. Fortunately @Unroll has a really clever trick up its sleeve. We can give the annotation a description string with placeholders for the parameters from the `where:` block, as is done in the following:

```
@Unroll("a new user cannot register with the username '#username'")
def "a new user cannot register with an invalid username"() {
```

Now, the test report can point us directly to a failing iteration:

Test	Duration	Result
a new user cannot register with the username	0s	passed
a new user cannot register with the username ''	0.001s	passed
a new user cannot register with the username @&%$+[	0.001s	passed
a new user cannot register with the username *null*	0.001s	passed
a new user cannot register with the username *spock*	0s	passed

@Unroll Tokens in Feature Method Names

In fact, it's possible to go further and embed the expression into the feature method name itself, as shown here:

```
@Unroll
def "a new user cannot register with the username '#username'"() {
```

Although embedding the expression in the feature method name like this is powerful, it makes sense to exercise caution. If you are using multiple where: block parameters, it can make your test name very difficult to read and understand because it might be largely comprised of parameter tokens. A good approach is often to use the feature method name to describe the general case and add an @Unroll expression via the annotation to describe a specific iteration. Sometimes, though, that's overkill because the feature method name remains perfectly understandable with a token or two in it. Take each feature method individually and use whichever approach makes it read better.

Class Level @Unroll Annotations

If you have multiple parameterized feature methods in a specification class and don't need to add explicit @Unroll expressions to any of them, you can move the @Unroll annotation up to class level, and it will apply to every feature method. Token replacement still works in the feature method name when @Unroll is placed on the class.

IDE Support for the where: Block

The IntelliJ IDEA IDE can offer autocompletion support and type inference for where: block parameters throughout the feature method. In addition, it can auto-complete tokens in an @Unroll expression. As of this writing, it doesn't work for expressions in the feature method name itself, only for annotation parameters.

If you're using an IDE that isn't aware of Spock's where: block, or if you're using a data pipe for which the type of the individual elements cannot be inferred, you can still get help from your IDE. You can define formal parameters to the feature method that match the where: block parameter names—this is in fact what Spock is doing anyway via a compile-time transformation:

```
@Unroll
def "a new user cannot register with the username '#username'"(
  String username
) {
```

Multiple Data Pipes

If a feature method needs more than one parameter, it's possible to add them to the `where:` block. Let's extend our test to verify that a more specific type of exception is thrown in response to various types of errors the user can make:

```
@Unroll
def "a new user cannot register with the username '#username'"() {
  given:
  dataStore.usernameInUse("spock") >> true

  when:
  service.register(username)

  then:
  thrown(exceptionType) ❷

  and:
  0 * dataStore.insert(_ as User)

  where:
  username << [null, "", "      ", "@&%\$+[", "spock"]
  exceptionType << [
    MissingUsernameException,
    MissingUsernameException,
    InvalidCharactersInUsernameException,
    InvalidCharactersInUsernameException,
    UsernameAlreadyInUseException
  ] ❶
}
```

❶ A second parameter has been introduced to specify the exception type that should be thrown for the various types of validation errors.

❷ The new parameter is used as the parameter to the `thrown` method.

 Spock will throw an error on initialization if data pipes have different lengths or if a data pipe is empty.

Data Tables

As you can imagine from looking at the previous example, it's easy for a `where:` block to become very confusing if there are more than a couple of data pipes. Because of this problem, Spock introduced another format for declaring `where:` block parameters: the data table. A data table allows you to lay out parameters in a simple text table with the parameter names as column headers and pipes separating each column. Each row in the table corresponds to a single iteration of the test, and each column in that row is a single parameter value. It's really just some syntactic sugar for multiple data pipes, and there are no differences in the semantics of the parameters created by using a data table from those created by using data pipes. Data tables are much easier to read and maintain, though.

Here's our registration specification rewritten to use a data table:

```
@Unroll
def "a new user cannot register with the username '#username'"() {
  given:
  dataStore.usernameInUse("spock") >> true

  when:
  service.register(username)

  then:
  thrown(exceptionType)

  and:
  0 * dataStore.insert(_ as User)

  where:
  username    | exceptionType ❶
  null        | MissingUsernameException ❷
  ""          | MissingUsernameException
  "    "      | InvalidCharactersInUsernameException
  "@&%\$+["   | InvalidCharactersInUsernameException
  "spock"     | UsernameAlreadyInUseException
}
```

❶ The first row in the table defines the parameter names.

❷ Subsequent rows define parameter values for a single iteration of the feature method.

It's now much clearer what constitutes the parameters for an iteration of the feature method. It's very easy to add further cases to the table to check for additional edge cases.

 IntelliJ IDEA can automatically format Spock data tables with the Reformat Code command, so there's no need to painstakingly align the table columns yourself.

Fields and Methods as Data Providers

There's a restriction on usernames we haven't enforced yet. We're ensuring that a user cannot register with a username that is already in use, but that check is supposed to be case-insensitive.

To enforce this, we'll define a `@Shared` field holding the existing username and then use some variants of it as parameters to the feature method:

```
@Shared usedUsername = "Spock"  ❶
def dataStore = Mock(DataStore)
@Subject service = new RegistrationService(dataStore)

def setup() {
  dataStore.usernameInUse({
    usedUsername.equalsIgnoreCase(it)
  }) >> true  ❷
}

@Unroll
def "a new user cannot register with the username '#username'"() {
  when:
  service.register(username)

  then:
  thrown(exceptionType)

  and:
  0 * dataStore.insert(_ as User)

  where:
  username                   | exceptionType
  null                       | MissingUsernameException
  ""                         | MissingUsernameException
  "     "                    | InvalidCharactersInUsernameException
  "@&%\$+["                  | InvalidCharactersInUsernameException
  usedUsername               | UsernameAlreadyInUseException  ❸
  usedUsername.toLowerCase() | UsernameAlreadyInUseException  ❹
  usedUsername.toUpperCase() | UsernameAlreadyInUseException
}
```

❶ The `usedUsername` field is defined as `@Shared`.

❷ The stub interaction is configured in a `setup` method and uses a `Closure` to match a parameter that is equal to `usedUsername`, irrespective of case.

❸ The `usedUsername` field can be used as a parameter value in the data table. This is possible only because the field is `@Shared` (although a `static` field would also work).

---

❹   It's also possible to use the result of a method call in the data table.

Derived Values

As well as data pipes and data tables, `where:` blocks can include straightforward assignments. Assignments can coexist with data pipes or tables. They are evaluated once per iteration and can refer to other parameters. Assignments are particularly useful for encapsulating repetitive value conversions and formatting values for use in @Unroll expressions.

Let's revisit the idea of a user having a timeline of messages. We'll take a slightly different approach to our previous example. This time, we'll post a message and make an assertion about whether that message appears in a user's timeline based on whether the user follows the message poster. Unlike the previous examples in Chapter 2, we'll be testing the persistent API using JDBI.

```
class TimelineSpec extends BasePersistenceSpec {

  @Shared @Subject User user
  @Shared User followedUser
  @Shared User notFollowedUser

  def setupSpec() {
    user = dataStore.newUser("spock")
    followedUser = dataStore.newUser("kirk")
    notFollowedUser = dataStore.newUser("khan")

    user.follow(followedUser) ❶
  }

  def cleanup() {
    handle.execute("delete from message")
  }

  @Unroll
  def "a user only sees messages from users they follow in their timeline"() {
    given:
    def message = new Message(postedBy, "Lorem ipsum dolor sit amet")
    dataStore.insert(message) ❸

    expect:
    user.timeline().contains(message) == shouldAppearInTimeline ❹

    where:
    postedBy         | shouldAppearInTimeline ❷
    user             | true
    followedUser     | true
    notFollowedUser  | false
```

```
    }
  }
```

❶ We set up three users. One is the @Subject, whose timeline the feature method will check. One of the others is followed by the subject, and one is not.

❷ The where: block contains a data table with two columns: the user who will post a message, and a Boolean indicating whether we expect to see the message in the subject user's timeline.

❸ As part of the given: block, we create a message and store it on the database.

❹ The feature method asserts that the message does or does not appear in the subject user's timeline according to the expectation from the where: block.

You can think of the Message instance created in the given: block as another parameter to the test. We could add another column to the data table to create the message, but because we don't really care about the message text, only the posting user, it wouldn't make sense to duplicate the constructor call on every row. However, Spock allows straightforward assignments in a where: block that can refer to the parameters of the current iteration. We can use that to construct the message.

```
@Unroll
def "a user only sees messages from users they follow in their timeline"() {
  given:
  dataStore.insert(message) ❷

  expect:
  user.timeline().contains(message) == shouldAppear

  where:
  postedBy          | shouldAppear
  user              | true
  followedUser      | true
  notFollowedUser   | false

  message = new Message(postedBy, "Lorem ipsum dolor sit amet") ❶
}
```

❶ The Message instance is constructed in the where: block. Note that the first parameter to the constructor is one of the parameters from the data table.

❷ The message parameter is accessible from the body of the feature method in exactly the same way as any other where: block parameter.

Clarifying @Unroll Expressions

Another important use for assignments in `where:` blocks is creating parameters that are used *only* as tokens in an `@Unroll` annotation. As we discussed earlier, it is extremely important to strike a balance between feature method names that are readable in the code and `@Unroll` descriptions that describe behavior well in the test reports. So far, we have not added an expression to the `@Unroll` annotation in `TimelineSpec`, so the output in the test report looks like this:

Test	Duration	Result
a user only sees messages from users they follow in their timeline[0]	0.006s	passed
a user only sees messages from users they follow in their timeline[1]	0.002s	passed
a user only sees messages from users they follow in their timeline[2]	0.001s	passed

Attempting to add an `@Unroll` expression using only the parameters we need for the feature method is not particularly easy. I find this is very often the case when using Boolean values in a data table. We could settle for something like this:

```
@Unroll("a message posted by #postedBy appears in the timeline? #shouldAppear")
```

Which would give us this test report:

Test	Duration	Result
a message posted by @khan appears in the timeline? false	0.001s	passed
a message posted by @kirk appears in the timeline? true	0.001s	passed
a message posted by @spock appears in the timeline? true	0.002s	passed

Although it's something of an improvement, reports like this bother me. They don't read very naturally and their awkward grammar can be difficult to interpret. I think it's worth making an effort to output a report that reads as proper, grammatical English. There's no reason we can't assign parameters in the `where:` block that are purely used to make the `@Unroll` expression read better in the test report. Here's how to do that:

```
@Unroll("a message posted by #postedBy #behavior in #whose timeline") ❸
def "a user only sees messages from users they follow in their timeline"() {
  given:
  dataStore.insert(message)

  expect:
  user.timeline().contains(message) == shouldAppearInTimeline

  where:
  postedBy        | shouldAppearInTimeline
  user            | true
```

```
        followedUser    | true
        notFollowedUser | false

        message = new Message(postedBy, "Lorem ipsum dolor sit amet")
        behavior = shouldAppearInTimeline ? "appears" : "does not appear" ❶
        whose = postedBy == user ? "their own" : "$user's" ❷
    }
```

❶ The Boolean value is translated into a phrase that describes the behavior it represents.

❷ The ownership of the *timeline* is described differently when testing whether the user sees their *own* message. Not doing this would leave us with "a message pos ted by @spock appears in @spock's timeline" in the report, which sounds slightly odd.

❸ The @Unroll expression uses the new behavior and whose parameters.

The report now reads very nicely:

Test	Duration	Result
a message posted by @khan does not appear in @spock's timeline	0.001s	passed
a message posted by @kirk appears in @spock's timeline	0.002s	passed
a message posted by @spock appears in their own timeline	0.003s	passed

It's wise in cases like this to keep the @Unroll expression separate from the feature method name. To anyone browsing the code, the method name should explain the general terms of the behavior being tested. If the @Unroll expression in this case were inlined into the method name, it would be difficult to make sense of without the actual test report to use as a reference.

Summary

In this chapter, you learned how to use Spock's where: block to reduce duplication in test code by iteratively running the same feature method with different sets of parameters. The where: block makes it very easy to test edge cases and boundary conditions by making generalized assertions and proving them against a variety of data.

We covered the use of data pipes to iterate feature methods against an Iterable data provider that can be anything from a *List* literal to a @Shared field or a helper method. You also saw how data tables can clarify multiparameter features.

With an emphasis always on generating good diagnostics in the case of test failures, we looked at the @Unroll annotation. You saw how and where you can apply it and how to use the parameters from the `where:` block to generate meaningful names for individual feature method iterations.

At this point, we've covered all the basics of Spock. You have the tools to write effective and expressive specifications for your code. Now it's time to go further and look at how you can creatively use Spock and the Groovy language it's built on to tackle more advanced scenarios.

PART II

Advanced Spock

Part I provided you with a good grasp of how to write a Spock specification. Now we'll move on to some more advanced topics. How do you design and write *good* specifications? How do you get the most out of the Groovy language that underlies Spock? How do you use the features of Spock in some less obvious ways?

CHAPTER 7

Idiomatic Spock

So far, we've looked at the mechanics of *how* to write specifications with Spock as well as all the core functionality. If you've read this far and followed along with the examples, you basically know how to write specifications.

However, it's easy to take Spock and write very verbose, Java-like, JUnit-like specifications that don't really get the best out of what Spock or Groovy have to offer. There's more to Spock than just the *given, when, then* structure and implicit assertions.

In this chapter, I want to explore a range of smaller topics that serve as tips on writing idiomatic Spock specifications. By "idiomatic," I mean that test code seamlessly uses the features and grammar of Spock and Groovy.

Let's begin at the highest level by looking at how to structure a suite of specification classes.

Organizing Tests

Many IDEs and frameworks will automatically generate stub test classes for you. For example, IntelliJ IDEA can generate a skeleton Spock specification based on a class. It can even generate a feature method for each public method in the class.

Perhaps because such tools encourage them down this path, many developers seem to become stuck in a rut in which each production class has a one-to-one correspondence with a test class. This doesn't need to be the case.

It's a perfectly acceptable way to begin, but there are many valid reasons why strictly maintaining a one-to-one relationship between production classes and text classes is a bad idea.

Refactoring can (and should) change the boundaries of production classes. For example, moving functionality from one class to another where it fits more appropriately. Does that mean the test classes should be changed to follow the new boundaries? Isn't that just creating unnecessary rework?

Tests can be usefully organized around behavior rather than units of code. Each test class can deal with a single behavioral aspect of the system that might cut across multiple units of code. When organized that way, refactoring doesn't necessarily require extensive busywork maintaining tests.

Common setup might apply to some feature methods and not others. Grouping tests into a single class without allowing for this can lead to the antipattern known as *The Cuckoo* (discussed next).

The Cuckoo Antipattern

The Cuckoo is a feature method that sits in the same specification class as others but doesn't really belong there.

Perhaps it's testing a different unit or behavior. Perhaps it's ignoring the shared setup used by the other feature methods, which can be very misleading for someone trying to understand the intent of the test. Worst of all, perhaps it's actively undoing some of the shared setup because it requires different preconditions to all the other feature methods.

The Cuckoo is often a result of a misguided assumption that all tests for an individual unit of code belong in a single test class.

This is not to say it's *never* appropriate to have a one-to-one relationship between test and production classes, simply that it shouldn't be something to which you are beholden. By all means, start your tests organized in that way. After you begin to feel that adding further tests to the same class is like trying to bash square pegs into a round hole, create a new test class.

When you're implementing a new feature of the system, consider adding new specification classes organized around the behaviors required to implement that feature rather than tacking new feature methods on to existing specification classes. That's not to say it's *always* wrong to add new feature methods to an existing specification. But you should at least consider the alternatives.

The "Test-per-Method" Antipattern

Although a one-to-one relationship between test and production classes is a reasonable starting point, a one-to-one relationship between test and production methods is almost always a bad idea. Even the simplest method is likely to have multiple paths through its code. There are pathological cases to cover—invalid inputs or system states. Trying to pack coverage for all of those aspects into a single feature method is either going to result in a violation of the *single responsibility principle* or missing coverage.

The single responsibility principle states that a unit of code should be concerned with one thing and one thing only. As Robert C. Martin says, "A class should have only one reason to change."

When he described the idea in his article *Principles of Object-Oriented Design* [pood], Robert C. Martin ("Uncle Bob") was talking about classes and modules, but the principle can be applied at all levels of software design.

When it comes to feature methods in Spock, I consider the principle to mean that a feature method should be responsible for testing a single aspect of behavior. Not that it should be responsible for exhaustively testing a single unit of code. As we've discussed earlier, units of code and the boundaries between them can change with refactoring and are therefore a shaky foundation upon which to build.

Required behavior changes, too, but it does so in response to the intent of the project as a whole. When requirements change, tests *should* change to specify the new behavior. When code is being refactored, ideally the tests should change very little, if at all, so that they provide assurance that the refactored code works as before.

Well-Factored Specifications

> Programs must be written for people to read, and only incidentally for machines to execute.
>
> —Abelson and Sussman, *Structure and Interpretation of Computer Programs*

One of the *most important* features of test code is its readability. This principle is about more than just failure diagnostics. New programmers joining your team, colleagues reviewing your code, even yourself six months from now, when you've forgotten the details of what you are implementing, all benefit from being able to read tests to understand the desired behavior of the system. Clear, concise, and descriptive test code helps immeasurably.

Feature methods can become very difficult to understand if they exhibit any of the following:

- They contain line upon line of complex setup establishing multiple preconditions.
- They use complex code to retrieve the values against which assertions are made.
- They perform multiple actions in order to exercise the behavior being specified.

- They need to walk through a number of steps to get the system to the point at which the behavior can be tested (this is common with end-to-end tests).

Remember that test code is still just code. We typically approach breaking down complexity in production code by refactoring long methods into multiple shorter ones. If you've read *Clean Code* by Robert C. Martin [cleancode], you will be very familiar with this technique and his mantra of "extract till you drop"; that is, keep breaking methods down into multiple smaller and simpler methods until each is so simple it's trivial to understand.

If the methods you extract are well-named, the resulting program reads as a layered description of the behavior. The higher-level methods deal in abstracts, calling lower-level methods that deal in details. It's possible to get a clear understanding of *what* the program does by just reading the higher-level methods. The lower-level methods deal with the *how*.

It's possible to break down Spock feature methods in the same way.

Sharing Helper Methods

Sometimes, you might find that helper methods can be useful across more than one specification class. When working with Spock, you have a number of options for sharing helper methods between classes.

Let's reconsider some of the testing we had around the user's message timeline. Our initial attempt at a specification looked like this:

```
@Subject user = new User("khan")
def followedUser = new User("kirk")
def otherUser = new User("spock")

def setup() {
  handle = dbi.open()

  userStore = handle.attach(UserStore)
  userStore.createUserTable()

  messageStore = handle.attach(MessageStore)
  messageStore.createMessageTable()

  followingStore = handle.attach(FollowingStore)
  followingStore.createFollowingTable()

  [user, followedUser, otherUser].each {
    userStore.insert(it.username)
  }
  followingStore.follow(user, followedUser)

  def now = now()
```

```
      messageStore.insert(
        otherUser,
        "His pattern indicates two-dimensional thinking.",
        now.minus(6, MINUTES))
      messageStore.insert(
        user,
        "@kirk You're still alive, my old friend?",
        now.minus(5, MINUTES))
      messageStore.insert(
        followedUser,
        "@khan KHAAANNNN!",
        now.minus(4, MINUTES))
      messageStore.insert(
        followedUser,
        "@scotty I need warp speed in three minutes or we're all dead!",
        now.minus(3, MINUTES))
      messageStore.insert(
        otherUser, "@bones I'm sorry, Doctor, I have no time to explain this.",
        now.minus(2, MINUTES))
      messageStore.insert(
        user,
        "It is very cold in space!",
        now.minus(1, MINUTES))
    }

    def "a user's timeline contains posts from themselves and followed users"() {
      expect:
      with(messageStore.timeline(user)) {
        size() == 4
        !postedBy.any {
          it == otherUser
        }
      }
    }

    def "a user's timeline is ordered most recent first"() {
      expect:
      with(messageStore.timeline(user)) {
        postedAt == postedAt.sort().reverse()
      }
    }
```

We're setting up three users and a number of messages posted by different users at different times. The code creating the messages is very repetitive and long-winded. One feature method ensures that only the messages from followed users appear. The other ensures that messages appear in the correct order. Because of the tedious nature of creating the messages, we've reused the same data in each feature method, but in fact the first feature method is concerned only with the user that posted the message, and the second is concerned only with the times at which the messages were posted. Because creating messages is awkward, we've inadvertently coupled the feature methods' fixtures. As the specification evolves, this might well turn out to be inconvenient.

Let's address the inconvenience of creating messages and define a couple of helper methods:

```
@Subject User user

def setup() {
  handle = dbi.open()

  userStore = handle.attach(UserStore)
  userStore.createUserTable()

  messageStore = handle.attach(MessageStore)
  messageStore.createMessageTable()

  followingStore = handle.attach(FollowingStore)
  followingStore.createFollowingTable()

  user = userStore.insert("khan")
}

def "a user's timeline contains posts from themselves and followed users"() {
  given:
  def followedUser = newFollowedUser("kirk")
  def otherUser = newUser("spock")
  [user, followedUser, otherUser].each { poster ->
    2.times { postMessageBy(poster) }
  }

  expect:
  with(messageStore.timeline(user)) {
    size() == 4
    !postedBy.any {
      it == otherUser
    }
  }
}

def "a user's timeline is ordered most recent first"() {
  given:
  (6..1).each { minutesAgo ->
    postMessageAt(minutesAgo)
  }

  expect:
  with(messageStore.timeline(user)) {
    postedAt == postedAt.sort().reverse()
  }
}

void postMessageBy(User poster) {
  messageStore.insert(poster, "aaaa", now())
}
```

```
void postMessageAt(int minutesAgo) {
  def timestamp = now().minus(minutesAgo, MINUTES)
  messageStore.insert(user, "aaaaa", timestamp)
}

User newFollowedUser(String username) {
  def newUser = newUser(username)
  followingStore.follow(user, newUser)
  return newUser
}

User newUser(String username) {
  userStore.insert(username)
}
```

We've now defined specialized helper methods for creating a new user, creating *and following* a new user, inserting a message posted by a particular user, and posting a message at a specific time. Each feature method can then conveniently set up only the data it cares about without having to specify unnecessary detail. The feature methods are no longer coupled by shared fixtures.

Sharing Methods by Using import static

The helper methods we've defined could easily be shared with other specifications. Although we could share methods by defining an abstract base specification class and extending that, it's probably more appropriate to *mix in* the fixture-creating behavior we're defining. The most straightforward way to share methods is by defining them as static methods in a new class and then use `import static` to include them in the specification classes, as demonstrated here:

```
class Fixtures {
  static void postMessageBy(MessageStore messageStore, User poster) {
    messageStore.insert(poster, "aaaa", Instant.now())
  }

  static void postMessageAt(MessageStore messageStore,
                            User poster,
                            int minutesAgo) {
    def timestamp = Instant.now().minus(minutesAgo, ChronoUnit.MINUTES)
    messageStore.insert(poster, "aaaaa", timestamp)
  }

  static User followNewUser(UserStore userStore,
                            FollowingStore followingStore,
                            User user,
                            String username) {
    def newUser = newUser(userStore, username)
    followingStore.follow(user, newUser)
    return newUser
```

```
  }

  static User newUser(UserStore userStore, String username) {
    userStore.insert(username)
  }
}
```

Unfortunately, because static methods in classes cannot share state via properties, we are forced to pass more parameters to the fixture methods than we did when they were members of the specification class itself.

Sharing Methods with Groovy Traits

Groovy 2.3 introduced traits, allowing multiple inheritance in the style of Scala. Traits are like interfaces in that a class can implement many traits. However, like the interfaces in Java 8, they can also contain nonabstract methods. Unlike Java 8 interfaces, traits can also be stateful and have their own fields.

Traits cannot have constructors, so any fields needed in the trait will need to be provided another way. Recall that properties in Groovy—defined like fields with no visibility keyword—have implied *getter* and *setter* methods. We can define abstract *getter* methods in our trait that will automatically be implemented by the properties already declared in the specification class:

```
trait FixturesTrait {

  abstract MessageStore getMessageStore() ❶
  abstract UserStore getUserStore()

  abstract FollowingStore getFollowingStore()

  abstract User getUser()

  void postMessageBy(User poster) {
    messageStore.insert(poster, "aaaa", Instant.now())
  }

  void postMessageAt(int minutesAgo) {
    def timestamp = Instant.now().minus(minutesAgo, ChronoUnit.MINUTES)
    messageStore.insert(user, "aaaaa", timestamp)
  }

  User followNewUser(String username) {
    def newUser = newUser(username)
    followingStore.follow(user, newUser)
    return newUser
  }

  User newUser(String username) {
    userStore.insert(username)
  }
```

```
  List<Message> getTimeline() {
    messageStore.timeline(user)
  }
}
```

❶ The trait defines abstract *getter* methods for the fields it will need that are implemented in the specification class by the fields we have already seen.

One inconvenient feature of traits is that the abstract *getter* methods defined in the trait cannot be implemented with @Shared fields due to the way Spock transforms the Java bytecode. Depending on your specification classes, this may or may not be a problem. Delegates have no such restriction and do work with @Shared fields.

Because they can encapsulate state, traits are more useful than static helper methods. However, having to define abstract methods introduces quite a lot of boilerplate.

Sharing Methods with Delegation

Another option instead of using traits is to declare the fixture methods in a delegate class that the specification initializes once:

```
@Delegate FixturesDelegate fixtures ❶

def setup() {
  fixtures = new FixturesDelegate(
    messageStore,
    userStore,
    followingStore,
    user
  )
}
```

❶ The delegate is created as a property of the specification class and annotated with @Delegate.

```
@TupleConstructor
❶
class FixturesDelegate {

  final MessageStore messageStore ❷
  final UserStore userStore
  final FollowingStore followingStore
  final User user

  void postMessageBy(User poster) {
    messageStore.insert(poster, "aaaa", Instant.now())
  }

  void postMessageBy(String posterName) {
    postMessageBy(userStore.find(posterName))
```

```
      }

      void postMessageAt(int minutesAgo) {
        def timestamp = Instant.now().minus(minutesAgo, ChronoUnit.MINUTES)
        messageStore.insert(user, "aaaaa", timestamp)
      }

      User followNewUser(String username) {
        def newUser = newUser(username)
        followingStore.follow(user, newUser)
        return newUser
      }

      void followExistingUser(String username) {
        def userToFollow = userStore.find(username)
        if (!userToFollow) throw new IllegalStateException("No such user $username")
        followingStore.follow(user, userToFollow)
      }

      User newUser(String username) {
        userStore.insert(username)
      }

      // tag::get-timeline-fixture[]
      List<Message> getTimeline() {
        messageStore.timeline(user)
      }
      // end::get-timeline-fixture[]
    }
```

❶   The `@TupleConstructor` annotation will create a constructor that accepts a
    parameter initializing each property in the class. Alternatively, you can just
    declare a constructor.

❷   Properties can (and I think *should*) be declared final because nothing in the dele-
    gate class or in the specification should reassign them.

You can think of delegation as a way to import instance methods of an object in much
the same way that `import static` imports static methods. Groovy's `@Delegate` annotation intercepts any unknown method calls and redirects them to the delegate object.
Because the delegate is just a regular class with instance methods, it can share properties between its methods.

A class can declare many delegates, and if there are any conflicts between their
declared methods, the first delegate with a matching method signature is used.

The Geb test framework uses `@Delegate` to provide specification classes with convenient access to the *page* and *browser* objects.

Helper Methods and Assertions

Remember that implicit assertions are processed *only* directly in the body of a feature method. It's not a good idea to extract the entire assertion into a helper method. Instead, extract the code required to derive the expected and/or actual values used in the assertion and leave the Boolean expression in the body of the test itself.

In a couple of the examples shown earlier, we extracted a `getTimeline()` method that's used in assertions. For example:

```
timeline.size() == 2
```

The property `timeline` there references this helper method:

```
List<Message> getTimeline() {
  messageStore.timeline(user)
}
```

We could wrap the `boolean` condition in a method:

```
boolean timelineSizeIs(int expectedSize) {
  messageStore.timeline(user).size() == expectedSize
}
```

Because the helper method returns `boolean` it can be used as an assertion in a `then:` block. But we lose all of the diagnostics provided by Spock's power assert. If the size is incorrect, the test result will not include the actual size report, only that the method returned `false`.

We could create a helper method that encapsulates the assertion.

We regain diagnostic information if we explicitly use the `assert` keyword, such as this:

```
void timelineSizeIs(int expectedSize) {
  assert messageStore.timeline(user).size() == expectedSize
}
```

However, doing the assertion like this is not very flexible, because it allows us to make only one specific assertion about the timeline.

Helper Methods and Mock Interactions

Although Spock's mocks rely on a special syntax interpreted in the context of a `then:` block, it is possible to set expectations for interactions in helper methods. To do so, it's necessary to call the helper in a closure passed to the `interaction` method. Let's take a look at an example from our earlier tests for the `PersistentUser` class that we saw in Chapter 5.

```
void insertsMessageOnce(String text) {
  1 * dataStore.insert({ it.text == text }) ❶
}

def "posting a message inserts it to the database"() {
  when:
  user.post(messageText, now())

  then:
  interaction {
    insertsMessageOnce(messageText) ❷
  }

  where:
  messageText = "Fascinating!"
}
```

❶ We define a helper method that performs a mock interaction check.

❷ Calls to the method are wrapped in an `interaction` block that informs Spock it needs to parse the mock expectation syntax within the method.

Comparing "Before" and "After" Values

A common case when writing tests is to compare a value after an action takes place to the same value before the action took place. Although it's possible to hardcode values in many circumstances, comparing old and new values can assist in separating test data from test logic.

If values are unpredictable, it's not really possible to use hardcoded values. Even if values *are* predictable, if they appear arbitrary, it can be more difficult for a reader to understand the intent of the specification.

For example, perhaps we want to test that a newly posted message appears first in a user's timeline:

```
def "when new messages are posted they appear in the timeline"() {
  given:
  def followedUser = followNewUser("kirk")

  and:
  postMessageBy(followedUser)

  expect:
  timeline.size() == 1
```

```
  when:
  postMessageBy(followedUser)

  then:
  // tag::assertion-helper[]
  timeline.size() == 2
  // end::assertion-helper[]
}
```

Here we compare the size of the timeline before and after posting a second message. This proves that the timeline becomes larger, but it doesn't ensure that the newer message appears first in the list. The postedAt timestamp of each message is unpredictable.

Sure, we *could* specify a relative or absolute timestamp for each message, but it's not really necessary. We can keep things simpler by just comparing the timestamps of the first timeline message.

```
def "when new messages are posted they appear in the timeline"() {
  given:
  def followedUser = followNewUser("kirk")

  and:
  postMessageBy(followedUser)
  def oldSize = timeline.size()
  def oldTimestamp = timeline.first().postedAt

  when:
  postMessageBy(followedUser)

  then:
  timeline.size() == oldSize + 1
  timeline.first().postedAt > oldTimestamp
}
```

This specification looks very much like the typical approach we'd use in a JUnit test. The "previous" values of the size of the message list and the timestamp of the first message are stored in variables and then compared with the updated values later.

Spock provides a convenient way to apply exactly this pattern without having to declare variables.

The old method can be used in a then: block. It takes a single expression parameter and returns the value that expression had *before* the preceding when: block ran.

The old method does clarify assertions nicely, as shown here:

```
def "when new messages are posted they appear in the timeline"() {
  given:
  def followedUser = followNewUser("kirk")

  and:
```

```
    postMessageBy(followedUser)

    when:
    postMessageBy(followedUser)

    then:
    timeline.size() == old(timeline.size()) + 1
    timeline.first().postedAt > old(timeline.first().postedAt)
  }
```

Now we're no longer cluttering up the feature method with local variables, and the relationship between the old and new values in the assertion is very clear.

The old method works with any type of value. It's not limited to simple types or unit tests. It's possible to use old with Geb, for example, to get the previous content of an element in the browser window.

The only restrictions are that old can be used only in a then: block and it cannot refer to any local variable declared in or after the preceding when: block.

How Does old Work?

If you're used to Java, the behavior of old probably seems remarkably odd.

In fact, it's a fairly simple trick. At compile time, Spock replaces the call to the old method with a variable assigned earlier in the method.

The actual bytecode executed is almost identical to the previous example in which we declared our own variables for storing the previous values.

If you follow execution of a feature method with a debugger, it becomes apparent what is going on. The debugger will jump ahead to the old method and then back to the when: block.

The Grammar of Blocks

We've seen what the different blocks do, but there are no hard and fast rules enforcing exactly how they are used. Good "grammar" makes a test easier to understand for the reader and modify later when requirements change.

Let's consider how blocks in a feature method can best communicate the intent of the test.

Separation of Logic and Data with where: Blocks

A typical unit test contains both logic describing the behavior being verified and example data used to trigger the behavior. In Spock, when you want to test a range of different values for the example data, you use a `where:` block. This has a neat side effect, though. With example data declared in the `where:` block and represented in the body of the test by symbolic variable names, we have a clean separation between the behavior verification logic and the example data we use to put that logic through its paces.

The body of the test describes a *general case* and reads like a formal description of the desired behavior.

In Chapter 6, we looked at using Spock's `where:` block to repeatedly run a feature method using different parameters. However, it's also possible to use the `where:` block even in tests that aren't run iteratively.

Remember that assigning to a `where:` block parameter using = rather than << will result in a parameter that is evaluated the same way for each iteration. If there *are* no iterable parameters, straightforward assignments in the `where:` block still work. I find them useful for separating example data from the logic of the feature method.

Let's take another look at one of the tests from Chapter 3. Here, we are testing that posts appear in reverse chronological order:

```
def "a user's posts are listed most recent first"() {
  when:
  user.post("It's life, Jim", now())
  user.post("but not as we know it", now())

  then:
  user.posts*.text == ["but not as we know it", "It's life, Jim"]
}
```

In this test, we see sample data mixed with the test logic. What's worse, the sample data is repeated. It would be fairly easy to break the test by making a mistake in one of the literal strings of sample data. We can use a `where:` block to tidy this up:

```
def "a user's posts are listed most recent first"() {
  when:
  messages.each {
    user.post(it, now())
  }

  then:
  user.posts().text == messages.reverse()

  where:
  messages = ["It's life, Jim", "but not as we know it"]
}
```

Not only have we now removed the duplication, we have also separated the sample data from the test logic. It's actually clearer that we expect the messages to be listed in reverse order because we're explicitly reversing the messages list. The where: block adds example data to drive the specification, but the when: and then: blocks deal only with the general case. When the main part of the feature method is read without the where: block, it reads as a pure logical description of the behavior being specified.

You might be asking why we couldn't just set up sample data in a given: block. That's certainly possible, but in many cases the given: block is already doing things related to the test logic. If we add sample data there, we're no longer achieving the separation from logic that using the where: block affords us.

Let's revisit another example, this time from Chapter 4.

```
def "can retrieve a list of user objects"() {
  given:
  def timestamp = LocalDateTime.of(1966, 9, 8, 20, 0).toInstant(UTC)
  ["kirk", "spock"].each {
    handle.createStatement("""insert into user (username, registered)
                              values (?, ?)""")
          .bind(0, it)
          .bind(1, timestamp)
          .execute()
  }

  when:
  def users = dataStore.findAllUsers()

  then:
  with(users.toList()) {
    username == ["kirk", "spock"]
    registered.every {
      it == timestamp
    }
  }
}
```

Here, we're inserting some records in the database before testing that data read by a data access object (DAO) is correct. Again, there's some repeated sample data in the given: and then: blocks. We can remove that duplication, but the given: block also contains the logic that writes the data to the database.

If we set up the sample data there, we're compounding the detail of the sample data itself (which is orthogonal to the logic of the test) with the fact that its existence in the database drives the behavior we're testing. By using the where: block, we clearly separate our sample data from the test logic:

```
def "can retrieve a list of user objects"() {
  given:
  usernames.each { ❷
```

```
        handle.createStatement("""insert into user (username, registered)
                                 values (?, ?)""")
             .bind(0, it)
             .bind(1, timestamp) ❸
             .execute()
    }

    when:
    def users = userStore.findAllUsers()

    then:
    with(users.toList()) {
      username == usernames ❹
      registered.every {
        it == timestamp
      }
    }

    where:
    usernames = ["kirk", "spock"] ❶
    timestamp = LocalDateTime.of(1966, 9, 8, 20, 0).toInstant(UTC)
}
```

❶ We provide a list in the `where:` block, but using the = operator rather than the <<
operator so that the feature method doesn't repeat.

❷ We iterate over the list of usernames and create a record in the database for each.

❸ We use the other `where:` block parameter to assign a registration timestamp to
each user.

❹ We use the `where:` block parameters again to assert the data returned by the
DAO is correct.

Of course, assignments in the `where` block can be mixed with data pipes and data
tables. Even if a feature method is iterating over a sample data set, if there are
unchanging bits of example data, consider extracting them to the `where:` block, as
well.

Using when/then or given/expect

We've talked about composing assertions, but we should also consider where they are
placed in the feature method.

Spock has two blocks that can contain implicit assertions—`then:` and `expect:`. Their
meaning is somewhat different if we think about the "grammar" of a specification.

A `then:` block naturally appears after some kind of action, such as the following:

- *When* a user posts a message, *then* it appears at the top of their timeline.

- *When* a user follows someone, *then* that person is sent a notification.

- *When* a user tries to follow someone they already follow, *then* an exception is thrown.

However, its also possible to think of examples that don't fit so neatly into the *when/then* structure:

- *When* a user is not following anyone, *then* their timeline contains only their own messages.

- *When* a user is logged out, *then* they cannot post messages.

- *When* a message contains an at sign (@) followed by a user's name, *then* it is rendered as a link to that user's profile.

You might think that all those sound reasonable, and indeed, it is of course possible to construct feature methods with such a structure. For example:

```
def "a user who does not follow anyone sees only their own messages"() {
  when:
  def user = newUser("spock")
  3.times { postMessageBy(user) }
  def other = newUser("kirk")
  3.times { postMessageBy(other) }

  then:
  user.timeline().postedBy.every {
    it == user
  }
}
```

But think about the action or behavior being tested in each case. The when: block should contain the action being tested. Are we testing creating users and posting messages? No, we're testing the algorithm that selects messages for the timeline. The creation of users and messages is a precondition for the behavior we expect to see. The test would read better as *"given a user is not following anyone, expect that their timeline contains only their own messages,"* as demonstrated in the following:

```
def "a user who does not follow anyone sees only their own messages"() {
  given:
  def user = newUser("spock")
  3.times { postMessageBy(user) }
  def other = newUser("kirk")
  3.times { postMessageBy(other) }

  expect:
  user.timeline().postedBy.every {
    it == user
```

```
    }
  }
```

This reads better. The `given:` block contains the preconditions that establish the con-text for the test. The `expect:` block contains an assertion of the behavior we should see.

Separating Preconditions

We can go further and divide the two preconditions—the existence of the user whose timeline we'll be checking and the existence of another user whose messages we should not see—into a `given:` and an `and:` block. We can even separate the test data (the usernames) out to a `where:` block, as shown here:

```
def "a user who does not follow anyone sees only their own messages"() {
  given:
  def user = newUser(username)
  3.times { postMessageBy(user) }

  and:
  def other = newUser(otherUsername)
  3.times { postMessageBy(other) }

  expect:
  user.timeline().postedBy.every {
    it == user
  }

  where:
  username = "spock"
  otherUsername = "kirk"
}
```

This reads much better to me. Even without block labels, the intent of the test is very clear. We have two clear and straightforward preconditions: a simple assertion and some test data parameters that are neatly separate from the test logic.

Separating Preconditions from Actions

Let's look at another of the *when/then* examples: "*when* a user tries to follow someone they already follow, *then* an exception is thrown."

We can begin with a specification like this:

```
def "a user cannot follow someone they already follow"() {
  when:
  def user = userStore.insert("spock")
  def other = userStore.insert("kirk")
  followingStore.follow(user, other)
  followingStore.follow(user, other)
```

```
then:
thrown UnableToExecuteStatementException
}
```

Again, think about what the action is that we're testing. In this case, it's that trying to follow a user we're already following is an error. In the feature method as it stands, we're conflating the preconditions—two users exist and one follows the other—from the action we're testing—trying to follow a user we're already following raises an exception.

This is a fairly common antipattern that can result in a feature method for which it's difficult to identify what the test is really about.

Our feature method becomes clearer if we separate the preconditions and keep the when: block very focused on the cause of the effect we're making an assertion about:

```
def "a user cannot follow someone they already follow"() {
    given:
    def user = userStore.insert("spock")
    def other = userStore.insert("kirk")
    followingStore.follow(user, other)

    when:
    followingStore.follow(user, other)

    then:
    thrown UnableToExecuteStatementException
}
```

We can further separate the two preconditions and parameterize the test data to keep it distinct from the logic:

```
def "a user cannot follow someone they already follow"() {
    given:
    def user = userStore.insert(username)
    def other = userStore.insert(otherUsername)

    and:
    followingStore.follow(user, other)

    when:
    followingStore.follow(user, other)

    then:
    thrown UnableToExecuteStatementException

    where:
    username = "spock"
    otherUsername = "kirk"
}
```

A fairly useful rule of thumb is that declaring variables (other than a result type that needs to be verified) is typically part of a precondition rather than a when: block. Like any such heuristic, there are certainly exceptions, but it's worth considering if you find yourself with an overlong when: block.

Method Parameter Capture with Mocks

1. Chapter 5 demonstrates how to use parameter predicates on a mock or stub to effectively assert that a method is invoked with a particular parameter or parameters. Sometimes, for more complex parameters, it's nice to have more fine-grained control than this mechanism affords. To get a good diagnostic of a failure, what we really want is to "capture" the parameters sent to the method and make individual assertions about them.

To show you what I mean, let's consider a simple example. In Squawker, when a user gets a new follower, we want to send the user an email notification. Let's create a service interface that can send arbitrary messages to users:

```
public interface EmailSender {
  void send(User to, EmailMessage message);
}
```

The sendEmail method simply accepts the User to whom the email should go and a Map containing the details of the message: *subject, from address*, and so on. Then, we'll create a class that will listen for an event raised when a new follower is added:

```
public class NewFollowerNotifier {

  private EmailSender emailSender; ❶

  @Subscribe ❷
  public void onNewFollower(NewFollowerEvent event) throws Exception {
    EmailMessage message = new EmailMessage( ❸
      "admin@squawker.io",
      "You have a new follower!",
      "new-follower",
      event.getNewFollower().getUsername()
    );
    emailSender.send(event.getUser(), message); ❹
  }

  public void setEmailSender(EmailSender emailSender) {
    this.emailSender = emailSender;
  }
}
```

❶ The EmailSender is an injected dependency.

❷   The onNewFollower method subscribes to an event.

❸   The message will need a *from* address, a subject, a template name for the body, and the username of the new follower.

❹   Finally, the sendEmail method is called.

To test that the message details are passed correctly, we could simply use a map literal as the parameter predicate:

```
@Subject notifier = new NewFollowerNotifier()

def "sends email to user when someone follows them"() {
  given:
  def emailSender = Mock(EmailSender)
  notifier.emailSender = emailSender ❷

  when:
  notifier.onNewFollower(event) ❸

  then:
  1 * emailSender.send(user1, new EmailMessage(
    "admin@squawker.io",
    "You have a new follower!",
    "new-follower",
    user2.username
  )) ❹

  where:
  user1 = new User("spock")
  user2 = new User("kirk")
  event = new NewFollowerEvent(user1, user2) ❶
}
```

❶   In the where: block, we set up an event object that simply contains the two users: the user spock and his new follower kirk.

❷   We inject a mock EmailService into the notifier.

❸   We send the event to notifier. There's no need to use a real event bus here, because we're just testing how the NewFollowerNotifier interacts with the Email Sender.

❹   The then: block asserts that the sendEmail method is called using two precise parameters: the user spock and a Map of message details.

This test certainly works but feels a bit overly strict. Maybe we don't want to exactly specify the *subject*, only that there is one. Using a map literal, we can't exactly match some properties and not others.

Using a Closure as a Parameter Predicate

Recall from Chapter 5 that you can use a closure as a parameter predicate on a mock or stub. We could use a closure here to match more flexibly:

```
then:
1 * emailSender.send(user1, {
  it.from == "admin@squawker.io" &&
    it.subject ==~ /.+/ && ❶
    it.template == "new-follower" &&
    it.follower == user2.username
})
```

❶ Now we're able to use a regular expression to simply assert that the *subject* contains something.

Again, this works but is quite ugly. Notice that we have to chain all of the individual conditions together using && because the closure must return a single Boolean value rather than making a series of assertions.

Another problem is the diagnostic output when the mock interaction does not occur as expected. If our NewFollowerNotifier mixes up its messages and sends a "__Wel come to Squawker!__" email by mistake, this is what the output will look like:

```
Too few invocations for:

1 * emailSender.send(user1, {
      it.from == "admin@squawker.io" &&
        it.subject ==~ /.+/ &&
        it.template == "new-follower" &&
        it.follower == user2.username
    })   (0 invocations)

Unmatched invocations (ordered by similarity):

1 * emailSender.send(@spock, ['template':'welcome', 'follower':'spock',
'subject':'Welcome to Squawker!', 'from':'admin@squawker.io'])
```

The information we need is all there so that we can debug the problem, but it's not obvious at a glance what's wrong. Also, remember that it's the default toString behavior of a Map that's giving us enough detail to go on. If we were using a different class to pass the message details, the diagnostics would be at the mercy of its toString method.

Using Hamcrest for Parameter Predicates

Another approach would be to use a Hamcrest matcher in place of the parameter. Hamcrest provides a library of matchers as static methods that you can import with the following:

```
import static org.hamcrest.Matchers.*

then:
1 * emailSender.send(
  user1, ❶
  allOf( ❷
    hasProperty("from", equalTo("admin@squawker.io")), ❸
    hasProperty("subject"), ❹
    hasProperty("template", equalTo("new-follower")),
    hasProperty("follower", equalTo(user2.username))
  ))
```

❶ Parameter literals can be mixed with matchers. Here, the to user is a literal.

❷ The Hamcrest allOf matcher is used to compose other matchers.

❸ The hasEntry matcher is used to assert that a key-value pair exists in a Map.

❹ It's possible to mix in a less strict assertion. Here, we're ensuring a subject exists but not validating its content.

Hamcrest matchers suffer some of the same problems as using closures, though. Primarily it's not always easy to determine what's wrong if a match fails. Diagnostic information tends to depend on the quality of the toString implementation used by the actual parameter value. Even here the failure message is not particularly easy to decipher:

```
Too few invocations for:

1 * emailSender.send(
      user1,
      allOf(
        hasEntry("from", "admin@squawker.io"),
        hasKey("subject"),
        hasEntry("template", "new-follower"),
        hasEntry("follower", user2.username)
      )) (0 invocations)

Unmatched invocations (ordered by similarity):

1 * emailSender.send(@spock, ['template':'new-follower', 'follower':'spock',
'subject':'You have a new follower!', 'from':'admin@squawker.io'])
```

Parameter Capture Using a Mock Responder

What would really be nice here is a way to make individual assertions about the content of the second parameter to sendEmail in the then: block. Luckily, there is a way to do it.

Remember that by using the >> operator, we can attach a return value to a mock method call or—what we'll do here—use a closure to provide a dummy implementation called a *"responder."* Remember also that Groovy closures *close over* a scope that includes variables local to the declaration of the closure. We can put these two things together to capture the sendMessage parameter like this:

```
def "sends email to user when someone follows them"() {
  given:
  def emailSender = Mock(EmailSender)
  notifier.emailSender = emailSender

  and:
  def message ❶

  when:
  notifier.onNewFollower(event)

  then:
  1 * emailSender.send(user1, _) >> { ❷
    message = it[1] ❸
  }

  and: ❹
  message.from == "admin@squawker.io"
  message.subject == "You have a new follower!"
  message.template == "new-follower"
  message.follower == user2.username

  where:
  user1 = new User("spock")
  user2 = new User("kirk")
  event = new NewFollowerEvent(user1, user2)
}
```

❶ We create a local variable message that will be used to capture the mock call parameter.

❷ We no longer apply a predicate to the second parameter because we'll be handling that separately. The _ wildcard means any parameter can be passed in that position. Then, we use the >> operator to assign a closure as a dummy implementation for the method.

❸ The closure's implicit parameter `it` is an array of all the parameters passed to the method. So, index *1* is the second parameter to `sendEmail`. We assign that to the `message` variable we declared earlier.

❹ After we've validated that the mock was invoked, we can make assertions directly on the captured parameter.

The code feels a lot less cluttered than when we were trying to cram four Boolean conditions into an parameter predicate. Also, a failing test now gives us much better output, as is illustrated here:

```
message.subject == "You have a new follower!"
|       |       |
|       |       false
|       |       18 differences (25% similarity)
|       |       (Welcom-)e (to---) (Squa-)w(k)er!
|       |       (You hav)e (a new) (follo)w(-)er!
|       Welcome to Squawker!
[template:welcome, follower:spock, subject:Welcome to Squawker!,
from:admin@squawker.io]
```

However, notice that we had to declare the `message` variable in the `given:` block. That's because Spock will do an early evaluation on the mock interaction, and the variable won't actually be in the closure's scope unless it was declared before the `when:` block. That might seem confusing and counterintuitive but remember that the behavior specified in the interaction needs to actually *happen* in the `when:` block.

I don't think the separation between the declaration of the `message` variable and the mock interaction is very tidy. It feels like we need to add a comment to explain why the `message` variable is declared there.

> The proper use of comments is to compensate for our failure to express ourself in code.
>
> —Robert C. "Uncle Bob" Martin, *Clean Code: A Handbook of Agile Software Craftsmanship [cleancode]*

The ability to declare mock interactions in a `then:` block is not a requirement; it's a convenience that Spock provides so that tests can be written in a more readable order. It's acceptable to have the interaction defined in the `given:` block, as we would do with a stub:

```
given:
def message
notifier.emailSender = Mock(EmailSender) { ❶
  1 * send(user1, _) >> { message = it[1] } ❷
}

when:
```

```
notifier.onNewFollower(event)

then:
message.from == "admin@squawker.io"
message.subject == "You have a new follower!"
message.template == "new-follower"
message.follower == user2.username
```

❶ The Mock and Stub methods can accept a closure as a second parameter that is used to declare interactions.

❷ We're declaring exactly the same interaction as before, but notice the mock variable is no longer required as the interaction is declared in the closure passed to the Mock(Class, Closure) method that creates the mock.

We've removed the confusing separation between the declaration of message and the interaction that initializes it. Generally, I much prefer declaring mock interactions in a then: block, but I think the tradeoff in clarity is worth it here. We could also use a stub rather than a mock because message will be assigned only if the sendEmail method is called. In that case, a failure to call the method at all would be detected by NullPointerException being thrown when we try to read any of the properties of message. As ever, consider what will make for a clearer diagnostic in the event of a failure. I don't think a NullPointerException does a particularly good job of pointing out the source of the error, so the mock should stay.

One small modification that might clarify things is to use explicit parameters in the closure used as the mock responder, as we've done here:

```
given:
def message
notifier.emailSender = Mock(EmailSender) {
  1 * send(user1, _) >> { _, msg -> message = msg }  ❶
}
```

❶ Instead of using the implied parameter it, we've declared two explicit parameters. Because we're not interested in the first, we can use Spock's 0 wildcard to ignore it.

If the uninitialized variable bothers you, it's possible to capture the values by using a container type instead. One obvious option is to use a map:

```
given:
def message = [:]
notifier.emailSender = Mock(EmailSender) {
  1 * send(user1, _) >> { _, EmailMessage msg -> message.putAll(msg.properties) }
}
```

It's easy to imagine using a list to collect parameters from multiple calls to a mocked method in a very similar way.

Java provides a class `AtomicReference` that's ideal for this case. It's simply a wrapper around any type. The underlying value can be read and written in a concurrency-safe manner. For typical parameter capture, we don't need the thread-safety features, but `AtomicReference` provides a neat container type that avoids the dangling uninitialized variable.

```
given:
def message = new AtomicReference<EmailMessage>()
notifier.emailSender = Mock(EmailSender) {
  1 * send(user1, _) >> { _, EmailMessage msg -> message.set(msg) }
}
```

Parameter capture is great if you need to verify multiple facets of a complex parameter passed to a collaborator. As with many techniques, I think it should be used sparingly. In many cases, there's probably a better way to break up the test coverage so that parameter capture is not necessary, but for cases like the example here, it's a useful technique to know.

Can't I Just Make Assertions in the Behavior Closure?

Yes, you can. And they will even fail and throw `AssertionError`. However, Spock's mocking framework catches errors thrown inside a result generator closure so that the assertion failure will not cause the feature method to fail.

Good thing we always ensure our tests fail, right?

Also, I really don't like placing raw `assert` keywords in Spock specifications. It doesn't feel like an idiomatic way to express the intent of the test.

We'll see in "Asynchronous Parameter Capture" on page 146 how method parameter capture can also be useful when dealing with interactions that happen asynchronously.

@Stepwise Specifications

As we've seen, a typical Spock specification should ideally have isolated feature methods that do not affect one another. An instance of the `Specification` class is created for each feature method to help avoid modifications to fields leaking between features. Theoretically, feature methods also can be run in any order. When using an IDE, it's possible to isolate a single feature method and run it without the others.

However, on very rare occasions it's actually desirable to create a specification whose feature methods are dependent on one another and need to run in order, and whose changes to shared state are maintained.

One typical example of when you might want to do this is to mitigate slow-running browser-based tests, particularly if a user needs to go through a long process in order to get to the stage being tested. A checkout workflow in an online store might be a good example of where you might want to optimize test-running time by verifying several things at once during a single pass through the checkout.

Another is to test some step-by-step process in which each step is naturally interdependent, but the entire process is too complex to fit neatly into a single feature method.

Spock accommodates this with the `@Stepwise` annotation. A `Specification` class annotated with `@Stepwise` will run each of its feature methods in source order. If any feature method fails, the subsequent ones are skipped on the assumption that the initial conditions they rely upon are likely incorrect.

How to Use @Stepwise

Let's look at a simple example based on the timeline specifications we've been using. Instead of setting everything up anew for each feature method, we can test several cases with the same fixtures using `@Stepwise`, as shown here:

```
@Stepwise
class TimelineSpec extends Specification {

  @Shared dbi = new DBI("jdbc:h2:mem:test")

  ❶
  @Shared Handle handle
  @Shared UserStore userStore
  @Shared MessageStore messageStore
  @Shared FollowingStore followingStore
  @Shared User user

  def setupSpec() {
    dbi.registerArgumentFactory(new TimeTypesArgumentFactory())
    dbi.registerMapper(new TimeTypesMapperFactory())

    handle = dbi.open()

    userStore = handle.attach(UserStore)
    userStore.createUserTable()

    messageStore = handle.attach(MessageStore)
    messageStore.createMessageTable()

    followingStore = handle.attach(FollowingStore)
    followingStore.createFollowingTable()

    user = userStore.insert("khan")
  }
```

```
def cleanupSpec() { ❷
  dbi.withHandle { handle ->
    handle.execute("drop table user if exists")
    handle.execute("drop table message if exists")
    handle.execute("drop table following if exists")
  }
}

@Delegate FixturesDelegate fixtures ❸

def setup() {
  fixtures = new FixturesDelegate(
    messageStore,
    userStore,
    followingStore,
    user
  )
}

def followedUsername = "kirk"
def otherUsername = "spock"

def "a user's timeline contains posts from themselves and followed users"() {
  given:
  def followedUser = followNewUser(followedUsername)
  def otherUser = newUser(otherUsername)
  [user, followedUser, otherUser].each { poster ->
    2.times { postMessageBy(poster) }
  }

  expect:
  timeline.size() == 4
  !timeline.postedBy.username.contains(otherUsername)
}

def "when new messages are posted they appear in the timeline"() {
  when:
  postMessageBy(followedUsername) ❹

  then:
  timeline.size() == 5
  timeline.first().postedAt > old(timeline.first().postedAt)
}

def "after following a user their posts appear in the timeline"() {
  expect:
  !messageStore.postsBy(otherUsername).empty

  when:
  followExistingUser(otherUsername)
```

```
    then:
    timeline.size() > old(timeline.size())
    timeline.postedBy.username.contains(otherUsername)
  }
}
```

❶ Because we'll no longer be destroying data between features, any data we need must set up only once using setupSpec.

❷ Similarly, we'll now delete data after all of the feature methods have completed by using cleanupSpec rather than after each one using cleanup.

❸ The @Delegate annotation cannot be used on @Shared fields, so the FixtureDelegate still needs to be created in setup.

❹ Data created in a previous feature method, such as the user posting a message here, can be relied on to be present in subsequent ones.

Reading the feature methods carefully, you should be able to see that the second and third rely on data created in the first. The first feature method sets up two additional users and has them post some messages. The second feature tests that if one of those users posts more messages, they appear in the timeline. The third tests that if we follow a user who has already posted messages, those messages will begin appearing in the timeline.

 Remember that setup and cleanup still run before and after each feature method in a @Stepwise specification. If a cleanup method (or @Autocleanup annotated field) has destructive side effects, it might break subsequent feature methods.

Disadvantages of @Stepwise

Now you know *how* to use @Stepwise; the question is whether you *should*.

Deciding to use @Stepwise is always a compromise. You should not do it without recognizing what is lost by having feature methods dependent on one another.

First, it's an extreme case of a test with too many assertions. We looked at the problem of assertions that fail-fast earlier in this chapter. A single feature method that contains multiple assertion statements can result in you playing whack-a-mole with failures. With a @Stepwise specification, the problem is even worse. Not only will multiple assertions in a single feature method fail-fast, but the feature methods in the specification will fail-fast, too.

It can be frustrating to deal with failures in a @Stepwise specification because each must be dealt with in turn, and fixing one might just move you on to the next error rather than getting you to a passing suite of tests.

This is particularly true for the case in which @Stepwise is used to mitigate a slow-running sequence of steps that would otherwise need to be repeated in each feature method. The time spent correcting successive failures and rerunning can become more of a burden than any inherent slowness of more isolated tests.

Another problem is that as systems evolve, tests that are coupled to one another are likely to be more difficult to change. A change to an earlier feature method will have a cascade effect on the subsequent ones in a @Stepwise specification, and it's much more likely you will need to make changes to downstream tests that are unrelated to the behavior on which you're actually trying to work.

The bottom line is that I don't think you should *never* use @Stepwise, but certainly it should be used only with justification and not as a matter of course.

Conditional Specifications

Like JUnit, Spock provides an @Ignore annotation that will cause the test runner to skip a particular feature method or specification class. There is also an @IgnoreRest that allows you to isolate a single feature method or specification class that should be executed while the rest of the suite is skipped.

The intention is that these annotations should be used only transiently to isolate a particular bit of functionality you're working on. It's definitely a bad sign if code with @Ignore or @IgnoreRest annotations ends up in source control.

Marking Pending Features

The @PendingFeature annotation is a variant of @Ignore that was added in Spock 1.1. Unlike with @Ignore, feature methods annotated with @PendingFeature *are* executed with the expectation that they will fail. If a feature method annotated with @Pending Feature actually passes, *that* is reported as an error.

This can be very useful when developing new functionality because, as we discussed earlier, tests should pass only for the right reason. If a feature method passes before it "should"—that is, before the functionality that ought to make it pass has been implemented—this means that the test is not correctly isolating the behavior it is validating. If a subsequent change breaks the correct behavior, the test might not detect it.

Selectively Executing Tests

Sometimes, a test is valid only under certain conditions. There might be a variant behavior on different operating systems, Java versions, or browsers, for example.

Spock provides two annotations that are useful in such cases: `@IgnoreIf` and `@Requires`. `@IgnoreIf` evaluates a condition and will skip the annotated feature method or specification class if the condition is true. `@Requires` is exactly the opposite: the annotated feature method or class will run only if the condition is true.

The conditions in these annotations are closures whose delegates have some special properties that are typically useful in determining whether a test should be evaluated:

`javaVersion`
 A floating-point value representing the Java version, for example `1.8`.

`os`
 The current operating system with subproperties for `name`, `family`, and `version`.

`env`
 A `Map` of the current environment variables.

`properties`
 The JVM system properties.

For example, you could skip certain tests if a particular environment variable is set.

```
@IgnoreIf({
  env.SKIP_INTEGRATION_TESTS == "yes"
})
```

When using the Geb browser-testing framework, you could skip a test that is known to be unreliable in certain browsers, as demonstrated in the following:

```
@IgnoreIf({
  properties."geb.env" == "ie"
})
```

If your test suite includes a smoke test for a web application, you could skip it if there is no internet connection available.

```
@Requires({
  available("http://spockframework.org/")
})
```

With the preceding example, it's worth mentioning that it's less than ideal if the conditional used in an `@IgnoreIf` or `@Requires` annotation is itself slow. For example, checking whether a URL is available is probably reasonably quick in the case of a successful result but may take a few seconds to time-out if it fails. We can mitigate this by ensuring the result of any repeated check is cached:

```
@Memoized
static boolean available(String url) {
  try {
    url.toURL().openConnection().with {
      connectTimeout = 1000
      connect()
    }
    true
  } catch (IOException e) {
    false
  }
}
```

The @Memoized annotation is part of the Groovy standard library and will cache the results of a method call. A separate cache is maintained for each unique set of parameters. In this case, that means each unique URL will be checked only once.

Automatically Cleaning Up Resources

Spock's @AutoCleanup annotation allows you to declaratively release resources after each test.

For example, our timeline specification could automatically close the Handle it uses for connecting to the in-memory database. Instead of explicitly calling close() at the end of the cleanup method:

```
Handle handle

def cleanup() {
  handle.execute("drop table user if exists")
  handle.execute("drop table message if exists")
  handle.execute("drop table following if exists")
  handle.close()
}
```

we can instead annotate the field with @AutoCleanup:

```
@AutoCleanup Handle handle

def cleanup() {
  handle.execute("drop table user if exists")
  handle.execute("drop table message if exists")
  handle.execute("drop table following if exists")
}
```

After the end of the cleanup method, any fields annotated with @AutoCleanup have their close method called. If the field is in @Shared, cleanup happens after the clea nupSpec method completes.

If the field uses a method named something other than close, you need to specify the name in the value of the @AutoCleanup closure.

Documenting Specifications

Previously, I discussed how the strings attached to block labels in a feature method are retained in the byte code and can be accessed by documentation tools.

In addition, Spock provides some annotations to aid in documenting specifications in a manner accessible to tooling. Let's take a look at them:

@Issue

> The @Issue annotation is used to provide a link to your issue tracker that relates to the feature method or specification class. Typically, you use this when a test is written in response to a bug report, but you also can use it for new features, in which case the annotation might well be placed on a specification class that tests various aspects of the feature.

@Subject

> The @Subject annotation indicates the unit under test. The examples we've seen so far in this book have used @Subject liberally. The annotation helps readers to understand the purpose of the test and could potentially be used by tools to provide links to the documentation for the unit under test. The annotation can be used in a couple of different ways:
>
> 1. On a field of the specification class or a local variable in a feature method, the annotation indicates the "instance under test"; that is, the object whose behavior is being verified.
>
> 2. On a specification class with a java.lang.Class parameter that indicates the class whose behavior is being specified.

@Title

> The @Title annotation is for attaching a natural language name to a specification class. Feature methods in Spock can have natural language names, but the specification classes themselves must conform to typical Java class name restrictions.

@Narrative

> Similar to the @Title annotation, @Narrative allows you to attach a long-form, natural language description to the specification class.

Summary

In this chapter, you hopefully learned a selection of tips and tricks that you can use to write better specifications. Nothing is set in stone and you should exercise your own judgment. I encourage you to at least consider readability and maintainability. A jumbled, confusing test will bite you down the line when you need to change it or it detects a regression. If the test is clear, concise, and provides good diagnostics, you'll be able to deal with things quickly. On the other hand, if you struggle to understand the intent of the author (which can happen even if "the author" was you), it can be a frustrating experience.

CHAPTER 8

Advanced where: Blocks

In Chapter 6, we saw how a Spock feature method can iterate over a data pipe defined in the where: block. The examples in that chapter showed where: blocks that used statically defined data and some using @Shared fields as data providers. In this chapter, we look at a couple of less typical examples of data providers backed by *external* data: first a database and then a set of files output by a previous build step.

A Primary Key Verifier

I once implemented a test that confirmed that every table in our database schema had a primary key defined. A couple of times, we had forgotten to do this when adding a new table to the application and had experienced data integrity issues and performance degradation. We wanted a simple test that would catch this for us automatically; that is, whenever a new table was added, the test would check it automatically without the need for anyone to inform it about the existence of the new table.

This was a great opportunity to use a dynamic data pipe in a Spock where: block. Recall that data pipes can use any Iterable value as their source. In this case, we want a list of the names of every table in the database.

This example uses a @Shared connection to a simple in-memory database and a Sche maBuilder object that uses the connection to create the application's database schema for us. The precise details of the schema itself aren't important for this discussion. Assume that the SchemaBuilder.createSchema() method creates some tables, foreign keys, and so on. The @AutoCleanup annotation will ensure the schema is destroyed at the end of the specification.

```
class PrimaryKeySpec extends Specification {

  @Shared @AutoCleanup Connection connection ❶
  @Shared @AutoCleanup("destroySchema") SchemaBuilder schemaBuilder

  def setupSpec() { ❷
    Class.forName("org.h2.Driver")
    connection = DriverManager.getConnection("jdbc:h2:mem:test", "sa", "")

    schemaBuilder = new SchemaBuilder(connection)
    schemaBuilder.createSchema()
  }

  private Iterable<String> readTableNames() { ❸
    def list = []
    def tables = connection.metaData.getTables(
      null, null, "%", ["TABLE"] as String[]
    )
    try {
      while (tables.next()) {
        list << tables.getString(3)
      }
    } finally {
      tables.close()
    }
    list.asImmutable()
  }

  @Unroll
  def "the #tableName table has a primary key"() { ❻
    expect:
    keys.next() ❼

    cleanup:
    keys.close()

    where:
    tableName << readTableNames() ❹
    keys = connection.metaData.getPrimaryKeys(null, null, tableName) ❺
  }
}
```

❶ The @AutoCleanup annotation ensures that the connection's close method is called at the end of the specification class without us having to do it explicitly in cleanupSpec.

❷ In the setupSpec method we establish the connection and create the database schema.

❸ We define a method that will retrieve the names of all the tables in the database.

---

❹ The method is used as the source for a data pipe in the `where:` block of a feature method. If there were more than one such feature method, it would make sense to use a `@Shared` field so that `readTableNames` is called only once.

❺ Using the table name for the current iteration of the test we fetch the table's primary keys.

❻ The `@Unroll` expression in the feature method name refers to the database table name of the current iteration.

❼ We assert that the `ResultSet keys` has at least one row. The test doesn't care about the details of the primary key, only that there *is* one.

Notice that the `readTableNames` method is used as the source for a data pipe using the ❹ operator so that the test will run once for each table in the database. The `where` block also contains an assignment that fetches the primary keys of the table for the current iteration of the test. The `getPrimaryKeys` method of `DatabaseConnectionMe taData` is part of the standard JDBC API. It returns a `java.sql.ResultSet` containing details of the primary key columns of the specified table.

This is a simple but very effective test. The real beauty of it is that no maintenance is required; as tables are added to the application, they will be checked automatically when the unit tests are run.

It's easy to imagine a more complex version of this specification that checks for foreign key definitions for relationships present in a set of ORM model classes or indexes on the columns used by queries.

A Static Site Link Checker

JBake (*http://jbake.org*) is a static site generator for the JVM. You can use it to write content in Markdown, Asciidoc, or plain HTML that JBake then merges with layout templates to build a static website. If we're building such a static site, we might want to test that we don't have any broken links.

In this section, we'll work up a Spock specification that can do just that. It will scrape the generated content for HTML anchors and verify that their `href` attributes contain valid URLs. Each link is tested with an individual iteration of a parameterized feature method. As more links are added to the site, the specification will pick them up and test them automatically.

Recall from Chapter 6 that a data pipe in a Spock `where:` block can be any `Iterable` including the result of a method call.

JBake Configuration

There is a Gradle plugin that enables the building of a JBake site as part of an application build. This example uses that plugin to build the static site along with the Groovy
plugin to execute Spock tests.

The Gradle build looks like this:

```
buildscript {
  repositories {
    jcenter()
  }

  dependencies {
    classpath "me.champeau.gradle:jbake-gradle-plugin:0.2"
    classpath "org.freemarker:freemarker:2.3.22"
    classpath "org.asciidoctor:asciidoctor-java-integration:0.1.4"
  }
}

apply plugin: "groovy"
apply plugin: "me.champeau.jbake"  ❶

dependencies {
  testCompile "org.spockframework:spock-core:1.1-groovy-2.4"
}

assemble.dependsOn jbake  ❷
```

❶   Here, we apply the JBake Gradle plugin.

❷   This forces the `assemble` task to depend on the `jbake` task, which means that the
    JBake site will be built before the tests run.

After that, the JBake site content is added to `src/jbake` and the specification class to
`src/test/groovy`. When the Gradle `jbake` task runs, the static site is built to `build/
jbake`. Here's a diagram of the resulting files:

```
build/jbake
├── about.html
├── archive.html
├── blog
│   └── 2013
│           ├── first-post.html
│           ├── fourth-post.html
│           ├── second-post.html
│           └── third-post.html
├── css
│   ├── …
├── favicon.ico
├── feed.xml
```

```
├── fonts
│   ├── …
├── index.html
├── js
│   ├── …
└── sitemap.xml
```

A Data Pipe Driven by a File

As a first step, the specification will verify external links from the site HTML files, ignoring any internal links.

The specification uses a `@Shared File` object representing the root directory of the JBake output. We'll recursively read the contents of that directory in `setupSpec`, looking for HTML files. Each file is parsed, and any links it contains are stored in a collection we can use as the source for the feature method's data pipe. For the time being, the test deals only with fully qualified URLs, most likely links to external websites. As the chapter progresses, we'll begin dealing with relative links, as well.

File.traverse()

`traverse` is a method Groovy adds to `java.io.File` that allows recursive traversal of a directory subtree. The method accepts a closure that is called for by each file in the subtree and passed that file as a parameter. Optionally, the files in the subtree can be filtered. In the example that follows, the callback closure is invoked once for every file below `rootDir` whose name matches the regular expression ❶.

```
@Shared rootDir = new File("build/jbake")
@Shared Set<String> links = new HashSet<>()  ❶

void setupSpec() {
  rootDir.traverse(nameFilter: ~/.*\.html/) { file ->
    $(file.text).find("a")*.attr("href").each { href ->  ❷
      if (href.toURI().absolute) {
        links << href
      }
    }
  }
}

@Unroll("link to '#link' is valid")
❸
def "site external links are valid"() {
  expect:
  Unirest.head(link).asBinary().status == HTTP_OK  ❺

  where:
```

```
    link << links ❹
  }
```

❶ A @Shared Set will store URLs extracted from the HTML documents. A Set is
   preferable to a List here so that multiple links to the same URL are tested only
   once.

❷ Jerry extracts all a[href] attributes from the document.

❸ The @Unroll expression uses the href value being tested on the current iteration.

❹ The where: block uses the @Shared field links as a data pipe.

❺ The feature method performs a *HEAD* request on the URL and ensures it
   receives a valid response.

Jerry

Jerry (*http://jodd.org/doc/jerry/*) is a part of the Jodd (*http://jodd.org*) library, a set of
lightweight tools and utilities for Java. Jerry is a component for HTML document
parsing and manipulation that closely mirrors the jQuery API. As such, the API is
likely familiar to most developers who have done any JavaScript development for
browsers.

To make Jerry even more jQuery-like, I like to alias its factory method as $ with
import static jodd.jerry.Jerry.jerry as $.

The factory method accepts an HTML document string and returns a Jerry object,
which, like a jQuery object, is a wrapper for a collection of DOM nodes. Here's a complete breakdown of the Jerry call in the LinkVerifierSpec class:

```
// Parse the HTML document returning a Jerry object that wraps the document
// root node.
$(file.text)
  // Find all <a> tags in the document.
  .find("a")
  // Use Groovy's spread operator to call Jerry's attr method on each node and
  // collect the results as a list.
  *.attr("href")
  // Use Groovy's `each` method on the list of href values.
  .each { href ->
```

A Filtered Data Pipe

So far, `LinkVerifierSpec` is only dealing with external URLs, but it should really check the internal links within the site, as well. Those will be relative URLs, but since the entire site is static, the test can simply check for the presence of a corresponding *.html* file.

It would be possible to rewrite the existing test so that it made a different assertion for absolute and relative URLs, making an HTTP *HEAD* request in the former case and checking for a local file in the latter. However, it would make more sense to treat those cases as two separate feature methods. In that case, the test will need to create two different data pipes: one containing external absolute URLs and the other containing local `file://` URLs.

```
// TODO: better way to supply this
@Shared rootDir = new File("build/jbake")
@Shared Set<URI> links = new HashSet<>() ❶

void setupSpec() {
  rootDir.traverse(nameFilter: ~/.*\.html/) { file ->
    $(file.text).find("a")*.attr("href").each { href ->
      if (href.toURI().absolute) {
        links << href.toURI()
      } else if (!href.startsWith("#")) { ❷
        links << new File(file.parentFile, href).toURI() ❸
      }
    }
  }
}

@Unroll("link to '#link' is valid")
def "site external links are valid"() {
  expect:
  Unirest.head(link.toString()).asBinary().status == HTTP_OK

  where:
  link << links.findAll { it.scheme == "http" } ❹
}
```

```
@Unroll("link to '#link' is valid")
def "site internal links are valid"() {
  expect:
  new File(link).exists() ❺

  where:
  link << links.findAll { it.scheme == "file" }
}
```

❶ Each link is now represented as a `java.net.URI` instead of a string. URI objects have an accessor method for their scheme, so it's easy to distinguish HTTP URIs from file URIs.

❷ The test is ignoring fragment links within the same document. Those will need to be handled another way.

❸ When a relative URL is found, the `setupSpec` creates a file URI relative from the directory of the file containing the link.

❹ The original feature method now uses Groovy's `findAll(Closure)` method to filter the data pipe so that it deals only with http URIs.

❺ A new feature method verifies file URIs by converting them back to `java.io.File` instances and using the `exists` method.

Relative Filepaths

One problem with `LinkVerifierSpec` currently is that the URI for an internal link is an absolute filepath, which is long and contains some irrelevant information that would be useful to exclude from the test report. As illustrated in the following report, the part of each filepath up to and including `build/jbake` is the same for each file and will vary when the test is run on different computers:

Test	Duration	Result
link to *file:/Users/rob/Development/site/build/jbake/* is valid	0s	passed
link to *file:/Users/rob/Development/site/build/jbake/about.html* is valid	0s	passed
link to *file:/Users/rob/Development/site/build/jbake/archive.html* is valid	0s	passed
link to *file:/Users/rob/Development/site/build/jbake/blog/2013/../../* is valid	0.001s	passed
link to *file:/Users/rob/Development/site/build/jbake/blog/2013/../../about.html* is valid	0s	passed
link to *file:/Users/rob/Development/site/build/jbake/blog/2013/../../feed.xml* is valid	0s	passed
link to *file:/Users/rob/Development/site/build/jbake/blog/2013/../../index.html* is valid	0.001s	passed
link to *file:/Users/rob/Development/site/build/jbake/blog/2013/first-post.html* is valid	0s	passed
link to *file:/Users/rob/Development/site/build/jbake/blog/2013/fourth-post.html* is valid	0s	passed

Test	Duration	Result
link to *file:/Users/rob/Development/site/build/jbake/blog/2013/second-post.html* is valid	0s	passed
link to *file:/Users/rob/Development/site/build/jbake/blog/2013/third-post.html* is valid	0s	passed
link to *file:/Users/rob/Development/site/build/jbake/feed.xml* is valid	0s	passed
link to *file:/Users/rob/Development/site/build/jbake/index.html* is valid	0s	passed
link to *http://example.org* is valid	0.090s	passed
link to *http://getbootstrap.com/* is valid	0.220s	passed
link to *http://jbake.org* is valid	0.021s	passed

Although it makes sense to use an absolute file URI for the test so that it's easy to resolve correctly, it would be neater to shorten the form output in the @Unroll expression so that it is relative to the root directory of the site. This is quite straightforward to achieve with a where: block assignment.

Recall from Chapter 6 that where: block assignments can reference *the current value* of a parameter assigned from a data pipe or data table. This is ideal for manipulating the parameter values of the where: block. In the case of LinkVerifierSpec, we can use an assignment to convert the absolute file URI in the link parameter to a relative form.

```
@Unroll("link to '#relative' is valid")
def "site internal links are valid"() {
  expect:
  new File(link).exists()

  where:
  link << links.findAll { it.scheme == "file" }
  relative = link.toString() - rootDir.toURI().toString() ❶
}
```

❶ The variable relative is assigned a relative form of link. The assignment is reevaluated on every iteration, and thus will contain the relative version of the link in the current iteration.

Groovy's Minus Operator and Strings

The assignment of `relative` in the previous example uses the *minus* operator on two strings. In Groovy, this will return a new string, which is the left argument with the first occurrence of the right argument removed. For example:

```
def rootDir = "file:/Users/rob/site/build/jbake/blog/"
def absolutePath =
  "file:/Users/rob/site/build/jbake/blog/2013/
  first-post.html"
assert absolutePath - rootDir ==
  "blog/2013/first-post.html"
```

The report now looks a lot better because we've removed the redundant directory path from each filename:

Test	Duration	Result
link to " is valid	0s	passed
link to *about.html* is valid	0.001s	passed
link to *archive.html* is valid	0s	passed
link to *blog/2013/../../* is valid	0s	passed
link to *blog/2013/../../about.html* is valid	0s	passed
link to *blog/2013/../../feed.xml* is valid	0s	passed
link to *blog/2013/../../index.html* is valid	0s	passed
link to *blog/2013/first-post.html* is valid	0s	passed
link to *blog/2013/fourth-post.html* is valid	0s	passed
link to *blog/2013/second-post.html* is valid	0s	passed
link to *blog/2013/third-post.html* is valid	0s	passed
link to *feed.xml* is valid	0s	passed
link to *http://example.org* is valid	0.090s	passed
link to *http://getbootstrap.com/* is valid	0.190s	passed
link to *http://jbake.org* is valid	0.025s	passed
link to *index.html* is valid	0s	passed

Summary

> **David St. Hubbins**: It's such a fine line between stupid, and uh…
> **Nigel Tufnel**: Clever.
> **David St. Hubbins**: Yeah, and clever.
>
> —Spinal Tap

Spock's `where:` block can be driven by data from all kinds of sources. We've seen examples here of using database metadata read by using JDBC and HTML files read from the filesystem. It's easy to imagine specifications driven by spreadsheet data, CSV files, rows in a database, data read over a network connection, and so on.

That being said, some of the most important characteristics of a good test are idempotence (by which I mean that a test will always behave in the same way regardless of when or how many times it is run or any other tests that might or might not run alongside it) isolation, and speed. Don't sacrifice those in order to do "clever" things with `where:` blocks.

The database example in this chapter does not attempt to test a live production database. Instead, it loads the production schema to an in-memory H2 database and tests it there. In the real-world project I worked on in which that test was used, that's exactly what we did. The schema was loaded to an in-memory database by the Grails database migration plugin (*http://grails.org/plugin/database-migration*). That means the test can execute fast and does not depend on external systems running, network availability, or anything else.

The link validator example needs to be run after the JBake site is generated, but we've made that as seamless as possible by configuring the Gradle build to do this for us. The test depends only on local resources; it does not attempt to validate a deployed version of the site. The only real external dependency is network availability and the availability of any sites linked to from the JBake pages. This is a tradeoff—it's not ideal that we need to connect to real URLs on the internet, but there's not a sensible way to isolate the test from that requirement. It's fine to make those kind of tradeoffs when you understand the implications, and in this case it makes sense.

Exercise: Diagnostics for Bad Links

Currently `LinkVerifierSpec` does not produce great information when an invalid link is found. The report will contain the invalid link URL but no information about where the link was found. Adapt the specification so that it reports the file or files where an invalid link occurred.

Exercise: Test Fragment Links

Extend `LinkVerifierSpec` so that it also tests fragment links within a document; for example, `<a href="#foo">Foo</a>`.

CHAPTER 9

Asynchronous Testing

One of the trickiest aspects of testing is dealing safely with asynchronous behavior; that is, things that happen on a different thread from the one executing the test. If handled badly, tests for off-thread behavior can be slow, brittle, or prone to leaking state.

The fundamental problem when dealing with asynchronous behavior is that assertions need to be delayed until the other thread has completed its work. A naïve approach is to simply sleep the main thread for long enough that other threads can complete their work. But how long is long enough? Sleeping the thread tends to result in tests that fail intermittently on different machines under different conditions or run unnecessarily slowly because they sleep far longer than is typically necessary.

Other, better approaches are to either block or poll until the result of the off-thread process is ready. Spock offers constructs that can help with both of those approaches.

Blocking Constructs

One simple and highly effective way to deal with asynchronous behavior is to use some kind of blocking construct that allows the test to ensure the asynchronous behavior has completed before making assertions about the result.

Spock has two blocking constructs in the `spock.util.concurrent` package that you can use to capture values generated by asynchronous processes: `BlockingVariable`, which captures a single value, and `BlockingVariables` (note the plural), which can capture multiple values.

BlockingVariable

`BlockingVariable` is a little like Java's `AtomicReference`. It is simply a container for a single generically typed value with `get` and `set` methods. The difference from `Atomi cReference` is that the `get` operation blocks until `set` has been called, presumably in a different thread.

The typical use for `BlockingVariable` is to have the code under test call `set` somewhere off the main thread while the Spock feature method calls `get` in its `then:` block. Because the call to `get` blocks the feature method, execution will pause exactly as long as necessary before making assertions about the value placed in the `Blocking Variable` instance.

BlockingVariables

The `BlockingVariables` class is similar to `BlockingVariable` except that it is a container for many values rather than just one. It is basically a map whose `get` operation blocks until `set` is called for the same key.

`BlockingVariables` awaits each key separately, so you can use it for scenarios with more than one asynchronous action that might complete at different times.

Testing Nonblocking APIs by Using Callbacks

A typical use for `BlockingVariable` is to substitute for a callback parameter when testing a nonblocking method.

Nonblocking Methods with Callbacks

Nonblocking methods are simply those that do not make the caller wait for a result, which might take some time to generate.

Nonblocking methods that generate a result will typically either return a `Future` or accept a *callback* parameter instead of having a return type.

A callback parameter is simply a function—for example, a Java single abstract method (SAM) type or a Groovy closure—that will be invoked and passed the result of the asynchronous operation when it is complete. The calling code does not then need to wait for the completion of the method before moving on and potentially releasing the thread. Such APIs are very common in JavaScript development and are becoming more so in Java, particularly with the addition of lambdas and the `java.util.func tion` package in Java 8.

Of course, callbacks are used not only by asynchronous, nonblocking methods. If you've used Groovy's `each`, `collect`, `find`, or any of the other common iterator

---

methods, you're used to providing closures as callbacks. Although those methods are not typically asynchronous, there's nothing in the API that prevents them from being implemented in a nonblocking way.

Let's imagine that we decided to provide a nonblocking implementation of the Messa geStore in Squawker. We can do so by simply wrapping nonblocking versions of the API methods around the existing MessageStore using a delegate pattern, as demonstrated here:

```java
public class AsyncMessageStore {

  private final MessageStore delegate; ❶
  private final ExecutorService executor; ❷

  public AsyncMessageStore(MessageStore delegate, ExecutorService executor) {
    this.delegate = delegate;
    this.executor = executor;
  }

  public void latestPostBy(String username, Consumer<Message> callback) { ❸
    executor.submit(() -> { ❹
      Message result = delegate.latestPostBy(username); ❺
      callback.accept(result); ❻
    });
  }
}
```

❶   The asynchronous implementation simply wraps around a delegate instance of the existing MessageStore.

❷   The asynchronous methods will use an ExecutorService to do work off the main thread.

❸   An asynchronous implementation of latestPostBy accepts a callback parameter, which is an instance of java.util.function.Consumer.

❹   The method submits a lambda to the ExecutorService. Note that this is itself an example of calling a method and passing a callback.

❺   Inside the lambda we call the existing, blocking implementation of latestPostBy to generate the result.

❻   Finally, the result is passed to our callback parameter.

The existing implementation of latestPostBy returns a Message instance and therefore must block until data is read from the database and the Message instance is constructed and mapped to the retrieved data.

Our new asynchronous implementation is void; that is, it does not require the calling code to wait for a result. Instead, as soon as a result is available, it passes it to the Consumer parameter. The Consumer interface is simply a SAM type with a single method accept that takes one parameter and does not return anything.

The invocation of the delegate's latestPostBy method and the passing of the result to the callback happen off the calling thread.

Nonblocking is great for performance-sensitive or high-throughput code, but when testing it, we almost certainly want to block. In fact, if we try a naïve implementation of a feature method for our new asynchronous latestPostBy implementation, it's easy to come up with something that appears to work but doesn't:

```
def "retrieves the latest post by a user"() {
  given:
  userStore.insert(username).with { user ->
    user.post(messageText, now())
  }

  expect:
  asyncMessageStore.latestPostBy(username) {
    assert it.text == messageText ❶
  }

  where:
  username = "spock"
  messageText = "Fascinating!"
}
```

❶ Here we attempt to assert that the result object is correct inside a closure passed as the callback parameter to latestPostBy.

This test will appear to work but in fact doesn't assert anything. Remember that the new implementation of latestPostBy does not block the calling thread. Therefore, there is a very good chance that the feature method will complete execution before the callback is invoked.

Closures and SAM Types

You might have noticed that we used a Groovy closure as the callback parameter to `latestPostBy` in the previous example when in fact that method expects an instance of `Consumer`, which is a Java 8 SAM type.

Java's SAM types are interfaces with a single abstract method. You can implement them by using inline lambdas in Java 8 code. Similarly, Groovy closures will be automatically coerced to the correct SAM type so long as the parameters of the closure match those in the SAM type method.

Using BlockingVariable in a Callback

Instead of trying to make assertions directly in the context of the other thread, we can use a `BlockingVariable` instance in our callback and then block until it receives the result.

```
def "retrieves the latest post by a user"() {
  given:
  userStore.insert(username).with { user ->
    user.post(messageText, now())
  }

  when:
  def result = new BlockingVariable<Message>() ❶
  asyncMessageStore.latestPostBy(username) { message ->
    result.set(message) ❷
  }

  then:
  result.get().text == messageText ❸

  where:
  username = "spock"
  messageText = "Fascinating!"
}
```

❶ We construct a `BlockingVariable` instance.

❷ In the callback closure, we set the `BlockingVariable` value.

❸ In the `then:` block, we can await the result and then make assertions as usual.

This is very straightforward and eliminates all the uncertainty about when the work thread will complete.

Using a Reference to BlockingVariable.set as a Callback

In fact, we can go one step further and avoid the use of a closure literal. Remember that the callback is an instance of `Consumer`—a SAM type with a `void` method that takes one parameter. Well, `BlockingVariable.set` is also `void` and takes one parameter!

We can use the Groovy `.&` operator to get a reference to the `set` method in much the same way as the `::` operator works in Java 8. The Groovy version predates the Java one by several years, which is why the syntax doesn't match:

```
when:
def callback = new BlockingVariable<Message>()
asyncMessageStore.latestPostBy(username, callback.&set)

then:
callback.get().text == messageText
```

This is a little neater and works in exactly the same way as before. We've simply avoided a layer of indirection.

Awaiting Multiple Values with BlockingVariables

The `BlockingVariable` construct is great for dealing with a single value generated asynchronously, but what about when we're testing multiple values in a similar way? Spock provides the class `BlockingVariables` (note the plural), which is effectively a `Map`-like container whose *get* operation blocks until a corresponding *set* operation has been performed.

Suppose that we implement a method `latestPostsByFollowed` on our `AsyncMessageStore` class. Given a user, it will fetch the latest message posted by each user they follow and pass them to a callback. There's no guarantee regarding the order in which the messages are retrieved. Further, there's no guarantee that they will all be retrieved at the same time. The fact that the latest post by follower *A* is passed to the callback does not mean the latest post by follower *B* has been retrieved yet.

A simple implementation might look like this:

```
public void latestPostsByFollowed(User user, Consumer<Message> callback) {
  user
    .following()
    .forEach(followed -> latestPostBy(followed.getUsername(), callback));
}
```

This implementation just repeatedly calls the asynchronous `latestPostBy` method we defined earlier. There are other ways we could solve this, such as doing a single join fetch, but this implementation will demonstrate multiple asynchronous invocations of the callback parameter.

Here, we can't use a single `BlockingVariable`, because the callback will be invoked many times—once for each user followed. Instead, we can assign each message retrieved to a key in a `BlockingVariables` object according to the username of the poster. We know that there will be one message per user followed.

We can write a feature method that exercises the functionality like this:

```
def "can retrieve latest message by all followers"() {
  given:
  def user = userStore.insert(username)
  followedUsernames.each {
    def followed = userStore.insert(it)
    user.follow(followed)
    followed.post("Older message", now().minusSeconds(5))
    followed.post("Hi @$username from @$it", now())
  }

  expect:
  user.following*.username.containsAll(followedUsernames)

  when:
  def messages = new BlockingVariables() ❶
  asyncMessageStore.latestPostsByFollowed(user) { message ->
    messages[message.postedBy.username] = message ❷
  }

  then:
  followedUsernames.every {
    messages[it].text == "Hi @$username from @$it" ❸
  }

  where:
  username = "spock"
  followedUsernames = ["kirk", "bones", "sulu"]
}
```

❶ We create a `BlockingVariables` instance to store the retrieved messages.

❷ Passing a closure as the callback, we store each individual message in the `Block ingVariables` instance keyed by the username of the poster.

❸ Using Groovy's `every` method, we assert that the latest message for each followed user corresponds to what we expect.

The key feature is that `messages[it]` used in the assertion will block until a value has been set under that key.

The assertion isn't coupled to the mechanism used to retrieve the messages. It doesn't concern itself with the order in which the messages are passed to the callback.

Whether the messages are retrieved all at once or each in a separate thread, the feature method will continue to work.

Improving diagnostics

One thing we've neglected in the assertion is that a failure is not going to produce a very good diagnostic breakdown of the error.

If the callback is *never* invoked the assertion will fail, as illustrated here:

```
BlockingVariable.get() timed out after 1.00 seconds
```

However, if the assertion itself is faulty, the failure message is not very informative. A small error in the assertion (see if you can spot it) will cause a failure:

```
followedUsernames.every {
    messages[it].text == "Hi @$username from $it"
}
```

But the failure message is not very helpful at all:

```
followedUsernames.every { messages[it].text == "Hi @$username from $it" }
|                       |
|                       false
[kirk, bones, sulu]
```

It's not clear if the expectation is incorrect, if the retrieved message text is not what we expected, or if we've simply attempted to read the wrong value from the message object.

A good way to provide additional diagnostic information in assertion failures is always to break down the top-level expression into additional steps. Here, we can transform the list of usernames we're interested in and the `BlockingVariables` object into a map of usernames to message text:

```
then:
followedUsernames
    .collectEntries { [(it): messages[it].text] } ❶
    .every { it.value == "Hi @$username from $it.key" } ❷
```

❶ The list of usernames is transformed to a map of each username to the message text posted by that user.

❷ The assertion can then operate on the map entries, which contain all of the information required.

If the assertion fails (that error is still present), we should have a much better chance of spotting what the problem is. Here's the assertion output now:

```
followedUsernames .collectEntries { [(it): messages[it].text] } .every { ... }
|                       |                                                   |
[kirk, bones, sulu]|                                                   false
                  [kirk:Hi @spock from @kirk, bones:Hi @spock from @bones, ...]
```

Don't neglect assertion diagnostics even if they're somewhat tricky to improve, as was the case here.

Polling for Eventual State

An alternative approach to the use of blocking constructs to capture values generated asynchronously is to poll for an expected result. Spock includes the PollingCondi tions class in order to accommodate this approach.

The PollingConditions class provides two methods: within(double, Closure) and eventually(Closure). Both methods return true if any assertions made within the closure pass before the timeout expires. The within method requires a specified timeout in seconds, whereas eventually uses the default timeout of the PollingCon ditions object.

Let's look at an alternate way to deal with the feature method we've been working on using PollingConditions instead of BlockingVariables:

```
when:
def messages = [] ❶
asyncMessageStore.latestPostsByFollowed(user) { message ->
  messages << message
}

then:
def conditions = new PollingConditions() ❷
conditions.eventually {
  assert messages.text.containsAll(expectedMessages) ❸
}

where:
username = "spock"
followedUsernames = ["kirk", "bones", "sulu"]
expectedMessages = followedUsernames.collect {
  "Hi @$username from @$it".toString()
}
```

❶ Instead of using a BlockingVariables instance, we'll just store messages in a list.

❷ We need to create an instance of PollingConditions. At this point, we could specify the timeout, polling frequency, and so on, but the default—timeout after one second, poll every tenth of a second—is fine.

❸ The eventually closure needs to contain assertion statements. Here, we're checking that sooner or later all the messages we expect are received.

 Within the closure it's necessary to use the `assert` keyword. A common mistake (one I frequently make) is to think `PollingConditions` is evaluating Boolean statements in the same way as a `then` block. This is not the case. Instead, it will execute the closure repeatedly until either all the assertions pass or the timeout expires.

Using PollingConditions as a Delegate

If you're using a `PollingConditions` instance in more than one feature method, instead of declaring it as a local variable, you can declare it as a delegate of the specification class. This cuts down on the verbosity and is an elegant way to extend Spock's grammar.

First, declare the delegate field. It's necessary for the type to be declared for the `@Dele gate` annotation to work because it can't infer the type from the assignment on the righthand side of the expression:

```
@Delegate PollingConditions conditions = new PollingConditions()
```

Then, in the feature method itself, we can treat the methods of `PollingConditions` as though they were methods of `Specification`:

```
then:
eventually {
  assert messages.text.containsAll(expectedMessages)
}
```

Removing the `PollingConditions` variable from the feature method reduces the clutter and could make the test easier to read.

If you have many specification classes that use `PollingConditions`, I'd even be tempted to define a trait to import this extension.

```
trait Polling {
  @Delegate PollingConditions conditions = new PollingConditions()
}
```

Any specification classes can then declare `extends Specification implements Polling` and do away with the need to declare its own `PollingConditions` delegate.

Asynchronous Interaction Testing

One of the limitations of Spock's interaction testing syntax is that it doesn't offer any way to make assertions about interactions that happen off the main thread.

Let's look at an example. Suppose that we want to automatically trigger an event any time a user in Squawker follows another user. This will allow the application to do things like send email or push a notification to a user's mobile device. Obviously, the event mechanism is not as time-sensitive as the actual updating of the database, so it's acceptable for the event to fire asynchronously. For example, the application could use a database trigger that fires any time an insert is made to the table linking users to followers, or a background process could poll for new data periodically.

To test such an asynchronous event, we want to register a mock event subscriber, make one user follow another, and assert that the mock subscriber is sent an event. That sounds simple enough, but it turns out that standard interaction cardinality assertions don't work very well if the interaction happens asynchronously, as demonstrated in the following:

```
def executor = newSingleThreadExecutor()
def eventBus = new AsyncEventBus(executor) ❶

interface Subscriber {
  @Subscribe
  ❷
  void onEvent(NewFollowerEvent event)
}

def "publishes event when a user follows another"() {
  given:
  def user1 = userStore.insert(username1)
  def user2 = userStore.insert(username2)

  and:
  def subscriber = Mock(Subscriber)
  eventBus.register(subscriber) ❸

  when:
  user2.follow(user1)

  then:
  1 * subscriber.onEvent(new NewFollowerEvent(user1, user2)) ❹

  where:
  username1 = "spock"
  username2 = "kirk"
}
```

❶ We begin by declaring an eventBus, which is used to publish events.

❷ Because EventBus requires annotated subscriber methods, we create a simple interface.

❸ A mock of that interface is registered with the EventBus.

❹ Finally, we assert that the subscriber is called with a matching event.

Some of the fine detail of the setup is omitted here; the eventBus will need to be injected into the underlying data persistence layer so that it publishes events when new followers are registered on a user. Attempting to use a Spock mock as a subscriber looks straightforward enough and would work if the event were triggered and published on the main thread. However, if the event is triggered asynchronously or published asynchronously, as it is in this example, the mock interaction is never tracked.

The Guava Event Bus

Guava's EventBus is a simple publish-subscribe event system. The EventBus class is used to publish events. Subscribers do not need to implement any interface; instead, they are identified by SAMs annotated with @Subscribe. This means that a single class can contain multiple subscriber methods for different types of events. Subscribers are registered with the event bus instance and will receive events that match the declared parameter type of their subscriber methods.

We can take a naïve approach to fixing this by sleeping the thread until the interaction happens, as shown here:

```
when:
user2.follow(user1)

and:
sleep 1000 ❶

then:
1 * subscriber.onEvent(new NewFollowerEvent(user1, user2))
```

❶ A one second delay before evaluating the mock interaction might be sufficient time for the asynchronous event to occur.

However, sleeping the thread is not a good solution for a number of reasons. Is one second too long or too short? If it's too long, by how much? How much time are we actually wasting? If we have many such tests, we could be unnecessarily slowing down the test suite a significant amount.

Asynchronous Parameter Capture

We looked at method parameter capture in "Method Parameter Capture with Mocks" on page 107. The technique is also a very effective way to verify interactions that happen off the main thread.

In the previous examples, we used simple variables or collections to capture parameters. When dealing with asynchronous interactions, we can use `BlockingVariable` instead:

```
def "publishes event when a user follows another"() {
  given:
  def user1 = userStore.insert(username1)
  def user2 = userStore.insert(username2)

  and:
  def event = new BlockingVariable<NewFollowerEvent>()  ❶
  def subscriber = Stub(Subscriber) {
    onEvent(_) >> { event.set(it[0]) }  ❷
  }
  eventBus.register(subscriber)

  when:
  user2.follow(user1)

  then:
  with(event.get()) {  ❸
    user == user1
    newFollower == user2
  }

  where:
  username1 = "spock"
  username2 = "kirk"
}
```

❶ We create a `BlockingVariable` instance.

❷ Instead of a mock subscriber, we use a stub that passes the event it receives to the `BlockingVariable`'s set method.

❸ The then block uses `BlockingVariable.get` to retrieve the value and make assertions about it.

This is much neater because we don't sleep unnecessarily. Instead, the test blocks until the interaction has occurred and we can examine the parameter value passed to the stub.

Extending BlockingVariable

We can make it even neater by just making the Subscriber type extend Blocking Variable, as in the following:

```groovy
static class AsyncSubscriber<T> extends BlockingVariable<T> {
  @Subscribe
  @Override
  void set(T event) {
    super.set(event)
  }
}

def "publishes event when a user follows another"() {
  given:
  def user1 = userStore.insert(username1)
  def user2 = userStore.insert(username2)

  and:
  def subscriber = new AsyncSubscriber<NewFollowerEvent>()
  eventBus.register(subscriber)

  when:
  user2.follow(user1)

  then:
  with(subscriber.get()) {
    user == user1
    newFollower == user2
  }

  where:
  username1 = "spock"
  username2 = "kirk"
}
```

Here, there's no need to even use a stub because the `EventBus` will send the event to our `AsyncSubscriber`'s annotated method directly.

Summary

Asynchronous testing remains a tricky proposition. It's always wise to separate the logic of your code from the asynchronous aspects as far as possible so that you can test that logic without having to deal with the added complexity of asynchrony.

However, at some point you obviously need to test that you are handling multiple threads and their shared data correctly. Spock's blocking and polling constructs provide a simple way to eliminate the uncertainty from dealing with asynchronous behavior.

Hopefully, with these tools you'll be able to eliminate the temptation to use `Thread.sleep` in your specifications!

CHAPTER 10

Extending Spock

Although Spock has a great selection of built-in features, it's always useful to have extensibility. In this chapter, we look at various ways by which you can extend the default capabilities of your Spock specifications. We'll look at composing assertions with Hamcrest matchers, providing reusable functionality with JUnit rules and Spock's own extension mechanism.

The Message Timeline

We'll refer back a couple of times in this chapter to a `TimelineSpec` specification class that tests the database queries and object marshalling around retrieving a user's timeline. We saw some variation on this earlier in the book, but let's just revisit it quickly here:

```
class TimelineSpec extends Specification {

  @Shared
  def dataSource = new JdbcDataSource(
    url: "jdbc:h2:mem:test;DB_CLOSE_DELAY=-1;DB_CLOSE_ON_EXIT=false"
  )

  DBI dbi = new DBI(dataSource)
  @AutoCleanup Handle handle

  UserStore userStore
  MessageStore messageStore
  FollowingStore followingStore

  @Subject User user
  User followedUser
  User otherUser
```

```
def setup() {
  dbi.registerArgumentFactory(new TimeTypesArgumentFactory())
  dbi.registerMapper(new TimeTypesMapperFactory())

  // tag::fixtures[]
  handle = dbi.open()

  userStore = handle.attach(UserStore)
  userStore.createUserTable()

  messageStore = handle.attach(MessageStore)
  messageStore.createMessageTable()

  followingStore = handle.attach(FollowingStore)
  followingStore.createFollowingTable()

  user = userStore.insert("khan")
  followedUser = userStore.insert("kirk")
  otherUser = userStore.insert("spock")
  user.follow(followedUser)

  def now = now()
  messageStore.insert(
    otherUser,
    "His pattern indicates two-dimensional thinking.",
    now.minus(6, MINUTES))
  messageStore.insert(
    user,
    "@kirk You're still alive, my old friend?",
    now.minus(5, MINUTES))
  messageStore.insert(
    followedUser,
    "@khan KHAAANNNN!",
    now.minus(4, MINUTES))
  messageStore.insert(
    followedUser,
    "@scotty I need warp speed in three minutes or we're all dead!",
    now.minus(3, MINUTES))
  messageStore.insert(
    otherUser, "@bones I'm sorry, Doctor, I have no time to explain this.",
    now.minus(2, MINUTES))
  messageStore.insert(
    user,
    "It is very cold in space!",
    now.minus(1, MINUTES))
  // end::fixtures[]
}

def cleanup() {
  dbi.withHandle { Handle handle ->
    handle.execute("delete from following")
    handle.execute("delete from message")
```

```
      handle.execute("delete from user")
    }
  }

  def "a user's timeline does not contains posts by users they do not follow"() {
    when:
    def timeline = messageStore.timeline(user)

    then:
    !timeline.empty

    and:
    !timeline.postedBy.any {
      it == otherUser
    }
  }

  def "a user's timeline is ordered most recent first"() {
    when:
    def timeline = messageStore.timeline(user)

    then:
    !timeline.empty

    and:
    timeline.postedAt == timeline.postedAt.sort().reverse()
  }

  def "a user's timeline can contain multiple messages from each user"() {
    when:
    def timeline = messageStore.timeline(user)

    then:
    timeline.postedBy == [user, followedUser, followedUser, user]
  }
}
```

The specification sets up three users: the primary one whose timeline we'll be testing, another that the primary "follows," and another that the primary does not follow. It also creates two messages posted by each of those users. The timeline should include the primary user's messages and the messages of the user the primary follows but *not* those of the third user.

The specification does some fairly complex setup and data management, which we'll clean up later. First, let's look at the assertion made in that last feature method and see if we can improve it.

Hamcrest Matchers

Although I'd argue that Spock's assertion syntax, with its simplicity, preference for Boolean expressions over assertion methods, and excellent diagnostics is one of Spock's most compelling features, it's not the only way to write assertions.

Hamcrest predates Spock by several years. It is a library for writing "matchers"—functional types that determine if expected and actual values *match* according to some criteria. Matchers are intended to make tests more readable and, crucially, to provide better failure diagnostics. JUnit 4 introduced the `assertThat` method, which relies on Hamcrest matchers.

Matchers are composable, so you can build up complex match conditions by combining them. Hamcrest also bundles a selection of standard matcher implementations, including `equalTo(T)` that checks for equality, `not(Matcher<T>)` that inverts conditions, `allOf(Matcher<T>...)` that aggregates matchers, `hasProperty(String, Matcher<T>)` that can be used to traverse object properties, and so on.

Let's look at that last feature method from the timeline specification. It's ensuring that a timeline can contain multiple messages from a given user. That's the kind of error that could happen if the SQL query is incorrectly de-duplicating rows from a join fetch; for example:

```
def "a user's timeline can contain multiple messages from each user"() {
  when:
  def timeline = messageStore.timeline(user)

  then:
  timeline.postedBy == [user, followedUser, followedUser, user]
}
```

In the preceding example, we're retrieving the timeline and then asserting that there are two instances of both `user` and `followedUser` in the list of message posters.

In this example, Groovy's implicit map operation is used to turn the `List<Message>` variable `timeline` into a `List<User>` using the `postedBy` property of each message in the list.

The expression `timeline.postedBy` is exactly equivalent to `timeline.collect { it.postedBy }`.

To make the test pass, however, it's necessary to order the expected elements correctly. This feels like it could be brittle. If the rules for ordering timelines change the test could break, even though the behavior it's testing is still correct.

What can we do to remove this brittleness? A first thing to try might be to ensure that the expected and actual lists are in a known order so that ordering becomes irrelevant to the success of the assertion:

```
then:
timeline.postedBy.sort() == [user, user, followedUser, followedUser]
```

Unfortunately, we're relying on the default sort order of the User class. If *that* changes, the test could again give us a false negative.

Of course, we can sort *both* sides of the expression:

```
then:
timeline.postedBy.sort() == [user, user, followedUser, followedUser].sort()
```

This solution removes the brittleness, but it feels rather cluttered and inelegant. A reader of the test might wonder why the values are being sorted.

Not only that, but this approach is only reliable if the items in the two lists implement Comparable. Groovy's sort method does not throw an exception if the list elements are not sortable. However, neither does it have any defined behavior, so we can't rely on its results.

 If we delve deep enough into the Groovy standard library, we discover that if the elements are not Comparable, they are sorted according to their hashCode values, but that's not something on which the correctness of the test should rely.

Instead of sorting, we can use another Groovy extension to Java's Collection. The countBy method takes a Closure<T> and turns a List<E> into a Map<T, Integer>, for which the keys are the distinct values returned by the closure and the values are the cardinality of those values.

That's perhaps an overly formal explanation that makes it sound more complicated that it actually is, so let's look at the example:

```
then:
timeline.countBy { it.postedBy } == [(user): 2, (followedUser): 2]
```

The closure passed to countBy returns the postedBy property for each message, so we end up with a Map<User, Integer> containing the cardinalities of each user.

This solution is much less brittle, but it requires good knowledge of Groovy, and some people might be confused by the syntax.

Hamcrest Support in Spock

We can also use a Hamcrest matcher to make the assertion.

Spock supports making assertions with matchers via the `HamcrestSupport` class that you can find in the `spock.util.matcher` package. It contains two static methods:

```
public static <T> void expect(T value, Matcher<? super T> matcher)
public static <T> void that(T value, Matcher<? super T> matcher)
```

The only difference between the two methods is their names—inside a `then:` block, `expect` reads better; and inside an `expect:` block, `that` reads better.

Using Hamcrest support and one of the standard matchers from the `hamcrest-all` library, we can write our assertion like this:

```
then:
HamcrestSupport.expect(
  timeline.postedBy,
  Matchers.containsInAnyOrder(user, user, followedUser, followedUser)
)
```

That's very long-winded and Java-like, but by using static imports and removing unnecessary braces, it's much less verbose:

```
then:
expect timeline.postedBy, containsInAnyOrder(
  user, user, followedUser, followedUser
)
```

The assertion is now expressive—the `containsInAnyOrder` matcher name tells the reader very clearly what is being verified—and is not prone to breaking due to changes in the timeline ordering or the default sort order of `User` objects.

Spock's assertion syntax means that Hamcrest matchers aren't always, or even often, necessary, but it's handy to be able to use them when they add clarity.

Hamcrest and Spock Mocks

As we saw in Chapter 7, Hamcrest matchers can also be used as predicates for parameters in a mock or stub interaction.

JUnit Rules

Rules are a reusable way to extend the `@Before` and `@After` semantics of JUnit tests. Rules are simply fields in a test class with an annotation that instructs JUnit how the rule fits in the test lifecycle. Rules annotated with `@Rule` can execute code before and after each test method; rules annotated with `@ClassRule` can execute code before and after a test class.

You probably noticed that these phases correspond to Spock's `setup`, `cleanup`, `setup Spec`, and `cleanupSpec` phases, and indeed because Spock runs using JUnit's test runner, JUnit rules are compatible with Spock specifications.

That opens up a variety of rules your tests can use. For example, JUnit's `Temporary Folder` rule is useful in tests that need to do filesystem IO.

Of course, you can write your own rules, as well.

Reusable Data Cleanup

In many of the specifications we've looked at so far, we've been careful to delete data from the in-memory database in the `cleanup` method. Because of referential integrity rules, the tests need to be careful to delete data in a particular order. Copy-and-paste errors could mean test data leaking and hard-to-debug failures. Cleaning up data seems an ideal candidate for some reusable code that we only need to write once.

Let's take a closer look at the data management in our timeline specification.

We have three fields involved in the management of the data source:

```
@Shared
def dataSource = new JdbcDataSource(
  url: "jdbc:h2:mem:test;DB_CLOSE_DELAY=-1;DB_CLOSE_ON_EXIT=false"
)

DBI dbi = new DBI(dataSource)
@AutoCleanup Handle handle
```

A `@Shared` in-memory database will persist between feature methods. A `DBI` bridges the data source to JDBI and the `Handle` is used to provide connections for the DAOs.

The `setup` method creates fixture data:

```
handle = dbi.open()

userStore = handle.attach(UserStore)
userStore.createUserTable()

messageStore = handle.attach(MessageStore)
messageStore.createMessageTable()

followingStore = handle.attach(FollowingStore)
followingStore.createFollowingTable()

user = userStore.insert("khan")
followedUser = userStore.insert("kirk")
otherUser = userStore.insert("spock")
user.follow(followedUser)

def now = now()
```

```
messageStore.insert(
  otherUser,
  "His pattern indicates two-dimensional thinking.",
  now.minus(6, MINUTES))
messageStore.insert(
  user,
  "@kirk You're still alive, my old friend?",
  now.minus(5, MINUTES))
messageStore.insert(
  followedUser,
  "@khan KHAAANNNN!",
  now.minus(4, MINUTES))
messageStore.insert(
  followedUser,
  "@scotty I need warp speed in three minutes or we're all dead!",
  now.minus(3, MINUTES))
messageStore.insert(
  otherUser, "@bones I'm sorry, Doctor, I have no time to explain this.",
  now.minus(2, MINUTES))
messageStore.insert(
  user,
  "It is very cold in space!",
  now.minus(1, MINUTES))
```

First, a handle is opened that maintains a dedicated database connection. The handle is then used to create the userStore, messageStore, and followingStore DAOs and ensure that the database tables they need are created.

The create...Table methods that set up the schema will be no-ops when called again because they use create table if not exists... in their DDL commands.

Finally, setup inserts user and message fixtures. The fixtures will violate uniqueness constraints if we do not clean them up after the first feature method.

At the end of each feature method, the data is torn down in the cleanup method.

```
def cleanup() {
  dbi.withHandle { Handle handle ->
    handle.execute("delete from following")
    handle.execute("delete from message")
    handle.execute("delete from user")
  }
}
```

Because in this specification we are sharing the in-memory database between all feature methods, if the data is not cleaned up, it will leak between tests. In this case, that will cause the setup method to fail because re-creating the same users will violate the uniqueness constraints on the user table. The cleanup method simply deletes data from the three tables that the specification uses.

However, it's important to note that the tables need to be cleaned up in this order (or at least the `user` table must be cleaned up last). The `following` and `message` tables have foreign keys referencing `user`, so trying to delete from `user` first would violate referential integrity constraints.

This is a little error-prone. In a more complex scenario, it could be extremely frustrating and time-consuming to identify exactly which tables need to be cleaned up, and in what order.

Why Not Just Drop the Database?

The problems we're seeing around data cleanup could be avoided here by simply not using a `@Shared` database. If I were writing exactly this test for real, that's what I'd do.

This example is simplified because what we're really interested in here is the way rules and extensions work in Spock.

However, don't assume that dropping the database is always possible. Dropping an H2 in-memory database is cheap and fast. If you're integration testing against a different product, that might not be the case.

Alternatively, the database might be a single component of an application container that itself is costly to re-create for every test. As we'll see in Chapter 12, when writing Spring integration tests, the database is managed by the Spring container and *is* retained between tests (along with the entire application context). The techniques we discuss in this chapter for cleaning up data are genuinely useful in that scenario.

Many specifications could conceivably require the same cleanup method, so this data cleanup seems like an obvious candidate for reuse. Because JUnit rules can act after each test method—or feature method when used with Spock—we can move the cleanup logic to a rule and share it between specification classes.

To apply the rule, we simply remove the `cleanup` method and declare a field annotated with `@Rule`, as shown here:

```
@Rule TruncateTablesRule dataCleanup = new TruncateTablesRule(dbi)
```

Explicit Types for Rule Fields

You might have noticed that I've declared the rule type on the left-hand side of the expression even though it's simply initialized with a constructor. Normally, I would just use `def` because the type can be inferred from the righthand side of the expression. However, when using JUnit rules, it's necessary to specify the type explicitly.

To implement the rule itself, we need to implement JUnit's `TestRule` interface, as follows:

```java
public class TruncateTablesRule implements TestRule {

  private final DBI dbi;

  public TruncateTablesRule(DBI dbi) {
    this.dbi = dbi;
  }

  @Override
  public Statement apply(final Statement base, Description description) { ❶
    return new Statement() { ❷
      @Override public void evaluate() throws Throwable {
        try {
          base.evaluate(); ❸
        } finally {
          truncateTables(); ❹
        }
      }
    };
  }

  private void truncateTables() {
    dbi.withHandle(handle -> {
      handle.execute("delete from following");
      handle.execute("delete from message");
      handle.execute("delete from user");
      return null;
    });
  }
}
```

❶ `TestRule` has a single abstract method, `apply`, that we need to implement. This method is passed a `Statement` that you can think of as a function parameter representing the feature method itself.

❷ The method returns another `Statement`, which in this case simply wraps a `try` / `finally` block around the invocation of the feature method.

❸ The `evaluate()` method on `Statement` executes the feature method.

❹ The `finally` block simply ensures that our `cleanup` routine runs regardless of whether the feature method passed, failed, or threw an exception.

Statements in Rules

JUnit rules are somewhat similar to Aspect-Oriented Programming (AOP) pointcuts in that they modify the original behavior by proxying a call.

In this case, we've wrapped the original `Statement` object in another `Statement`, effectively wrapping a `try` block around it. It's easy to imagine rules that do other things with the original statement; for example:

- Allowing the feature method to pass even if certain types of exceptions are thrown
- Conditionally returning the original statement or a no-op statement, meaning that the feature method is skipped
- Evaluating the original statement more than once

Simplifying the Rule by Using ExternalResource

The pattern of wrapping the original statement passed to a rule in a `try` / `finally` block is so common that JUnit provides a base class that we can extend to avoid dealing with `Statement` objects and anonymous inner classes. Instead of implementing `TestRule`, we can extend `ExternalResource`:

```
public class TruncateTablesRule extends ExternalResource {

  private final DBI dbi;

  public TruncateTablesRule(DBI dbi) {
    this.dbi = dbi;
  }

  @Override protected void after() {
    dbi.withHandle(handle -> {
      handle.execute("delete from following");
      handle.execute("delete from message");
      handle.execute("delete from user");
      return null;
    });
  }
}
```

The `ExternalResource` base class has two methods, `before()` and `after()`, that are no-ops by default. We don't need to do anything before the feature method, so we don't need to override `before()`. Any logic in `after()` is executed in a `finally` block after the original statement is evaluated.

Making the Cleanup Logic Generic

So far, we have a reusable rule that cleans up some specific tables. That's fine if we always create the same set of tables in any specification. However, our original specification only created the three tables it needs. Other specifications might create more or a completely different set of tables. When we get into the integration testing chapters later, we'll be adding new tables, and it would be nice to be able to use the same rule again.

Using database metadata available from a `java.sql.Connection`, it's actually fairly easy to write a function to delete data automatically. The function should find all database tables and delete data from each in turn. If any table has exported foreign keys, the related tables should be processed first recursively.

```
public class TruncateTablesRule extends ExternalResource {

  private final DBI dbi;

  public TruncateTablesRule(DBI dbi) {
    this.dbi = dbi;
  }

  @Override protected void after() {
    dbi.withHandle(handle -> {
      truncateTables(handle.getConnection());
      return null; ❶
    });
  }
}
```

❶ The lambda returns `null` simply because it's standing in for a non-void SAM type—JDBI's `HandleCallback`.

Implementing `truncateTables(Connection)` is left as an exercise for you to complete. However, after that's been done, we have a highly reusable component that you can use not just for a specific set of tables, but across the entire suite of specifications, as well as in other projects.

I encourage you to try writing the implementation yourself. Test drive it. What issues do you run into when testing a JUnit rule or extension? Does it make sense to implement the `truncateTables` method as a separate component that you can test in isolation from its integration with the scope of the test lifecycle? Can you extend the rule so that it works with other types of properties—a `javax.sql.DataSource`, for example?

You can use `DatabaseMetaData.getTables` to discover tables and `DatabaseMetaData.getExportedKeys` to find exported foreign keys. Armed with that information, you should be able to automatically work out the order to delete tables so that no foreign key constraints are violated.

Spock Extensions

Spock specifications are not limited to using JUnit rules; Spock also has its own extension mechanism with annotation-driven and global extensions.

Annotation-driven extensions are triggered by the presence of an annotation in the specification class. Depending on the extension, the annotation might appear in the specification class itself, a field, or method. Many of the features of Spock we've looked at—for example, `@Unroll`, `@Ignore`, and `@AutoCleanup`—are implemented as annotation-driven extensions.

Global extensions are attached to every specification if they are present on the class-path. Spring integration testing support is implemented as a global extension in the `spock-spring` library that you'll meet in Chapter 12. The integration that allows Spock to use JUnit rules is also implemented as a global extension!

Data Cleanup as a Spock Extension

Instead of using a JUnit rule, we could implement our cleanup routine as an annotation-driven extension.

Because the crucial `truncateTables` method requires a `java.sql.Connection` it makes sense to apply an annotation to a field that can supply the connection. In the case of our specification, that will be the `DBI`. The field in the specification will end up looking like this:

```
@TruncateTables
DBI dbi = new DBI(dataSource)
```

We'll need to build three components:

- The `@TruncateTables` annotation itself, obviously
- An extension class implementing `IAnnotationDrivenExtension` that has a callback Spock will invoke when it finds our annotation on a field
- An interceptor implementing `IMethodInterceptor` that runs in the cleanup phase of the test lifecycle and actually does the work of deleting data from tables

First, we need to define the annotation itself:

```
@Retention(RetentionPolicy.RUNTIME)
@Target({ElementType.FIELD}) ❶
@ExtensionAnnotation(TruncateTablesExtension.class) ❷
public @interface TruncateTables {
}
```

❶ This particular annotation specifies that it's valid only when applied to a field.

❷ The @ExtensionAnnotation defines the extension class *this* annotation activates.

There's not a whole lot to the annotation itself. The crucial thing is that it defines the extension class that actually supplies the extension's behavior.

Next, let's look at the extension class that will discover the annotation and apply the behavior to any feature methods.

In the org.spockframework.runtime.extension, Spock includes the interface IAnno tationDrivenExtension<T extends Annotation>, which is the base for any annotation-driven extensions. The interface defines the following methods:

```
void visitSpecAnnotation(T annotation, SpecInfo spec);
void visitFeatureAnnotation(T annotation, FeatureInfo feature);
void visitFixtureAnnotation(T annotation, MethodInfo fixtureMethod);
void visitFieldAnnotation(T annotation, FieldInfo field);
void visitSpec(SpecInfo spec);
```

The visitSpec method is called for any extension and provides hooks for intercepting the various phases of the specification lifecycle. The remaining methods are called when Spock finds an annotated component.

In our case, we'll only need to implement visitFieldAnnotation because our annotation can be applied only to fields.

 In theory, multiple fields could be annotated with the same annotation, although it doesn't really make sense in our case. Other annotations—for example, @AutoCleanup—work in exactly the same way, and you *can* sensibly apply them to any number of fields.

```
public class TruncateTablesExtension
    extends AbstractAnnotationDrivenExtension<TruncateTables> { ❶

    @Override
    public void visitFieldAnnotation(TruncateTables annotation, FieldInfo field) {
        SpecInfo spec = field.getParent(); ❷
        spec.addCleanupInterceptor(new TruncateTablesInterceptor(field));
    }
}
```

❶ We extend `AbstractAnnotationDrivenExtension`, which provides default implementations of all the callback methods we *don't* need, so our implementation needs to override only the one method.

❷ The `parent` property of the `field` parameter is the specification itself, which has the hooks we need to attach an interceptor to the cleanup phase.

 The default implementations of the `visit...Annotation` methods in `AbstractAnnotationDrivenExtension` throw an exception that tells developers the annotation should not be used on that particular element type. In our case, for example, it makes no sense to annotate a fixture method (`setup` or `cleanup`), a feature method, or the specification class itself.

As you can see, the extension class really just attaches the interceptor to the specification. The interceptor itself does the actual work.

Let's take a look at that implementation now.

The interceptor implements Spock's `IMethodInterceptor` interface, which has a single method `intercept(IMethodInvocation)`:

```
public class TruncateTablesInterceptor implements IMethodInterceptor {

  private final FieldInfo field;

  TruncateTablesInterceptor(FieldInfo field) {
    this.field = field;
  }

  @Override
  public void intercept(IMethodInvocation invocation) throws Throwable {
    try {
      invocation.proceed(); ❶
    } finally {
      DBI dbi = (DBI) field.readValue(invocation.getInstance()); ❷
      if (dbi != null) {
        try (Connection connection = dbi.open().getConnection()) {
          truncateTables(connection);
        }
      }
    }
  }
}
```

❶ The `IMethodInvocation` parameter in a method interceptor is similar to the `Statement` parameter passed to a JUnit rule's `apply` method: by calling `proceed()`, the original method is run. You can do this either before or after any additional code is executed. In this example, we're letting the original cleanup proceed first before truncating database tables.

❷ The interceptor accesses the actual value of the annotated field and can use that to acquire a database connection and run the same `truncateTables` method that we saw in the JUnit rule version.

As you can see, the interceptor implementation is conceptually quite similar to the JUnit rule we created earlier. Remember, though, that the method we're intercepting here is not a feature method but the `cleanup` method.

At this point, we have a fully functional Spock extension.

Further Steps

The extension is straightforward to implement but is also pretty basic. We could definitely take it further. Here are some ideas:

- The interceptor is always attached to the cleanup phase. If the annotated field is also `@Shared`, the interceptor should probably be attached by using `SpecInfo.add CleanupSpecInterceptor`.

- What happens if more than one field is annotated with `@TruncateTables`? This likely won't happen, but the extension doesn't explicitly prevent it.

- Currently, the extension assumes that the annotated field will be an instance of `DBI`, but we could make the extension more generally useful by supporting other types such as `javax.sql.DataSource`, as well.

- We could also allow the annotation to be applied to a factory method for connections rather than just to fields.

- Although the implementation so far doesn't need to do so, the interceptor can access the annotation itself from the `field` parameter. This means it is possible to customize the extension behavior by using fields on the annotation class. For example, we could provide a list of tables to ignore in cleanup (perhaps they contain static data that does not need to be torn down) or we could use the Boolean properties of the annotation to ignore errors or log activity to the console.

Global Extensions

Unlike annotation-driven extensions, global extensions do not rely on annotated elements in the specification. Instead, any global extensions found on the classpath are applied to every specification.

Global extensions are detected and loaded due to the existence of a file named org.spockframework.runtime.extension.IGlobalExtension in META-INF/serv ices. That file can be part of a *.jar* that bundles an extension or can exist under src/ test/resources in a standard Gradle project layout if the extension is local to the project.

Let's take a look at how a global extension works by writing our own. We'll create an extension that does some simple reporting by generating a Cucumber style .feature file for each specification run. The file will contain a summary of the specification in Cucumber's Gherkin syntax.

Gherkin Syntax

Gherkin is a human-readable way to express specification requirements using a simple structure and a few keywords. When used with Cucumber, specifications written in Gherkin are mapped to executable implementations.

A Gherkin file begins with a Feature: line and some free-form descriptive text describing the behavior being specified. It then has one or more scenarios beginning with the Scenario: keyword. Each scenario is roughly analogous to a feature method in Spock. Scenarios are comprised of lines starting with the keywords Given, When, Then, or And, which should feel pretty familiar by now!

Scenarios are indented within features; Given, When, and Then lines are indented within the scenario; and And lines are indented after the preceding line (unlike typical Spock formatting).

This structure maps to Spock's in a pretty straightforward way.

We'll need to write two classes to implement our extension. First, the extension class itself and then a listener that implements IRunListener, an interface that provides callbacks invoked before and after specs, feature methods, and blocks.

Global extensions implement the IGlobalExtension interface, which is very simple:

```
public interface IGlobalExtension {
  void start();
  void visitSpec(SpecInfo spec);
  void stop();
}
```

The start and stop methods are callbacks for the start and end of a test suite. The visitSpec method, like the one in IAnnotationDrivenExtension, is called for each specification as it is run. For convenience, there is also a AbstractGlobalExtension base class that provides no-op implementations of all the methods from the interface.

We can simply write a separate file for each spec executed so that we don't need to worry about implementing start and stop at this time. Our visitSpec implementation will just create an output file and pass it to a listener that does the actual work of generating the Gherkin syntax file:

```java
public class GherkinExtension extends AbstractGlobalExtension {

  @Override public void visitSpec(SpecInfo spec) {
    File file = new File(format(
      "./build/reports/gherkin/%s.%s.feature",
      spec.getPackage(),
      spec.getName()
    ));

    try {
      file.getParentFile().mkdirs();
      Writer writer = new FileWriter(file);
      spec.addListener(new GherkinListener(writer));
    } catch (IOException e) {
      throw new ExtensionException("Error writing to file", e);
    }
  }
}
```

The listener implements Spock's IRunListener interface, which provides callbacks for the start and end of specifications, feature methods, iterations (when a feature method uses a where: block), errors, and skipped features. We won't need to implement all of those, so again, we can extend a convenient base class AbstractRunLis tener that provides no-op implementations for those methods that we don't need:

```java
class GherkinListener extends AbstractRunListener {

  private final Writer writer;

  GherkinListener(Writer writer) {
    this.writer = writer;
  }

  @Override public void beforeSpec(SpecInfo spec) { ❶
    writeFeature(spec);
    writeNarrative(spec);
  }

  @Override public void beforeFeature(FeatureInfo feature) { ❷
    writeScenario(feature);
    feature
      .getBlocks()
      .stream()
      .filter(this::isSupportedBlockType)
      .forEach(this::beforeBlock);
  }
```

```java
@Override public void afterFeature(FeatureInfo feature) { ❸
  appendLine("");
}

@Override public void afterSpec(SpecInfo spec) { ❹
  try {
    writer.close();
  } catch (IOException e) {
    throw new ExtensionException("Cannot close writer", e);
  }
}

private void beforeBlock(BlockInfo block) {
  List<String> lines = block.getTexts(); ❺
  if (!lines.isEmpty()) {
    writeStep(block.getKind(), lines.get(0));
    lines
      .subList(1, lines.size())
      .forEach(this::writeAndStep);
  } else {
    writeStep(block.getKind(), "DESCRIPTION MISSING");
  }
}

private void writeFeature(SpecInfo spec) {
  appendLine("Feature: %s", spec.getName());
}

private void writeNarrative(SpecInfo spec) {
  String narrative = spec.getNarrative(); ❻
  if (narrative != null) {
    stream(narrative.split("\n"))
      .forEach(line -> appendLine("\t%s", line));
  }
  appendLine("");
}

private void writeScenario(FeatureInfo feature) {
  appendLine("\tScenario: %s", feature.getName());
}

private void writeStep(BlockKind blockKind, String description) {
  String keyword = keywordFor(blockKind);
  appendLine("\t\t%s %s", keyword, description);
}

private void writeAndStep(String description) {
  appendLine("\t\t\tAnd %s", description);
}

private boolean isSupportedBlockType(BlockInfo block) {
```

```
      List<BlockKind> supported = Arrays.asList(SETUP, WHEN, THEN, EXPECT);
      return supported.contains(block.getKind());
    }

    private String keywordFor(BlockKind block) {
      switch (block) {
        case SETUP:
          return "Given";
        case WHEN:
          return "When";
        case THEN:
        case EXPECT:
          return "Then";
        default:
          throw new IllegalArgumentException(
            format("Block kind %s not supported", block)
          );
      }
    }

    private void appendLine(String format, Object... args) {
      try {
        writer
          .append(format(format, args))
          .append("\n");
      } catch (IOException e) {
        throw new ExtensionException("Unable to write", e);
      }
    }
  }
}
```

❶ When the specification is started, we can extract the Gherkin `Feature:` line and a description if a `@Narrative` annotation is present on the specification.

❷ When a feature method starts, we can write the Gherkin `Scenario:` using the feature method name and then iterate over the blocks. We're actually interested in only certain block types—Gherkin has no syntax equivalent to Spock's `cleanup:` or `where:` blocks so we'll ignore those.

❸ After each feature method, we insert a blank line.

❹ After the specification is done, we simply close the writer.

❺ `BlockInfo.getTexts()` returns a `List<String>` of any description added to the block and those of any following `and:` blocks. Note that `FeatureInfo.get Blocks()` does *not* return separate `BlockInfo` instances for `and:` blocks. If there is no text attached to a block, the list returned by `getTexts()` might be empty.

❻ The `SpecInfo.getNarrative()` method will return the text supplied in a `@Narra`
   `tive` annotation. If there is no such annotation, it will return `null`, so we need to
   allow for that possibility.

Running the specification from earlier in the chapter with this extension in place produces a `TimelineSpec.feature` file:

```
Feature: TimelineSpec

    Scenario: a user's timeline contains posts from themselves and followed users
      When DESCRIPTION MISSING
      Then DESCRIPTION MISSING

    Scenario: a user's timeline is ordered most recent first
      When DESCRIPTION MISSING
      Then DESCRIPTION MISSING
```

We can certainly improve the results by adding `@Title` and `@Narrative` annotations
and adding label text to the blocks in our feature methods, as demonstrated here:

```
@Title("Timeline")
@Narrative("""
A user can access a 'timeline' -- a reverse-chronologically ordered list
of messages posted by themselves and any users they follow.
Messages posted by users they do not follow should not appear in the timeline.
""")
class TimelineSpec extends Specification {

  // ...

  def "a user's timeline does not contains posts by users they do not follow"() {
    when: "a user retrieves their timeline"
    def timeline = messageStore.timeline(user)

    then: "it contains some messages"
    !timeline.empty

    and: "it does not contain any messages posted by users they do not follow"
    !timeline.postedBy.any {
      it == otherUser
    }
  }

  def "a user's timeline is ordered most recent first"() {
    when: "a user retrieves their timeline"
    def timeline = messageStore.timeline(user)

    then: "it contains some messages"
    !timeline.empty

    and: "the messages are ordered most recent first"
    timeline.postedAt == timeline.postedAt.sort().reverse()
```

```
    }

    def "a user's timeline can contain multiple messages from each user"() {
      when: "a user retrieves their timeline"
      def timeline = messageStore.timeline(user)

      then: "it may contain multiple messages from the same user"
      expect timeline.postedBy, containsInAnyOrder(
        user, user, followedUser, followedUser
      )
    }
  }
```

After running the tests again, the Gherkin output looks a lot better:

```
Feature: Timeline
  A user can access a 'timeline'—a reverse-chronologically ordered list
  of messages posted by themselves and any users they follow.
  Messages posted by users they do not follow should not appear in the timeline.

  Scenario: a user's timeline contains posts from themselves and followed users
    When a user retrieves their timeline
    Then it contains some messages
      And it does not contain any messages posted by users they do not follow

  Scenario: a user's timeline is ordered most recent first
    When a user retrieves their timeline
    Then it contains some messages
      And the messages are ordered most recent first
```

Taking it Further

Try improving the Gherkin extension so that it can do the following:

- Write to a file or to the console as the tests run
- Handle tests that use the @Unroll annotation

Summary

You now have several options for moving beyond the core functionality of Spock when writing your Spock specifications.

To make complex assertions while retaining readability, Hamcrest matchers can be very helpful.

When it comes to sharing or abstracting away setup and cleanup code, you can use JUnit rules. Numerous rules are available, and they work seamlessly with Spock.

You should also now have a good headstart on writing your own annotation-driven or global extensions. If you find yourself repeating or copy-pasting setup or cleanup code between multiple specification classes, it's well worth considering whether an extension is appropriate.

CHAPTER 11

Test-Driven Development: The Diamond Kata

The *Diamond Kata* is a well-known test-driven development (TDD) exercise. In this chapter, we work our way to a solution demonstrating the use of Spock in a TDD workflow.

As we work through the exercise, we'll always implement a test before implementing the code that makes it pass. Thus, until we have implemented tests for every condition and made them pass, we will have an incomplete solution—but with each test, it will inch closer to completeness. As we add tests, we'll see how we can simplify what we need to assert at each step because of the conditions in place.

The Diamond Kata

In case you haven't come across the Diamond Kata prior to this, let's review what is involved. The aim is to create a function that accepts a single character as input and returns a matrix of characters in a specific pattern. The matrix should be a perfect square whose dimensions depend on the input character. Starting at A, each row in the pattern uses the next letter of the alphabet up to the argument character and then back down to A. The letters in the matrix form a diamond. The first row should include A, vertically centered surrounded by padding. The second row should include two B characters in the center, separated by a single padding character.

Here are some examples of the pattern:

```
-A-
B-B
-A-

---A---
--B-B--
-C---C-
D-----D
-C---C-
--B-B--
---A---
```

The simplest form is the diamond of A.

```
A
```

As you can see, all diamonds exhibit vertical and horizontal, but not rotational, symmetry.

Implementation

We'll implement the diamond function in Java as a `java.util.Function<Character, List<String>>`. Each row in the matrix is represented by a string element in the result list; each column is represented by a character in that string.

Our implementation will accept only characters in the range A..Z, throwing `Illegal ArgumentException` in all other cases.

First Step: The Pathological Case

When test-driving code, it makes sense to divide the requirements up into discrete behaviors exhibited by the correct solution. Each behavior is tackled in order from the simplest to the most complex.

Frequently, the simplest behaviors to start with are those that can be termed *pathological cases*: what happens when the input or the preexisting state is invalid?

In the case of our `Diamond` function, we can start by asserting that characters outside the valid range are rejected, as shown in the following code:

```
@Shared char aChar = 'A'
@Shared char zChar = 'Z'
@Shared Range<Character> validRange = aChar..zChar

@Unroll("rejects '#c'")
def "rejects characters outside the range A-Z"() {
  when:
  diamond.apply(c)
```

```
    then:
    thrown IllegalArgumentException

    where:
    c << Gen.character
            .filter { !validRange.contains(it) }
            .take(50) ❶
}
```

❶ We use *spock-genesis* to generate up to 50 unique characters and test that each is rejected.

The implementation that makes this first test pass couldn't be simpler:

```
public List<String> apply(Character c) {
    throw new IllegalArgumentException(c + " is outside the valid range A..Z");
}
```

We just always throw an exception, regardless of what character is passed. Clearly this is wrong, but our test should continue to pass as we implement the actual solution.

The Simplest Valid Diamond

Where should we go next? Looking at the algorithm we're going to require, it's clear that we're going to need some way to verify the leading and trailing padding and that the correct character appears on each row. However, it seems that we have a very simple special case that we could handle without having to think about anything very much.

Diamond(A) is simply a single-element array with a single character string containing A. It's a case that stands alone because there is no padding to verify, and because it's a boundary condition, it might be tricky to implement the math we'll use to divide up the diamond without falling afoul of fencepost errors.

So in our next test, we'll just check the special case of *diamond(A)* without diving into any complex paramaterized tests.

```
def "The diamond of A is 'A'"() {
    expect:
    diamond.apply(aChar) == ["A"]
}
```

You can force this test to pass by returning the *diamond(A)* for *any* valid input character:

```
public List<String> apply(Character c) {
    if (c < 'A' || c > 'Z') {
        throw new IllegalArgumentException(c + " is outside the valid range A..Z");
    } else {
        return singletonList("A"); ❶
```

```
      }
   }
```

❶ The static method `java.util.Collections.singletonList` returns a single element `List`.

The previous test for invalid input still passes, and now so does the new test for *diamond(A)*.

Enforcing Invariants

It would be tedious to approach the solution by writing 26 individual tests for each character from A to Z. At this point, we need to start thinking about how to really implement a *generic* diamond solution. We probably don't have much idea of where to begin. It's clear that there is an algorithm generating each line in the diamond, but it's probably not immediately obvious what it is. It's also not immediately obvious how we should write a single test that covers every aspect of every possible diamond matrix. Even if we could figure out how to write such a test, it seems highly unlikely that it would be very readable.

We can begin to break the problem down in the hopes that by implementing a step-by-step process, the tests will guide us to a solution that works correctly. There are a number of things we know to be true about any diamond. They are symmetrical, their size is a function of the input character, and perhaps simplest, *they are always square*.

That seems pretty straightforward to test. All we need to do is assert that the width and the height of the matrix are equal. In other words, the length of the result list is the same as the length of every string *in* the list, as demonstrated here:

```
@Shared char bChar = 'B'
@Shared Range<Character> testRange = bChar..zChar ❶

@Unroll
def "diamond('#c') is square"() {
  given:
  def result = diamond.apply(c)

  expect:
  result.every {
    it.length() == result.size()
  }

  where:
  c << testRange ❷
}
```

❶ Because we already have a comprehensive test for *diamond(A)*, there's no need to test it again. Instead, we'll create a shared range that we can use to drive subsequent tests.

❷ Our test will assert that every possible diamond is square.

Running this, we might be surprised to find that it *already passes*. Remember that all our diamond function does so far is return the *diamond(A)* matrix. We need to add another test as a forcing function to make our test for "squareness" work against some other sized matrices.

The size of a diamond is a pretty simple formula. It should be $2x + 1$, where x is the index of the argument character, treating 'A' as zero. Thus, *diamond(B)* should have $(2 \times 1) + 1 = 3$ rows; *diamond(D)* should have $(2 \times 3) + 1 = 7$ rows; and so on.

Let's implement that test next, which will force us to produce diamonds of varying heights.

```
@Unroll("diamond(#c) should have #expectedHeight rows")
def "a diamond's height is determined by the character argument"() {
  given:
  def result = diamond.apply(c)

  expect:
  result.size() == expectedHeight

  where:
  c << testRange ❶
  expectedHeight = ((c - aChar) * 2) + 1 ❷
}
```

❶ We'll use the same B..Z range as before because we know the height of *diamond(A)* is correct.

❷ Calculating the expected height here allows us to use it in the @Unroll expression. Note that Java's char type is a scalar numeric, so we can perform math operations that will promote the result to int.

Now, to make the new test pass, we can simply create a list of the correct size.

If we naïvely do that by just putting a single character in each list element, we'll also see that the "squareness" test begins to fail. Good!

Let's fill out the implementation to make both tests pass:

```
public List<String> apply(Character c) {
  if (c < 'A' || c > 'Z') {
    throw new IllegalArgumentException(c + " is outside the valid range A..Z");
  } else {
```

```
      final int size = (2 * (c - 'A')) + 1; ❶
      List<String> result = new ArrayList<>();
      while (result.size() < size) {
        StringBuilder row = new StringBuilder();
        while (row.length() < size) {
          row.append('A'); ❷
        }
        result.add(row.toString());
      }
      return result;
    }
  }
```

❶ We calculate the desired size using our formula and then use loops to build the width and height of the matrix to the same size.

❷ Because none of our tests other than the test for *diamond(A)* are yet checking the *content* of the rows, we'll just fill each row with 'A' characters.

Matrix Content

We now have an implementation that produces matrices of the correct size. We haven't yet made any attempt to insert the correct characters into the pattern. We'll need to come up with a way to calculate the positions at which a character should appear in each row.

We know that the first line should contain 'A' in the center, the second should contain two 'B' characters separated by a single space, the third should contain two 'C' characters separated by three spaces, and so on. Each character should appear at four coordinates:

topLeft
> *x: (length ÷ 2) – row, y: row,* where *length* is the length of the row string and *row* is the zero-indexed row number determined by subtracting the character from the ASCII value of 'A'

topRight
> *x: (length – 1) – topLeft.x, y: row*

bottomLeft
> *x: topLeft.x, y: (height – 1) – row*

bottomRight
> *x: topRight.x, y: bottomLeft.y*

In the center line, `topLeft` and `bottomLeft` will be the same coordinate as will `top Right` and `bottomRight`. In the first line `topLeft` is the same as `topRight`. In the last line `bottomLeft` is the same as `bottomRight`.

Let's try to implement that with the following test:

```
@Unroll
def "the appropriate character appears in each row and column in diamond(#c)"() {
  given:
  def result = diamond.apply(c)

  expect:
  int lastIndex = result.size() - 1
  int midpoint = result.size().intdiv(2) ❶

  for (rowChar in aChar..c) { ❷
    int rowIndex = (rowChar - aChar) ❸

    def topLeft = [x: midpoint - rowIndex, y: rowIndex] ❹
    def topRight = [x: lastIndex - topLeft.x, y: rowIndex]
    def bottomLeft = [x: topLeft.x, y: lastIndex - rowIndex]
    def bottomRight = [x: topRight.x, y: bottomLeft.y]

    assert result[topLeft.y].charAt(topLeft.x) == rowChar ❺
    assert result[topRight.y].charAt(topRight.x) == rowChar
    assert result[bottomLeft.y].charAt(bottomLeft.x) == rowChar
    assert result[bottomRight.y].charAt(bottomRight.x) == rowChar
  }

  where:
  c << testRange
}
```

❶ We need to know the last valid index and the midpoint of the matrix in order to work out some of the coordinates, so we might as well calculate them once upfront. Groovy's `intdiv` method will discard the noninteger part of the result.

❷ It's generally not a good idea to use loops to make Spock assertions. We can look at refactoring this later. For now, we want to test every character from `'A'` to the argument character and verify that it appears in the correct positions.

❸ We work out in which row the character should first appear.

❹ We calculate the x and y coordinates where we expect to find the character. There will be some overlap on these coordinates for `'A'` and c, but we won't worry about that for now.

❺ Finally, we make some assertions that the expected character appears in each coordinate. Because we're inside a for loop, we need to use the assert keyword.

This test isn't ideal. Making assertions in loops means that the test will fail-fast on the first failing character, as we'll see, if we run the test against our current implementation. Because for the moment we're filling the entire matrix with 'A' characters, the test will fail when it gets to 'B':

```
Condition not satisfied:

result[topLeft.y].charAt(topLeft.x) == rowChar
|      ||     |  |      |      |  | |
|      ||     1  A      |      1  | B
|      |[x:1, y:1]      [x:1, y:1] false
|      AAAAA
[AAAAA, AAAAA, AAAAA, AAAAA, AAAAA]
```

Because of the complexity of the assertion we're making, using every will ruin any diagnostic information. We could replace the for loop with (aChar..c).every, but an assertion failure wouldn't reveal anything about what is wrong with the diamond. We could try iterating over the rows of result instead, but it's actually really difficult to compose the relevant assertions because we need so many different values: the row index, the expected character, and whether we're past the midpoint of the matrix.

For now, we'll acknowledge that this test could use some improvement, but it is at least verifying things correctly, so we'll move on to the implementation:

```java
public List<String> apply(Character c) {
  if (c < 'A' || c > 'Z') {
    throw new IllegalArgumentException(c + " is outside the valid range A..Z");
  } else {
    final int size = (2 * (c - 'A')) + 1;

    char nextChar = 'A'; ❶
    boolean pastHalfWay = false; ❷

    List<String> result = new ArrayList<>();
    while (result.size() < size) {
      StringBuilder row = new StringBuilder();
      while (row.length() < size) {
        row.append(nextChar); ❸
      }
      result.add(row.toString());

      if (pastHalfWay) { ❹
        nextChar--;
      } else {
        nextChar++;
        if (nextChar == c) {
          pastHalfWay = true;
```

```
      }
    }
  }
  return result;
}
```

❶ We'll need a variable to track the character we're going to use to fill each row.

❷ We also need to know when we've gone past the halfway point in the diamond, because we'll need to start reversing the order of the characters at that point.

❸ Instead of appending a literal 'A' to each row, we now append our nextChar value.

❹ Finally, at the end of each row we increment or decrement nextChar to get it ready for the next row. If nextChar is equal to the argument character, we know we're at the halfway point and need to decrement nextChar until it's back down to 'A' again.

Note that we haven't actually attempted to put *only* the characters in the correct positions in each row. For our test, it's sufficient to fill each row with the desired character given that nothing is yet asserting that the row is padded correctly. This means that we'll now be generating "diamonds" like this:

```
AAAAA
BBBBB
CCCCC
BBBBB
AAAAA
```

It's definitely progress, but before we go any further, it's probably time for some refactoring.

Symmetry

In the latest test, we're working out four coordinates for each character and verifying all of them. In addition, in the implementation, we're incrementing all the way up to c and then decrementing all the way back down to 'A'. If we consider another invariant behavior of the diamond, this is completely unnecessary.

Diamonds are symmetrical both horizontally and vertically. If we simply build the top half of the diamond and then fill the remaining rows with a mirror image of the top half we will get the same result.

We can also save a lot of effort on testing multiple coordinates if we first write another test that ensures the diamond is symmetrical. After we know *that*, we actually only need to check character positions in one quadrant of the diamond because we will know the other quadrants must be correct, too.

The test for symmetry is very easy to write:

```
@Unroll
def "diamond(#c) is symmetrical"() {
  given:
  def result = diamond.apply(c)

  expect:
  result == result.reverse()  ❶

  and:
  result.every {
    it == it.reverse()  ❷
  }

  where:
  c << testRange
}
```

❶ Groovy decorates `java.util.List` with a `reverse` method that returns a copy of the list in reverse order. Because list equality is dependent on every element being equal, we can easily check for vertical symmetry by asserting that the diamond is identical if its rows are reversed.

❷ Similarly, Groovy also adds `reverse` to `java.lang.String`, so we can assert that every row is horizontally symmetrical in exactly the same way.

Now that we know all diamonds are symmetrical, we can simplify the previous test to only look at the one quadrant of the diamond:

```
@Unroll
def "the appropriate character appears in each row and column in diamond(#c)"() {
  given:
  def result = diamond.apply(c)

  and:
  int midpoint = result.size().intdiv(2)

  expect:
  for (rowChar in aChar..c) {
    int y = (rowChar - aChar)
    int x = midpoint - y
    assert result[y].charAt(x) == rowChar
  }

  where:
  c << testRange
}
```

It's remarkable how much we are able to simplify and clarify this test now that the symmetry is handled separately. Instead of four separate coordinates, we need only one.

Most important, if we try running this improved test against the previous iteration of the diamond function, the assertion failure gives a very good breakdown of what is wrong:

```
Condition not satisfied:

result[y].charAt(x) == rowChar
|    || |      | | |
|    |1  A     1 | B
|     AAAAA      false
[AAAAA, AAAAA, AAAAA, AAAAA, AAAAA]
```

We've taken advantage of the symmetry of the diamond pattern in the tests; now, it's time to do so in the implementation itself:

```java
public List<String> apply(Character c) {
  if (c < 'A' || c > 'Z') {
    throw new IllegalArgumentException(c + " is outside the valid range A..Z");
  } else {
    final int size = (2 * (c - 'A')) + 1;

    List<String> result = new ArrayList<>();
    for (char nextChar = 'A'; nextChar <= c; nextChar++) {  ❶
      StringBuilder row = new StringBuilder();
      while (row.length() < size) {
        row.append(nextChar);
      }
      result.add(row.toString());
    }

    ❷
    final int index = result.size();
    for (int i = 0; i < (index - 1); i++) {
      result.add(index, result.get(i));
    }

    return result;
  }
}
```

❶ Instead of looping *while* the number of rows is less than the desired size, we can iterate from 'A' up to the argument character. We've removed a couple of local variables including the Boolean that tracked whether we should increment or decrement the character at the end of the loop. The loop now builds the rows only up to the halfway mark.

❷ After the top half of the diamond is built, we simply mirror all but the last row.

There are a number of ways to approach the vertical mirroring, and it doesn't particularly matter exactly how you do it. This implementation definitely looks more straightforward than the previous one. We haven't actually pushed the solution any further, but we've clarified the tests and simplified the in-progress solution.

Eliminating the Assertion Loop

In the previous test that deals with validating the characters in one quadrant of the diamond, we used a `for` loop with a nested `assert`, which is not very idiomatic Spock style. Assertion loops are not ideal for a couple of reasons. First, it's very easy to forget to use the `assert` keyword and inadvertently write a test that doesn't really verify anything. Second, the test will fail-fast on an earlier iteration of the loop without running the subsequent ones.

We can eliminate the loop by moving the iteration of the character we're looking for into the `where` block. In effect, we want a *nested* iteration. Currently, we iterate over the characters B through Z, which are the valid parameters for the diamond function (omitting the simple case of A). However, for each of those characters, we also want to iterate from A to the character and run the feature method once for that individual character.

We need two parameters in the `where` block: the character c as we have now, and rowChar. The values of c and rowChar will be the same for numerous iterations of the feature method, but we want to test each unique combination.

If we draw this out as a data table, it's simple enough:

```
c   | rowChar
'B' | 'A'
'B' | 'B'
'C' | 'A'
'C' | 'B'
'C' | 'D'
'D' | 'A'
'D' | 'B'
...
'Z' | 'Y'
'Z' | 'Z'
```

Unfortunately, the full table has 350 rows!

We can solve this by collecting all the combinations for each value of c and performing a *flat-map* operation over them. A flat-map operation is simply taking a collection that contains other collections and iterating over all of the nested collections as if they were concatenated.

Groovy's implementation of flat-map is called collectMany. Let's look at that here to see how we can use it to finally get rid of the assertion loop in our feature method:

```
@Unroll
def "#rowChar appears in the correct row and column in diamond(#c)"() {
  given:
  def result = diamond.apply(c)

  and:
  int midpoint = result.size().intdiv(2)
  int y = (rowChar - aChar)
  int x = midpoint - y

  expect:
  result[y].charAt(x) == rowChar

  where:
  row << testRange.collectMany { c2 -> ❶
    (aChar..c2).collect { new Tuple(c2, it) } ❷
  }
  c = row[0] ❸
  rowChar = row[1]
}
```

❶ The combinations forming our previous table are generated by collectMany operating on the range of valid characters, B to Z.

❷ Inside the collectMany closure, we do a nested collect call that generates tuples with each combination for that value of c. So, each iteration of the feature method will have a single Tuple instance as the value for row.

❸ For convenience, we can unpack the tuple into the c and rowChar parameters we want.

The assertion itself has not changed from the previous version of the feature method; we have simply moved the iteration outside the body of the test itself. When you run this feature method, it will execute 350 times!

Adding Padding to the Rows

We now know that we have the correct characters in the correct diamond formation. However, our solution is incomplete because we haven't yet checked that the coordinates—other than the "interesting" ones that form part of the diamond—are filled with padding characters.

We can approach this assertion with a similar feature method as the last one. In fact, the where block is identical. Instead of checking the character at a particular *x* position in each row, we'll simply *remove* the character at that position and check that everything remaining is a padding character.

The key to keeping this feature method simple is in remembering what we *don't* need to prove. Here's what we know from the previous feature methods:

- The correct character appears in the correct place, so we don't need to make any consideration for what character we *remove* from the row.
- The diamond is symmetrical, so we can save some complexity by checking only the first half of the row.
- The diamond is the correct size, so we don't need to worry about how long the row is.

```
@Unroll
def "areas around the character `#rowChar` in diamond(#c) are padded"() {
  given:
  def result = diamond.apply(c)

  and:
  int midpoint = result.size().intdiv(2)
  int y = (rowChar - aChar)
  int x = midpoint - y

  expect:
  new StringBuilder(result[y][0..midpoint])
    .deleteCharAt(x)
    .toString()
    .every { it == '-' }

  where:
  row << testRange.collectMany { c2 ->
    (aChar..c2).collect { new Tuple(c2, it) }
  }
  c = row[0]
  rowChar = row[1]
}
```

The feature method is pretty straightforward. We use the `deleteCharAt` method of `StringBuilder` to remove the known character, and then Groovy's `every` method to ensure that everything remaining is padding.

At last, we can implement a change to the diamond algorithm that makes it generate the correct pattern:

```
public List<String> apply(Character c) {
  if (c < 'A' || c > 'Z') {
    throw new IllegalArgumentException(c + " is outside the valid range A..Z");
  } else {
    final int midpoint = c - 'A';  ❶
```

```java
    List<String> result = new ArrayList<>();
    for (char nextChar = 'A'; nextChar <= c; nextChar++) {
      final int x = midpoint - result.size(); ❷
      StringBuilder row = new StringBuilder();
      while (row.length() < x) { ❸
        row.append('-');
      }
      row.append(nextChar); ❹
      while (row.length() <= midpoint) { ❺
        row.append('-');
      }

      row.append(new StringBuilder(row.substring(0, midpoint)).reverse()); ❻

      result.add(row.toString());
    }

    int index = result.size();
    for (int i = 0; i < (index - 1); i++) {
      result.add(index, result.get(i));
    }

    return result;
  }
}
```

❶ Instead of the size of the diamond, we work out the index of the center row or column.

❷ The x position where the A..Z character belongs is derived from the center index and the current index.

❸ Before the character position, we add padding characters.

❹ Now we add a single instance of the A..Z character.

❺ If we're not at the center yet, we add more padding until we are.

❻ Finally, the row is mirrored horizontally in a similar way to the vertical mirroring we did previously.

Refinement

We now have a correct diamond implementation. However, looking at the last test we wrote, it seems overspecified. We're removing a character from *a specific index* in the row and verifying that we're left with only padding. But we already verified that the index was correct in a previous test. Instead of calculating the index again, we could simplify things by just removing *any* single instance of the character. In fact, because we've already verified that the correct character is placed on the correct row, we could just remove the first instance of *any* uppercase character, as shown in the following:

```
@Unroll
def "areas outside diamond(#c) are filled with padding"() {
  given:
  def result = diamond.apply(c)

  expect:
  upperLeftQuadrant(result)*.replaceFirst(/[A-Z]/, "").every {
    it ==~ /-+/
  }

  where:
  c << testRange
}

private List<String> upperLeftQuadrant(List<String> result) {
  int midpoint = result.size().intdiv(2)
  result[0..midpoint].collect { row ->
    row[0..midpoint]
  }
}
```

We've also introduced a helper method to allow us to get the truncated List<String> representing just the upper-left quadrant of the diamond from the full result.

Summary

In this chapter, we explored implementing some code in a test-driven manner by dividing a problem into behavioral *slices* and incrementing toward a complete solution. Each step along the way brought us closer and kept existing tests passing.

We saw how we can reduce complexity by using multiple tests that complement one another so that behavior covered by another test can be assumed.

We also saw how to use where blocks to exhaustively test a range of possible inputs with either predetermined or generated data.

Exercise: Customizable Diamonds

Modify the diamond implementation so that it has a constructor that accepts a character range, making it possible for you to do things like create numeric or lowercase diamond patterns.

Try to drive the changes with tests so that you write a test before introducing the corresponding change into the implementation.

PART III

Integrating Spock

In the third part of this book, we look at how to integrate Spock with other software. We examine end-to-end testing of REST applications, testing applications written using the Spring framework, and end-to-end testing web applications using Geb (*http://www.gebish.org*) among other things.

CHAPTER 12

Spock and Spring

In this chapter, we dive into integration testing with the Spring application framework.

In the examples in this chapter, we use Spring Boot 1.4 and Spock 1.1, which include some new features that streamline integration testing. In particular, until Spock 1.1, mocking beans in the application context of an integration test was awkward.

What Do We Mean by "Integration Tests"?

In unit tests, the specification class deals with a unit of code in isolation. Collaborators are mocked or stubbed.

With integration tests, the entire application—or a subset of it—is started and the behavior of the system as a whole is tested. Integration tests typically deal with the larger-scale behavior exhibited by units of code working together.

Integration tests are also a useful way to protect against incorrect assumptions about the way units interact that might have been made in unit tests. For example, if a mock collaborator in a unit test does not behave the way the *real* collaborator does, the unit test might be incorrect, and without any kind of integration test, this would not be obvious until someone tries to use the application.

Container Tests

Container tests are similar to integration tests in that the application or some subset of it is started; however, their intent is a little different. Container tests focus on how units of code interact with the functionality of the container or framework in which they run. They ensure the framework features have been properly understood and are being applied correctly.

For example, we'll see some examples of testing annotation-driven behavior in Spring. Without the Spring framework annotations such as @Transactional have no effect. To ensure that we're using those kinds of features correctly, it's necessary to exercise the code in the context of a Spring application.

There is a fine line between container-testing code and testing the container itself. Container tests should deal with the behavior we want our code to exhibit that is implemented via the container, not whether the container itself works as documented.

For the purposes of this chapter the distinction between integration and container tests is not particularly important. We're going to deal with some practical examples and techniques that you can apply in either context.

Should You Run Integration Tests in a Separate Test Suite?

Some people advocate splitting integration tests into a separate test suite that you can run separately from the unit tests. Some frameworks even enforce such a separation. For example, the Grails framework has separate unit, integration, and functional test phases. Tests that run in each phase are placed in separate source trees.

Spring Boot, on the other hand, uses annotations to define integration test behavior that needs to start the application container. Annotated tests can be mixed with regular unit tests in the same source tree.

However, just because Spring Boot doesn't require separation, there's nothing to prevent you from deciding to keep integration tests separate. You just need to define a separate test phase in a Gradle build. Many people advocate such a separation because integration tests are typically slower-running than unit tests.

So which is the correct approach?

Getting fast feedback from unit tests while developing and then running the integration suite less frequently might save some time. But I lean toward the school of thought that says if the integration tests are so slow that there would be a real benefit from running them separately, the problem is not how the tests are run but the fact they're so slow the question even arises. Fix the cause of the slowness before resorting to separate test suites.

Spring Compatibility

Spring Boot provides several annotations to support JUnit tests, and because Spock runs using the JUnit test runner, they are compatible with Spock. To hook in correctly to the Spring test framework, you need to add the *spock-spring* module to your build.

For example, the examples in this chapter declare the following dependency:

```
testCompile("org.spockframework:spock-spring:+")
```

With that module in place, Spock will automatically detect Spring-based tests based on the presence of one or more Spring test annotations. As we'll see later, the *spock-spring* module also provides support for defining Spock mocks and stubs as Spring beans.

Older versions of Spring Boot provided a variety of different annotations. `@Integra tionTest` or `@WebIntegrationTest` specify whether just the application context or the entire application including the HTTP listener need to be started. `@SpringAppli cationConfiguration` specifies the configuration classes or XML files to load.

In Spring Boot 1.4, these annotations were deprecated in favor of an all-in-one `@SpringBootTest` annotation. The `@SpringBootTest` annotation is what the examples in this chapter use.

@SpringBootTest

Just adding `@SpringBootTest` to a specification class will mean the Spring container is started. Spring will search for a root configuration class or XML file and initialize the application context.

This is done once for all annotated tests that share the same configuration, so the time cost of starting Spring is not compounded every time you add a new test to the suite.

Testing Annotation-Driven Transactions

Spring uses aspect-oriented programming (AOP) in various ways to provide cross-cutting behavior defined by the presence of annotations. One of the most commonly used AOP annotations is `@Transactional`. When applied to a method on a Spring-managed bean class, the `@Transactional` annotation wraps invocations of the method in a proxy that will start a transaction at the start of the method call and commit it at the end. If any runtime exception is thrown by the method, the transaction will be rolled back.

Transactions 101

You're probably familiar with database transactions, but if not, here's a quick overview.

If you have a number of operations that you need to run on a database that must be performed as an atomic unit, you should use a transaction. For example, if when inserting a new inventory item into a warehouse system you need to add pricing information in several currencies, you might do so like this:

```
insert into inventory (name) values ('Tricorder');
insert into prices (inv_id, currency, price)
        select id, 'USD', 199.95
          from inventory
         where name = 'Tricorder';
insert into prices (inv_id, currency, price)
        select id, 'GBP', 154.2
          from inventory
         where name = 'Tricorder';
insert into prices (inv_id, currency, price)
        select id, 'ZAR', 2747.02
          from inventory
         where name = 'Tricorder';
```

If any single insert operation fails, you want none of the operations to take effect; otherwise, you would have invalid data in the database—missing prices, or worse, prices referring to a nonexistent row on the inventory table.

Using a transaction guarantees that atomicity. The operations executed within a transaction are pending until the transaction completes. If an error occurs, the transaction is *rolled back* and all pending operations are undone. If the operations complete successfully the transaction is *committed* and the pending operations are made permanent.

Tracking Who Is Mentioned in a Message

Let's introduce some transactional behavior into Squawker.

Because users might want to easily access a list of messages that mention them directly, we'll create a new table to index "mentions." When a message is inserted, its text is scanned for references to usernames, and for each match, a row is inserted in the mention table.

For example, let's assume that the user table contains the following rows:

id	username
1	kirk
2	spock
3	bones

If the user @kirk posts a message—*"have @spock, @bones, and @redshirt report to the transporter room."*—we should insert the message itself and two rows on the mention table so that the data looks like the following two tables, respectively:

id	posted_by_id	text
1	1	have @spock, @bones, and @redshirt report to the transporter room.

user_id	message_id
2	1
3	1

Only two rows are inserted because part of the message looks like it mentions a user, @redshirt, but no such user actually exists on the user table. Any such "phantom" mentions should just be ignored.

If any of those inserts fails we don't want to be left with missing entries from the men tion table or, worse, rows on the mention table that don't refer to a valid row on the message table. This is something we should definitely handle as a transaction.

To do that, we can define a Spring bean that's at a slightly higher level than our existing MessageStore DAO. The new MessageService class will delegate the lower-level operations to MessageStore and a new DAO MentionStore that manages the entries on the mention table:

```
public void insert(String username, Message message); ❶

public List<Message> mentionsOf(User user); ❷
```

❶ insert adds a row to the mention table if username refers to a valid user and a row does not already exist linking the particular user and message; in other words, it silently ignores duplicates.

❷ mentionsOf simply returns all the messages that mention a particular user.

```
@Transactional
public Message postMessage(User user, String text); ❶
```

❶ postMessage is the higher-level method that will insert rows to the message and mention tables.

When MessageService.postMessage is called, it should in turn call MessageS tore.insert once and MentionStore.insert zero or more times, depending on how many users are mentioned in the message text.

Non-Spring-Dependent Tests

We can begin with some unit tests that validate the basic functionality of `MessageSer vice.postMessage`. To test most of the functionality, we don't need a Spring container, as demonstrated here:

```
class MessageServiceSpec extends Specification {

    def messageStore = Mock(MessageStore)
    def mentionStore = Mock(MentionStore)

    @Subject
    def messageService = new MessageService(messageStore, mentionStore)

    def "inserts a mention if the text mentions another user"() {
      when:
      messageService.postMessage(user, messageText)

      then:
      1 * mentionStore.insert(mentionedUsername, _)

      where:
      user = new User("kirk")
      mentionedUsername = "spock"
      messageText = "Strike that from the record, Mr. @$mentionedUsername!"
    }

    def "does not insert a mention if the text mentions a nonexistent user"() {
      when:
      messageService.postMessage(user, messageText)

      then:
      0 * mentionStore.insert(mentionedUsername, _)

      where:
      user = new User("kirk")
      mentionedUsername = "spock"
      messageText = "Strike that from the record, Mr. @$mentionedUsername!"
    }

    def "does not count multiple mentions in a single message"() {
      when:
      messageService.postMessage(user, messageText)

      then:
      1 * mentionStore.insert(mentionedUsername, _)

      where:
      user = new User("kirk")
      mentionedUsername = "spock"
      messageText = "@$mentionedUsername, come in! @$mentionedUsername, report!"
    }
```

```
def "inserts multiple mentions if necessary"() {
  when:
  messageService.postMessage(user, messageText)

  then:
  1 * mentionStore.insert(mentionedUsernames[0], _)
  1 * mentionStore.insert(mentionedUsernames[1], _)

  where:
  user = new User("kirk")
  mentionedUsernames = ["spock", "bones"]
  messageText = "Mr @spock, @bones... to the transporter room."
}
}
```

However, we begin to run into some problems with a mock and stub approach here. The two feature methods, "does not insert a mention if the text mentions a nonexistent user" and "does not count multiple mentions in a single mes sage", fail. In both cases, unexpected calls to MentionStore.insert are made. In fact, the functionality described in those cases is implemented by MentionStore itself.

Let's look at the SQL command used by MentionStore.insert:

```
INSERT INTO mention (user_id, message_id)
  SELECT
    u.id,
    :message.id
  FROM user u
  WHERE u.username = :username AND NOT EXISTS(
    SELECT 1
    FROM mention
    WHERE user_id = u.id AND message_id = :message.id
  )
```

If the subselect finds no user with a matching username, zero rows will be inserted. Likewise, the AND NOT EXISTS clause prevents duplicates from being inserted.

This means that MessageService is free to call MentionStore.insert for usernames that do not exist on the user table or multiple times for the same username. It simpli fies the implementation required in MessageService—no de-duplication or lookup of usernames is required. It's not an error for a user to post a message with text that includes an "@" character followed by something that is not actually a valid user name. The right thing to do is just ignore such cases when recording mentions.

Testing a Transaction Rollback

Now, let's try to write a feature method that should result in a transaction rollback and see what happens:

```
def "if mention insert fails a message is not persisted"() {
  given:
  mentionStore.insert(*_) >> {
    throw new RuntimeException("test")
  }

  when:
  messageService.postMessage(user, messageText)

  then:
  def e = thrown(RuntimeException)
  e.message == "test"

  and:
  // ... what do we do here?

  where:
  user = new User("kirk")
  mentionedUsernames = ["spock", "bones"]
  messageText = "@${mentionedUsernames[0]}, @${mentionedUsernames[1]}" +
    " meet me in the transporter room!"
}
```

First, we ensure that an exception will occur by trying to insert a mention, which should result in a transaction rollback. But what can we do to prove the message was not inserted?

We can't assert that messageStore.insert is not called because it *will* be called; we just expect the result of that call to be backed out.

Although this test will start and run fast because it is not dependent on the Spring context being initialized properly or even existing at all, it's not really sufficient for what we need. There are end-to-end scenarios that can't be validated using a mock MentionStore, and when it comes to testing the transactional behavior provided by Spring, the test can't prove anything without Spring's transactional proxy wrapping the MessageService.

Instead, we'll need to start a Spring container and test the MessageService after it's wrapped with a transactional proxy.

We should absolutely leave the working unit tests in place. There's really nothing to gain from replicating those tests in an integration test, and the more functionality we can test without requiring Spring, the better.

Setting Up the Spring Application

Spring Boot uses a Main class to boot the application. The class can declare beans just like any other configuration class, but instead of being annotated with @Configura tion, it is annotated with @SpringBootApplication:

```
@SpringBootApplication(scanBasePackages = {"squawker.jdbi", "squawker.mentions"})
public class Main {
  public static void main(String... args) {
    SpringApplication.run(Main.class, args);
  }
}
```

The static `main` method allows the application to run as an executable jar after it's packaged.

A First Integration Test

When writing an integration test, we can actually avoid a lot of the setup necessary for a unit test. After all, the integration test uses the context and configuration defined for the actual production application. There's no need to configure a data source or wire up DAOs to the data source and the service because the test will use the beans from the application context. Spring's test framework will automatically provide a data source connected to an in-memory database.

Let's take a detailed look at how we can write the test for transactional rollback:

```
@SpringBootTest(classes = Main)
❶
class MessageServiceSpec extends Specification {

    @Autowired @Subject MessageService messageService ❷
    @Autowired @TruncateTables(DBIConnector) DBI dbi ❸
    @Autowired UserStore userStore
    @Autowired MentionStore mentionStore

    def "does not insert a mention if the text mentions a nonexistent user"() {
      given:
      def user = userStore.insert(username)

      expect:
      !userStore.find(mentionedUsername)

      when:
      messageService.postMessage(user, messageText)

      then:
      count("mention") == 0 ❹

      where:
      username = "kirk"
      mentionedUsername = "spock"
      messageText = "Strike that from the record, Mr. @$mentionedUsername!"
    }

    def "does not count multiple mentions in a single message"() {
      given:
```

```
        def user = userStore.insert(username)
        userStore.insert(mentionedUsername)

        when:
        messageService.postMessage(user, messageText)

        then:
        count("mention") == 1

        where:
        username = "kirk"
        mentionedUsername = "spock"
        messageText = "Mr. @$mentionedUsername, come in! " +
          "@$mentionedUsername, report!"
    }

    def "if mention insert fails a message is not persisted"() {
        given:
        def user = userStore.insert(username)
        mentionedUsernames.each {
          userStore.insert(it)
        }

        and:
        dbi.withHandle { handle ->
          handle.execute("drop table mention") ❺
        }

        when:
        messageService.postMessage(user, messageText)

        then:
        thrown(DBIException)

        and:
        count("message") == 0

        where:
        username = "kirk"
        mentionedUsernames = ["spock", "bones"]
        messageText = "@${mentionedUsernames[0]}, @${mentionedUsernames[1]}" +
          " meet me in the transporter room!"
    }
}
```

❶ The first difference is that the test is annotated with `@SpringBootTest` and pro-
    vided a reference to the `Main` application class.

❷ Notice that instead of instantiating instances of the classes we'll need for the test,
    we have Spring autowire them.

❸ We can reuse the @TruncateTables annotation we developed in Chapter 10 on an injected bean.

❹ count(String tableName) is a helper method that returns the number of rows on a database table using a SELECT COUNT(*) FROM... query.

❺ Instead of having a mock MentionStore throw an exception, we need to force an error in another way. Dropping the mention table will certainly do that! However, as we'll see shortly, this is not actually a good idea and should not be emulated.

The two cases that failed in our unit test now work. Instead of attempting to validate whether MentionStore.insert is called for nonexistent users or multiple mentions, we can simply look at the resulting rows on the database. The behavior is abstracted from implementation. With this test, it really doesn't matter whether MessageService validates and de-duplicates usernames before calling MentionStore.insert or whether MentionStore simply ignores invalid usernames and repeated calls. What we care about is that data is not incorrectly persisted, and that's what the test verifies.

In addition, the transaction rollback test now works. We have a transactional proxy around the autowired MessageService instance and therefore a transaction is started when the test calls postMessage in the when: block. When the method returns, the transaction is committed or if the method throws an exception, as it does here, the transaction is rolled back.

 You can autowire any bean into a Spock specification. This could mean that beans that are explicitly declared by the application, such as the MessageService and the various DAOs in our specification or beans registered by the framework itself such as the DataSource. Specifications can also use the @Value annotation to wire-in values from a Spring configuration.

Because of the way Spock's lifecycle integrates with Spring's test support, it is not possible to combine the @Autowired and @Shared annotations in a single field.

Convenience and Cost

The convenience of autowiring dependencies directly into the specification is considerable. This convenience comes at a cost, though: the test is significantly slower to run than a unit test. On my laptop, the integration test takes more than four seconds to run, whereas the unit test—with more feature methods—takes far less than a second. Although Spring mitigates this by starting the application context only once and sharing it between multiple feature methods or specifications, that comes with its own disadvantages, which we'll discuss a little later.

The thing to take away is to test as much as possible in simple unit tests and only use integration tests where it's really necessary. That is, where you're testing interdependencies between components, configuration, or, as here, the way components interact with the application framework.

Unexpected Side Effects

In the previous integration test for transaction rollback, we dropped a database table in order to provoke an error. It's actually tricky to craft a scenario in which referential integrity is violated. If we construct the service properly, data integrity issues should be avoided. A more likely cause of failure might well be some kind of error connecting to the database.

Regardless of how realistic it is and the fact that it works, this turns out to be a pretty bad idea.

As I mentioned previously, Spring caches application contexts between tests to avoid the time cost of reinitializing the application for every feature method. Unfortunately, this means that the table we just dropped as a cute way to cause our transactional method to roll back...well, it's still dropped when the next feature method starts. It's not much fun to debug an error with the message `org.h2.jdbc.JdbcSQLException: Table "MENTION" not found` in a completely different test than the one causing the problem.

That's a classic example of leaking side effects between tests.

We can certainly fix the leak by adding a `cleanup:` block to the feature method, like this:

```
cleanup:
mentionStore.createMentionTable()
```

Forcing Spring to Re-Create the Application Context

As we've seen, Spring caches application contexts used by tests and reuses them if another test declares the same configuration; this typically means that the combination of configuration classes in the `@SpringBootTest` annotation is the same. Because of this any modifications to the application context (e.g., by mutating singleton beans) or any resources it manages (such as an embedded in-memory database) will leak into other tests.

Spring provides an annotation to help us here—`@DirtiesContext`. When applied to a feature method, it will mark the application context in the cache as dirty so that when the next test runs using the same context configuration, it will actually be re-created.

The annotation can also be applied to the specification class so that it will mark the context as dirty after all the feature methods run (think of it as part of the `cleanup`

Spec phase), or if written as @DirtiesContext(classMode = AFTER_EACH_TEST_METHOD) after each feature method runs (think of it as part of the cleanup phase).

Instead of using a manual cleanup specification that re-creates the table, we can simply annotate the feature method:

```
@DirtiesContext
def "if mention insert fails a message is not persisted"() {
  given:
  def user = userStore.insert(username)
  mentionedUsernames.each {
    userStore.insert(it)
  }

  and:
  dbi.withHandle { handle ->
    handle.execute("drop table mention")
  }

  when:
  messageService.postMessage(user, messageText)

  then:
  thrown(DBIException)

  and:
  count("message") == 0

  where:
  username = "kirk"
  mentionedUsernames = ["spock", "bones"]
  messageText = "@${mentionedUsernames[0]}, @${mentionedUsernames[1]}" +
    " meet me in the transporter room!"
}
```

Obviously, there is a cost associated with this. The startup time of a Spring application context is nontrivial in the *best* of scenarios, and preventing Spring from optimizing that time by reusing contexts will add to the time it takes to run the suite.

Where possible, it's best to avoid having to use @DirtiesContext, but it's useful for certain scenarios in which modifying the application context is inevitable or is the point of the test.

In the scenario we're dealing with here, it feels like we really need a better way to provoke that error, though.

A Better Way to Force Errors

In a typical unit test, we'd probably generate that kind of error using a stub, and that seems like a much saner way to go about things. Could we do that in a Spring integration test? Ideally, the test should look like this:

```
def "if mention insert fails a message is not persisted"() {
  given:
  def user = userStore.insert(username)
  mentionedUsernames.each {
    userStore.insert(it)
  }

  and:
  mentionStore.insert(*_) >> {
    throw new RuntimeException("test") ❶
  }

  when:
  messageService.postMessage(user, messageText)

  then:
  def e = thrown(RuntimeException)
  getRootCause(e).message == "test" ❷

  and:
  count("message") == 0 ❸

  where:
  username = "kirk"
  mentionedUsernames = ["spock", "bones"]
  messageText = "@${mentionedUsernames[0]}, @${mentionedUsernames[1]}" +
    " meet me in the transporter room!"
}
```

❶ Instead of dropping a table, we ensure that the MentionStore stub will throw an exception when invoked.

❷ In the interest of ensuring the test is actually doing what we think it is, it's prudent to check that the exception thrown by MessageService was caused by our stub and not something else.

❸ As before, we can validate that the rollback happened by checking that no rows exist on the mention table.

The crucial thing the test needs to know is whether the data created on the message table was rolled back. For that reason, we can't use a mock MessageStore, because MessageStore.insert *is* called, as we saw in the unit test earlier. But MentionStore doesn't need to be a real object.

This is indeed possible. In the next part of this chapter, we explore how you can use Spock's mocks and stubs as beans in the Spring application context.

Mock and Stub Beans

Until Spock 1.1, writing Spring integration tests that used mock and stub beans was tricky. Spock's mocks are tied closely to the specification lifecycle. This enables the seamless expectation syntax used in then: blocks. Mocks have (or had) to be defined in the context of a specification, either as a local variable in a feature method or as a nonshared field of the specification class. However, because Spring beans are defined in configuration classes or XML configuration files, they need to be defined independent of the specification context.

Spock 1.1 introduced the idea of *detached mocks*—mocks (or stubs, spies, etc.) defined outside of the context of the specification class that can then be "attached" to the specification lifecycle and used as normal. Defining mock and stub Spring beans is now actually very easy!

Let's take a look at some examples.

Mention Events

To tie in with the "mention" mechanism that we've been working on, it would also be good to send users a notification when someone mentions them in a message.

To implement this, we can use Spring's application event mechanism. Whenever a mention is inserted, we'll raise an application event, and at some point we can plug event listeners in that will email or send push notifications to users who are the subject of a mention.

Spring Application Events

Spring's application event mechanism is pretty simple. A bean class ApplicationE ventPublisher is available in the application context. Components can autowire the publisher and then use its publishEvent method to publish events.

Any component that needs to be notified of events can then implement the Applica tionListener<E> interface. Any event object that is in the bounds of the generic type on the listener is passed to its onApplicationEvent method.

It's also possible in recent versions of Spring to define listener methods using annotations rather than by implementing ApplicationListener. That is convenient when a component needs to respond in different ways to multiple event types.

Events themselves can either extend `ApplicationEvent` or just be defined as simple Plain Old Java Objects (POJOs). POJO event types are wrapped in a `PayloadApplica tionEvent` when passed to the listener.

We're going to inject a `ApplicationEventPublisher` dependency into `MessageSer vice` and then trigger an event every time a mention is inserted.

Our new specification is going to test that events are triggered correctly. The obvious way to do that is to register a mock `ApplicationListener<MentionEvent>` bean and assert that its `onApplicationEvent` method is called.

Mock Beans Before Spock 1.1

Before Spock 1.1, there were a couple of options for registering mock beans in a Spring application context.

- Drop Spock mocks and use another library such as Mockito
- Abandon annotation-driven tests and register the mock beans programmatically
- Register bean delegates into which mocks are injected by the specification

We'll skip over the first option, but take a brief look at the second and third.

If we don't mind losing some of the simplicity of annotation-driven integration tests, we can just set up an application context by hand and wire-up whatever beans we need:

```
class MentionNotificationSpec extends Specification {

  def applicationContext = new AnnotationConfigApplicationContext() ❶

  ApplicationListener<MentionEvent> mentionListener = Mock() ❷

  @Autowired MessageStore messageStore
  @Autowired MentionStore mentionStore

  def setup() {
    applicationContext.with {
      register(Main) ❸
      beanFactory.registerSingleton("mentionListener", mentionListener) ❹
      refresh() ❺
      beanFactory.autowireBean(this) ❻
    }

    userStore.createUserTable() ❼
    messageStore.createMessageTable()
    mentionStore.createMentionTable()
  }
```

```
// everything below this point is common in the next few examples

@Autowired @TruncateTables(DBIConnector) DBI dbi
@Autowired UserStore userStore
@Autowired MessageService messageService

def "registered listeners are notified of mentions"() {
  given:
  def user = userStore.insert(postingUsername)
  userStore.insert(mentionedUsername)

  and:
  def event = new BlockingVariable<MentionEvent>()
  mentionListener.onApplicationEvent(_) >> { MentionEvent it ->
    event.set(it)
  }

  when:
  def message = messageService.postMessage(user, messageText)

  then:
  with(event.get()) {
    mentionedUsername == mentionedUsername
    message.id == message.id
  }

  where:
  postingUsername = "kirk"
  mentionedUsername = "spock"
  messageText = "Report, Mr @$mentionedUsername!"
  }
}
```

❶ Instead of using @SpringBootTest, the specification creates its own application
   context.

❷ The mock listener bean is created just like any other mock.

❸ applicationContext.register tells Spring the base class to use to configure the
   application. It's possible to register multiple configuration classes or XML files,
   much as @SpringBootTest accepts an array for its classes property.

❹ We then register the mock listener as a singleton bean—a preconfigured object
   rather than one created by the Spring container.

❺ We call applicationContext.refresh() in order to initialize the container
   properly. This will wire our mock beans in to any other beans that depend on
   them.

❻   We need to explicitly autowire the specification class itself.

❼   Unfortunately, because we're not using the Spring Boot bootstrap, we also need to initialize the data source ourselves.

Obviously, this is fairly complex and although it works, we're also missing some of the enhancements @SpringBootTest gives us. We've had to initialize the database tables because we've lost the automatic bootstrapping done by Spring Boot. If the startup was more complex, we'd have had to do even more manual steps, and the process of figuring out exactly what is necessary and how to do it is crude and error prone.

Perhaps the most crucial thing lost is the reuse of the application context. As we add more feature methods to this specification, it will become slower and slower because a new application context is started for every feature method.

Mock Bean Delegates

Instead of this approach, we can define a bean delegate that will wrap a mock.

```
@SpringBootTest(classes = [
  Main,
  DelegatingApplicationListener ❶
])
@DirtiesContext
class MentionNotificationSpec extends Specification {

  @Autowired DelegatingApplicationListener listener ❷

  ApplicationListener<MentionEvent> mentionListener = Mock()

  def setup() {
    listener.delegate = mentionListener ❸
  }

  static class DelegatingApplicationListener
    implements ApplicationListener<MentionEvent> {
    @Delegate ApplicationListener<MentionEvent> delegate ❹
  }

  // ...
```

❶   In this case, we *are* using @SpringBootTest, but we're adding an extra class: our DelegatingApplicationListener to the context.

❷   We can then autowire the delegate bean into the specification.

❸   In the setup method, we inject our actual mock into the delegate bean.

❹ The `DelegatingApplicationListener` class is very simple; it's not intended for use outside the context of this specification.

The actual feature method in this example is identical to the one in the previous example; we've just simplified the setup a little.

This is better, but it's not always convenient to define bean delegate classes for everything. If a specification needs more than one mock or stub, or the interface being mocked is complex, it can result in a lot of boilerplate code.

Another issue is that by adding the mock to the delegate we're modifying a bean managed by the application context. We need to be very careful here; otherwise, we could start leaking state into other tests that happen to share the same application context. It's not a problem for other feature methods within this specification that will run the same `setup` method and therefore reset the delegate property, but having this state change leak out of the `Specification` class and break another test could be very frustrating to debug. For that reason, using `@DirtiesContext` at the specification level makes sense here.

Detached Mocks in the Spring Context

Detached mocks are potentially useful in a number of scenarios, but the *spock-spring* library provides special support for automatically attaching mocks registered as beans to the specification when running a Spring integration test.

Registering mock beans is now fairly transparent. Instead of needing a bean delegate, we can use a test configuration class that directly creates a mock or stub bean:

```
@SpringBootTest(classes = [
  Main,
  Config ❶
])
class MentionNotificationSpec extends Specification {

  @Autowired ApplicationListener<MentionEvent> mentionListener ❷

  static class Config {
    private final mockFactory = new DetachedMockFactory() ❸

    @Bean
    ApplicationListener<MentionEvent> mentionListener() {
      mockFactory.Mock(ApplicationListener)
    }
  }

  // ...
```

❶ Instead of specifying a mock delegate, we're going to use a test-specific configuration class.

❷ Now the mock listener is directly autowired into the specification.

❸ In the configuration class, we use a `DetachedMockFactory` to create mock instances as beans.

Spring Autoconfiguration and Test Configuration Classes

If you're accustomed to working with Spring configuration classes you might notice that the `Config` inner class in the previous specification was not annotated with `@Configuration`. Also, look back at the example with the bean delegate and notice that `DelegatingApplicationListener` is not annotated with `@Component`. There's a good reason for this.

The `@Configuration` and `@Component` annotations are used to expose classes to Spring's configuration autoscanning. If we annotate classes that are intended for use only in a single specification, they can accidentally be picked up and loaded into the application context used by another specification. Needless to say, this can be very confusing.

It's not necessary to annotate classes if you directly refer to them in the `@SpringBootTest` annotation.

Mock Beans in XML Configuration

It's also possible to define Spock mock beans in XML configuration if you need to:

```
@ContextConfiguration(locations = "mention-notification-spec.xml")
❶
@SpringBootTest(classes = Main)
class MentionNotificationSpec extends Specification {

  @Autowired ApplicationListener<MentionEvent> mentionListener

  // ...
}
```

❶ `@SpringBootTest` does not offer a way to specify XML configuration files, so it's necessary to add a `@ContextConfiguration` annotation.

The XML bean definition uses `SpockMockFactoryBean` to create mock instances. Like the ones we've seen so far, you can autowire them into specifications where they are automatically attached to the specification lifecycle:

```xml
<?xml version="1.0" encoding="UTF-8"?>
<beans xmlns="http://www.springframework.org/schema/beans"
       xmlns:xsi="http://www.w3.org/2001/XMLSchema-instance"
       xmlns:spock="http://www.spockframework.org/spring"
       xsi:schemaLocation="http://www.springframework.org/schema/beans
           http://www.springframework.org/schema/beans/spring-beans.xsd
           http://www.spockframework.org/spring
           http://www.spockframework.org/spring/spock.xsd">

    <spock:mock id="mentionListener"
                class="org.springframework.context.ApplicationListener"/>

</beans>
```

In addition to the `<spock:mock>` element shown in this example, there are also `<spock:stub>` and `<spock:spy>` elements.

It's also possible to use `SpockMockFactoryBean` in a configuration class, although there's no particular reason to prefer it over creating mocks with `DetachedMockFac tory`.

```
static class Config {
  @Bean
  FactoryBean<ApplicationListener<MentionEvent>> mentionListener() {
    new SpockMockFactoryBean(ApplicationListener)
  }
}
```

Replacing Application Beans with Mocks

Now that we've covered the use of mocks and stub beans in the Spring application context, let's revisit the original transactional spec and see if we can use a stub version of `MentionService` to provoke the exception we need to cause a transaction rollback.

We'll separate the transaction test out into its own class, `MessageServiceTransac tionSpec`, because the other test cases rely on `MentionStore` *not* being a mock and actually writing rows to the database:

```
static class Config {
  private final DetachedMockFactory mockFactory = new DetachedMockFactory()

  @Bean
  MentionStore mentionStore() {
    mockFactory.Stub(MentionStore)
  }
}
```

Instead of using the `Mock` method of `DetachedMockFactory`, the config here uses `Stub`. These methods are exactly equivalent to those available inside a specification and produce test doubles with the same characteristics.

One other thing to note is that there's an interdependence between the mock configuration and the "real" application configuration:

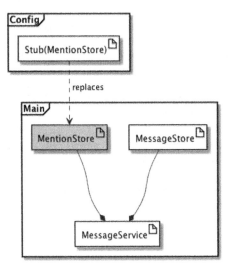

The two DAOs, `MessageStore` and `MentionStore`, are autowired into `MessageSer vice`. However, the test overrides the "real" `MentionStore` bean with a stub.

Because Spring handles all the autowiring, after beans are defined there's no need for the test config class to worry about the relationship between `MentionStore` and `Messa geService`. Because the `MentionStore` bean is replaced with a stub, it is the stub that is autowired into `MessageService`.

You might be wondering how Spring determines which of the two definitions of `Men tionStore` takes precedence. In this example, it's simply due to the declared order of the configuration classes.

```
@SpringBootTest(classes = [Main, Config])
```

The stub *should* take precedence because its bean definition is loaded last. In practice, I've found that sometimes bean precedence is nonintuitive. For example, if the bean name is not speicified in a `@Bean` or `@Component` annotation, it is derived from the class or bean method name. If your mock needs to replace a bean that exists in the "real" application context, the bean name needs to be identical.

Assuming two beans have the same name, the last one loaded should take precedence. Alternatively, if one of the beans is annotated with `@Primary`, it should take precedence.

Spock provides a way to actually assert whether an object is a Spock test double. We can use that to verify that our bean override is working as expected:

```
def "mock beans are auto-wired"() {
  expect:
  new MockUtil().isMock(mentionStore)
}
```

We can make this assertion fail by just reversing the declared order of the configuration classes in our example:

```
@SpringBootTest(classes = [Config, Main])
```

Now, the mock `MentionStore` bean is loaded first and then replaced with the real one from the main application context.

To make the bean precedence a little more explicit, there are a couple of approaches we can take. One is to annotate the mock bean definition method with `@Primary`. Another is to have our test configuration depend on the main configuration in a heirarchical relationship rather than specifying them both in the `@SpringBootTest` annotation.

First, we change the annotation on the specification class:

```
@SpringBootTest(classes = Config)
```

Then we import the main configuration in the test configuration class:

```
@Import(Main)
static class Config {
  private final DetachedMockFactory mockFactory = new DetachedMockFactory()

  @Bean
  MentionStore mentionStore() {
    mockFactory.Stub(MentionStore)
  }
}
```

Now the bean order is explicit: the main configuration is always loaded first and the test configuration extends it. The specification class depends only on the test configuration and inherits the main application configuration transitively.

Declarative Test Data

A suite of tests can have common data requirements, in which case Spring provides a couple of convenient ways to define fixtures.

Until now, we've been using our JDBI DAO classes such as `UserStore` and `MessageStore` to create test data. There's nothing wrong with this approach; in fact, I think the advantages of abstracting the tasks of creating data from the raw SQL used to insert rows to the database are considerable.

However, sharing fixtures in the form of SQL scripts can be a useful approach.

Using the @Sql Annotation for Data Fixtures

You can place Spring's @Sql annotation on a specification class or feature method, where it will use Spring's data source to execute SQL commands before the feature method runs (or before each feature method if the annotation is placed at the class level):

```
@Sql(statements = ["""
  insert into user (username, registered)
            values ('kirk', current_timestamp),
                   ('spock', current_timestamp),
                   ('bones', current_timestamp);
"""])
def "mentions are persisted with message"() {
  given:
  def user = userStore.find(username)

  when:
  def message = messageService.postMessage(user, messageText)

  then:
  count("mention") == mentionedUsernames.size()
  mentionedUsernames.every {
    mentionStore.mentionsOf(userStore.find(it)) == [message]
  }

  where:
  username = "kirk"
  mentionedUsernames = ["spock", "bones"]
  messageText = "@${mentionedUsernames[0]}, @${mentionedUsernames[1]}" +
    " meet me in the transporter room!"
}
```

Here, instead of creating data using the DAOs, we set it up directly by using SQL statements.

This is not much of an advantage when talking about the data for a single test. We've lost the type safety afforded to us by the DAOs and have had to specify some values—the timestamps—that the DAO handled for us. We've also lost the ability to tie values in the data to parameters from the where: block.

So, given all these disadvantages, why would you want to use @Sql? Well, mainly because it makes it easy to share fixtures between tests.

If we move that setup script to a file in src/resources/fixtures, we can refer to it from the @Sql annotation:

```
@Sql("/fixtures/users.sql")
def "mentions are persisted with message"() {
    // ...
```

Or we can even load it at a class level so that the same fixture is shared by all feature methods in the specification:

```
@SpringBootTest(classes = Main)
@Sql("/fixtures/users.sql")
class MessageServiceSpec extends Specification
```

Common Fixtures or Per-Test Data?

Scripts can be convenient, but I still worry that they divorce the test data from the context in which it is used. In the previous examples, we've relied on the fact that we haven't misspelled the values for username and mentionedUsernames in the where: block. They're simply repeated from the values in the fixture SQL script.

Another danger of using fixtures shared between many tests is that they tend to become overly generalized. Rather than having data fine-tuned to each case, they might contain data that many of the individual feature methods do not need. Trying to write new tests and adapt the fixtures to new requirements becomes increasingly difficult over time.

Unless the test requires a large volume of data, I much prefer to manage test data in individual feature methods or setup methods rather than with fixtures. As always, that's a preference that comes with valid exceptions.

Global Fixture Data

Spring Boot will automatically run a script found at src/test/resources/data.sql to populate the database. Alternately, you can override the spring.datasource.data property in application.properties or application.yml to specify a different script or multiple scripts.

This approach is really intended for bootstrapping reference data or running simple migration scripts rather than for integration testing. Although it is possible to create a Spring profile that will run a special integration test fixture, doing so comes with significant disadvantages.

Defining a profile that sets up our user data is straightforward:

```
---

spring:
  profiles: integration
```

```
datasource:
  data: classpath*:fixtures/users.sql
```

We can then use the `@ActiveProfiles` annotation to have a specification use the new profile:

```
@SpringBootTest(classes = Main)
@ActiveProfiles("integration")
```

However, when using this approach, we can't truncate the tables between each feature method, because the fixture data will *not* be re-created. It might be appropriate if you have tables with static data that does not need to be torn down between tests.

Cleaning Up Test Data Spring-Style

Because the Spring test framework maintains application contexts between tests for performance reasons, and because those application contexts typically contain an embedded in-memory database, data cleanup is vitally important.

We looked at this in some detail in Chapter 4. Nothing is particularly different in Spring. We can still clean up data manually:

```
def cleanup() {
  dbi.withHandle { handle ->
    handle.execute("delete from mention")
    handle.execute("delete from message")
    handle.execute("delete from user")
  }
}
```

We can still use the `@TruncateTables` annotation we developed in Chapter 10:

```
@TruncateTables
@Autowired DataSource dataSource
```

The only difference is that these two approaches use a dependency-injected method to connect to the database—either a JDBI `DBI` instance or Spring's `DataSource` bean.

Spring also provides a `JdbcTemplate` class that we can inject into specifications and use to execute SQL:

```
@Autowired JdbcTemplate jdbcTemplate

def cleanup() {
  jdbcTemplate.with {
    execute("delete from mention")
    execute("delete from message")
    execute("delete from user")
  }
}
```

Another option is to use the @Sql annotation again, this time specifying an execution phase so that the commands run *after* each feature method:

```
@SpringBootTest(classes = Main)
@Sql(executionPhase = AFTER_TEST_METHOD, statements = [
  "delete from mention",
  "delete from message",
  "delete from user"
])
```

Even better, use a cleanup script in src/test/resources that can be shared by many tests:

```
@SpringBootTest(classes = Main)
@Sql(executionPhase = AFTER_TEST_METHOD, scripts = "/cleanup.sql")
```

I like our @TruncateTables solution because it doesn't require any maintenance; it just figures out the order in which it needs to clean up tables and will automatically truncate any new tables we might add to the application as it grows. However, if you have certain tables that should not be cleaned up or other special requirements, using @Sql is a good approach.

Tests in Transactions

Another way to approach data cleanup is to run each feature method in a transaction that is automatically rolled back at the end. Spring's test framework supports doing so by just adding a @Transactional annotation to the specification class or an individual feature method.

Recall our very first integration test earlier in the chapter. We verified that mentions were not inserted for unknown usernames or more than one mention of the same username in a single message. With those scenarios, a transactional test works very well.

We can modify the specification to remove the explicit database cleanup and instead add a @Transactional annotation to the class:

```
@Transactional
@SpringBootTest(classes = Main)
class MessageServiceSpec extends Specification {

  @Autowired MessageService messageService
  @Autowired UserStore userStore
  @Autowired MessageStore messageStore
  @Autowired MentionStore mentionStore

  def "does not insert a mention if the text mentions a nonexistent user"() {
    given:
    def user = userStore.insert(username)
```

```
    expect:
    !userStore.find(mentionedUsername)

    when:
    messageService.postMessage(user, messageText)

    then:
    count("mention") == 0

    where:
    username = "kirk"
    mentionedUsername = "spock"
    messageText = "Strike that from the record, Mr. @$mentionedUsername!"
  }

  def "does not count multiple mentions in a single message"() {
    given:
    def user = userStore.insert(username)
    userStore.insert(mentionedUsername)

    when:
    messageService.postMessage(user, messageText)

    then:
    count("mention") == 1

    where:
    username = "kirk"
    mentionedUsername = "spock"
    messageText = "Mr. @$mentionedUsername, come in! " +
      "@$mentionedUsername, report!"
  }
}
```

Propagated Transactions

However, if we make the same change to our mock-using specification that verifies
the transaction rollback, things don't go as smoothly.

```
@Transactional
@SpringBootTest(classes = Config)
class MessageServiceTransactionSpec extends Specification {

  @Autowired MessageService messageService
  @Autowired UserStore userStore
  @Autowired MessageStore messageStore
  @Autowired MentionStore mentionStore

  def "if mention insert fails a message is not persisted"() {
    given:
    def user = userStore.insert(username)
    mentionedUsernames.each {
```

```
        userStore.insert(it)
      }

      and:
      mentionStore.insert(*_) >> {
        throw new RuntimeException("test")
      }

      when:
      messageService.postMessage(user, messageText)

      then:
      def e = thrown(RuntimeException)
      e.message == "test"

      and:
      count("message") == 0

      where:
      username = "kirk"
      mentionedUsernames = ["spock", "bones"]
      messageText = "@${mentionedUsernames[0]}, @${mentionedUsernames[1]}" +
        " meet me in the transporter room!"
    }

    @Import(Main)
    static class Config {
      def mockFactory = new DetachedMockFactory()

      @Bean
      MentionStore mentionStore() {
        mockFactory.Stub(MentionStore)
      }
    }
  }
```

This test will fail on the assertion that there are no messages:

```
count("message") == 0
|                   |
1                   false
```

Why is that? Well, because the feature method itself is wrapped in a transaction, the transactional proxy wrapped around `MessageService.postMessage` *inherits* the transaction from the test rather than creating its own. This means that the call to `post` `Message` is no longer the transaction boundary: the end of the feature method is. At the point at which we make the assertion about the size of the `message` table, the transaction has not been rolled back yet.

It's possible to make this work by changing the annotation on `MessageService.post` `Message` to specify that a *new* transaction is always required:

```
@Transactional(propagation = Propagation.REQUIRES_NEW)
```

This would mean that a new transaction is always created by the transactional proxy even if there's an existing transaction active before the call is made.

However, now we're starting to modify the behavior of production code to make testing easier. Depending on how the application handles errors and manages wider transactions, requiring a new transaction at that point may not be desirable.

Although it seems convenient, I find that wrapping tests in transactions can often lead to some confusion. Because of the simplicity of our `@TruncateTables` annotation, it doesn't benefit us very much.

Summary

You should now have a good grasp of integration and container tests with Spring. In this chapter, we looked at the following:

- How to test transactional behavior in Spring components
- How to trigger and respond to Spring application events
- How to register mocks and stubs as Spring beans
- How to override Spring beans with test configuration
- How to manage test data
- How to run tests in a transactional context
- How to ensure changes to the application context don't leak between tests

Building on the integration testing in this chapter, the next two chapters explore end-to-end testing REST APIs and web applications. We'll build out the Squawker application, exposing a REST API and then a JavaScript web application that uses it.

CHAPTER 13

Testing REST APIs

REST (*Representational State Transfer*) is an architectural style for managing data over HTTP. In the past decade, REST—or approximations of it—have become one of the default mechanisms for interapplication communication. With the increasing popularity of stateful browser applications and microservice architectures, REST has become a fundamental component of internal- and external-facing applications. Although we would want to test as much application behavior as possible using simple, fast-running unit tests, end-to-end testing REST applications is a common requirement. Spock is more than equal to the task.

In this chapter, we look at building and testing a REST frontend for the Squawker application. The examples build on the Spring Boot application we've been building but are equally applicable to any platform.

The general approach for testing REST APIs is to use an HTTP client to connect to a running instance of the application, send realistic requests, and make assertions about the HTTP headers and response data that come back. That approach is applicable using any one of the many HTTP client libraries available (or even just a plain old `java.net.HttpUrlConnection`). Spring Boot includes a built-in HTTP client, `TestRestTemplate`, that the examples in this chapter use; however, it should not be difficult to translate lessons learned here to a different HTTP client API. There are numerous HTTP client libraries available for the JVM and their abstractions over HTTP vary a little, but the examples in this chapter should be easy enough to translate.

Defining the Application URL

Because we'll be starting an actual HTTP server and connecting to it via its URL, we'll need to know what that URL is, or at least what the port number is, given that the application will run on `localhost`. Obviously, we don't want to hardcode the port number, because there's no guarantee some other process isn't using the port we choose, which would cause the tests to fail. It would also make it more difficult to share the tests between different team members who might have their machines configured differently as well as make it difficult to parallelize test suite execution on a continuous integration server.

Spring Boot, like most frameworks, allows an application to start on a random unallocated port. We just need a way to determine what port is actually being used so that our HTTP client can construct request URLs correctly. The details of how you can do this will vary depending on what web application framework you use.

The Root URL in Spring Boot REST Specifications

Tests for the REST or web API of a Spring Boot application are annotated with `@SpringBootTest` just as integration tests are. To run the embedded server on a random port we need to add `webEnvironment = SpringBootTest.WebEnvironment.RAN DOM_PORT`.

Spring's HTTP client `TestRestTemplate`, which the examples in this chapter use, can automatically convert relative URLs to absolute ones. But in some places, we'll be constructing the request outside the context of the `TestRestTemplate`, so we'll need to be able to figure out the port in order to construct absolute URLs.

We can inject the actual assigned port into the specification class by providing an `int` field annotated with `@LocalServerPort`.

I also like to create a simple private method that turns a relative URL into an absolute one so that each feature method can ignore the base URL and port number:

```
@LocalServerPort int port

protected URI url(String relativeUrl) {
  "http://localhost:$port$relativeUrl".toURI()
}
```

A First Specification

We'll begin with a very simple failure case. A *GET* request to a URL such as `spock/messages` should retrieve a list of messages posted by the user *@spock*. If the username in the URL is not valid—because no such user actually exists—the server should return a *404 not found* status.

We can write the specification for this behavior and make it pass before really implementing much code, and keep it passing as we add more functionality.

Remember the embedded web application is managed by Spring Boot because of the `@SpringBootTest` annotation. If you're using another platform, you'll need a way to start and stop the embedded server.

The example also uses the `TestRestTemplate` HTTP client provided by Spring Boot to make requests and decode responses:

```
@SpringBootTest(
  webEnvironment = RANDOM_PORT,
  classes = [Main] ❶
)
class MessageEndpointSpec extends Specification { ❷

  @Autowired TestRestTemplate client ❸

  def "returns a not found response for a nonexistent user"() {
    when:
    def entity = client.getForEntity("/api/$username/messages", Map) ❹

    then:
    entity.statusCode == NOT_FOUND ❺
    entity.body.message == "No user $username found"

    where:
    username = "spock"
  }
}
// tag::failure-case[]
```

❶ We specify the root configuration class or classes that will start the Spring Boot application.

❷ No special superclass is required; the class just extends `spock.lang.Specification`.

❸ The `client` field is the HTTP client that the specification uses to communicate with the application. Here, we're using an autowired instance of `TestRestTemplate`, which is provided by the Spring test environment.

❹ The feature method uses the client to make an HTTP *GET* request to the *messages* endpoint. Don't worry about the final parameter: that's specifying the type to which the response should be deserialized, but because we're not expecting a response, it's not particularly important here.

❺ The application should return a *404* status. I like to use constants when testing HTTP response codes rather than raw integers, so they are statically imported from `org.springframework.http.HttpStatus` in this example.

Because we haven't defined any endpoints in the application yet, this test should pass right away! Starting with a negative case like this is often very easy and doesn't require writing any application code. It will be important to keep this feature method passing as we develop the functionality.

 Because we've autowired the TestRestTemplate and we're using the getForEntity method that accepts a relative URL string here, we don't need to worry about the port and base URL of the application.

Web Application Lifecycle

The lifecycle of the embedded application in this example is managed by Spring Boot's test support. Because application initialization can take a few seconds Spring starts the application once for the entire test suite. This is a reasonable approach because the application itself—the contents of the Spring application context, in this case—are typically immutable.

With other application frameworks, it might be practical to start and stop the embedded server for each feature method. Ratpack applications, for example, are lightweight and start extremely fast.

Starting the server clean for each feature method is ideal but not always practical unless the application's startup time is extremely fast. The crucial concern is that the application itself is not left in a different state at the end of any individual feature method. That means clearing caches, invalidating HTTP sessions, and obviously, cleaning up test data.

Creating Data for End-to-End Tests

We've tested a case that doesn't require any data to exist, but the vast majority of specifications will need to create data to exercise the behavior they're testing. Managing data in end-to-end tests is a different proposition compared to unit and integration tests. Tests need to be able to create the data they require and clean up afterward so that state does not "bleed" between individual tests.

One solution is to run the application in the same JVM as the test and simply access the object-relational mapping (ORM) classes or underlying database directly from the test. The only downside is that it makes it impossible to run the tests against an external instance of the application on a virtual or physical server.

Another common solution is to provide a series of special endpoints for setting up and tearing down data. Although simple to do, you need to give thought to security in so much as production applications should not expose such endpoints. Accidentally hitting an endpoint that creates or destroys test data in a production environment can be catastrophic.

In addition, it's very easy to end up with a mess of endpoints that provide inconsistent capabilities for customizing the data created or end up being shared inappropriately by multiple tests because it's easier than writing hundreds of individual test data endpoints for many tests. There's a loss of cohesion, too, between the test and the fixture that creates its data. It's easy to break tests by making changes to test data construction that is not obviously associated with a specific test.

Bleeding Data Between Tests

Test data is said to "bleed" between tests when the data created for one test is not cleaned up or only partially cleaned up and still exists when the subsequent tests run. Because some unpredictable quantity of data exists, the subsequent tests can behave differently. For example, subsequent tests might fail when attempting to create their own test data due to database constraint violations or the code under test might behave differently due to the additional data.

Data bleeding between tests can be harmless, or it can be catastrophic and extremely difficult to debug. Typically, it can result in a test that fails when run as part of a suite but passes in isolation.

In the worst cases, the affected test is far downstream of the one causing the problem, potentially making it very difficult to identify the offending test that isn't cleaning up data properly.

Bleeding between tests can also be caused by long-lived caches or meta-programming that changes the behavior of application classes at runtime.

Disposable Persistence

Another factor to consider when isolating test data is that if data persists after the entire test suite completes, it will still be there for the next run. For this reason, it's a very good idea to either ensure that you are using an in-memory database, such as H2, rather than persisting to a real on-disk store or re-creating the entire database schema from scratch at the start of the suite.

Creating Test Data on Demand

Because we're using the @SpringBootTest annotation, Spring Boot allows beans from the application to be injected into our test classes. That makes it extremely easy to create and tear down test data.

It will allow our tests to set up very fine-grained and specific data without having to rely on monolithic shared data fixtures or requiring us to create custom endpoints for managing test data.

Let's use that to create a test that does retrieve and verify some data:

```
@Autowired UserStore userStore ❶

def "returns an empty array for a user who has not posted any messages"() {
  given:
  userStore.insert(username) ❷

  when:
  def response = template.getForEntity("/api/$username/messages", List) ❸

  then:
  response.statusCode == OK ❹
  response.body == [] ❺

  where:
  username = "spock"
}
```

❶ Using Spring's @Autowired annotation we can acquire an instance of the User Store DAO class.

❷ The feature method can then create a new User object and insert it in the database. Note that the username variable is not local to the closure; it's a where: block parameter. Any variable references that can be serialized will be accessible in the closure. Trying to access a nonserializable value here would have caused an error.

❸ The same request is made as in the previous test. Note that this time we expect a List rather than a Map.

❹ This time an HTTP *200* successful response is expected.

❺ The endpoint should return an empty JSON array.

Cleaning Up Test Data

Something is missing in the previous test case that will rapidly become a problem. The data created in the given: block is never cleaned up again. Let's do that now by autowiring another bean that we can use to directly destroy data in the database:

```
@Autowired DBI dbi

def cleanup() {
  dbi.open().withCloseable { handle ->
    handle.execute("delete from user")
  }
}
```

This time, we'll inject an instance of JDBI's *DBI* rather than a DAO class. In the `cleanup` method, we can then simply truncate the relevant tables.

The example uses Groovy's `withCloseable` method, which is analogous to Java's *try-with-resources* construct.

The `open()` method in `DBI` acquires an instance of *Handle*, which is a wrapper around a database connection. Closing the *Handle* closes the underlying connection or returns it to the pool depending on what kind of data source is being used.

Cleanup like this could just as well be done with a DAO method, but in this case it's easy enough to just access the table directly.

Java's try-with-resources and Groovy's withCloseable

Java's *try-with-resources*, introduced in Java 7, automatically calls a `close` method in an implied `finally` block, as shown here:

```
try (Handle handle = dbi.open()) {
  handle.execute("delete from user");
}
```

Although Groovy does not support the *try-with-resources* syntax, its `withCloseable` method does the same thing to the object it was called on. Both the `withCloseable` call shown in the listing and the preceding *try-with-resources* example are simply a more convenient way to do this:

```
Handle handle = dbi.open();
try {
  handle.execute("delete from user");
} finally {
  handle.close();
}
```

Requests with Data

REST APIs distinguish different actions on the same object by using the HTTP *verb*. So far, we've used HTTP *GET* requests, which don't require a message body, but in order to create new data, we'll use an HTTP *POST*:

```
def "can post a message"() {
  given:
  createUser(username)

  when:
  def request = RequestEntity
    .post(url("/api/$username/messages"))
    .contentType(MediaType.TEXT_PLAIN)
    .body(messageText) ❶
  def response = client.exchange(request, Message) ❷

  then:
  response.statusCode == CREATED ❸

  where:
  username = "spock"
  messageText = "@kirk That is illogical, Captain!"
}
```

❶ We'll use Spring's request builder to construct a *POST* request with a *Content-Type* header of *text/plain* and a message body consisting of the message we'd like to post.

❷ The request is executed using the HTTP client.

❸ The response code should be an HTTP *201* to indicate that new data was created.

Fixture Methods

Since the same code is required to set up a user as in the previous feature method it makes sense to extract a helper method createUser.

```
protected void createUser(String username) {
  userStore.insert(username)
}
```

Testing for HTTP Errors

When a REST client receives an invalid request, it should respond with a status code in the 400 to 499 range. It's a good idea to test edge cases and error scenarios to ensure that your REST service is handling invalid requests cleanly and returning the correct information to the client.

Some HTTP client libraries will throw exceptions if the response has an HTTP status code of *400* or higher. Spring Boot's TestRestTemplate does not do this, but Apache HttpClient does by default, for example. That might make sense in production code when connecting to remote APIs, but it's not what you want when explicitly testing for error conditions. When your specification *expects* the request to be rejected it's a good idea to turn this behavior off and make assertions about the response code rather than trapping the exception that's thrown.

HTTP Status Ranges

HTTP status codes are divided into ranges, which give a general indication of the class of response. Let's take a look at them:

100–199
> Indicates that the request has been received but the server is not yet ready to respond.

200–299
> Indicates a successful request. For example, *200* is the default *"OK"* code, and *201* indicates data was successfully created.

300–399
> Indicates that the client needs to go to a different URL to complete the request. For example, *301* and *302* are permanent and temporary redirects, respectively.

400–499
> The client has made an error such as requesting a nonexistent URL (*404*), using the wrong HTTP verb (*405*), or sending data that fails validation (*422*).

500–599
> The request was valid but the server failed to deal with it. Typical examples are *500* indicating a general error such as an uncaught exception on the server or *503* indicating the server is not available.

More simply put…

> HTTP status ranges in a nutshell:
>
> 1xx: hold on
> 2xx: here you go
> 3xx: go away
> 4xx: you fucked up
> 5xx: I fucked up

—Steve Losh, *https://twitter.com/stevelosh/status/372740571749572610*

If we attempt to post a Squawker message with no content, the server should reject our request. We can test that very easily:

```
def "cannot post a message with no text"() {
  given:
  createUser(username)
```

```
when:
def request = RequestEntity
  .post(url("/api/$username/messages"))
  .build() ❶
def response = client.exchange(request, Map)

then:
response.statusCode == BAD_REQUEST ❷

where:
username = "spock"
}
```

❶   We build a *POST* request without a request body.

❷   The server should respond with an HTTP *400*.

Verifying Response Data

In the earlier example when we successfully posted a message, we simply asserted that an HTTP *201* is returned. We didn't do any verification of the response headers or content. A REST endpoint will typically include a `Location` header pointing to the new entity and/or a response body with the entity's data.

It would make sense to verify that the entity data looks correct based on the request the specification sent.

A successful POST to our message endpoint should return a JSON response something like this:

```
{
  "message": {
    "id": 1,
    "text": "@kirk That is illogical, Captain!",
    "postedBy": {
      "username": "spock",
      "registered": "2016-02-05T09:13:19.744Z"
    },
    "postedAt": "2016-02-05T09:13:19.751Z"
  }
}
```

It's never a good idea to verify structured response data such as JSON, XML, or HTML by using string matching. Always parse the response and make assertions about individual properties. Many HTTP client libraries provide automatic parsing of known response types, and indeed that is the case with Spring Boot's `TestRestTemplate`.

The `exchange` we've been using thus far takes two parameters—the request and the type of the expected response:

```
def "a user can post a message"() {
  given:
  createUser(username)

  when:
  def request = post(url("/api/$username/messages"))
    .contentType(TEXT_PLAIN)
    .body(messageText)
  def response = client.exchange(request, Message) ❶

  then:
  response.statusCode == CREATED

  and:
  with(response.body) { ❷
    postedBy.username == username ❸
    text == messageText
  }

  where:
  username = "spock"
  messageText = "@kirk That is illogical, Captain!"
}
```

❶ We can specify `Message` as the response type, which will parse the JSON into an actual `Message` instance for us.

❷ Spock's `with(Object, Closure)` method makes the first parameter the delegate of the closure and treats every statement as an assertion.

❸ We can then assert that each property of the JSON response is correct.

We could specify `Message` instead of `Map` as the response type, but that would require us to be able to deserialize JSON to instances of `Message`. Because there isn't anywhere in the API that we need to do that, it seems unnecessary to configure JSON deserialization just for the tests.

Typed Response Entities

Until now, we've specified only `List` or `Map` as the return type from an API request. Now, however, because the *POST* endpoint will actually return a JSON representation of the message that is inserted, the call to `client.exchange` can specify a return type of `Message`. Right now we're not doing anything with it but we'll see examples shortly where the returned data is verified.

Of course, it would be possible to just specify Map, which will result in a nested Map that corresponds to the JSON structure. However, it's often simpler to verify a typed response. Consider that Message has a postedAt timestamp property. If we want to write a test that verifies that timestamp, it's easier to do so with a real Message object with a postedAt property that is a java.time.Instant than a Map for which the postedAt property would be a string. We need to ensure that the assertion formatted the expected timestamp correctly:

```
def "message endpoint renders correct timestamp"() {
  given:
  createUser(username)
  def messageId = createMessage(username, messageText, timestamp)  ❶

  when:
  def response = client.getForEntity("/api/messages/$messageId", Map)  ❷

  then:
  response.statusCode == OK
  response.body.postedAt == ISO_INSTANT.format(timestamp)  ❸

  where:
  username = "spock"
  messageText = "@kirk That is illogical, Captain!"
  timestamp = now()
}
```

❶ First, we specify a known timestamp when creating the message fixture so that the feature method does not fail sporadically because the assertion is made a few milliseconds after the message is inserted.

❷ A response type of Map will work, but any timestamps will be represented as strings.

❸ We need to format the expected timestamp in the same way as the one in the response.

If the intent is to test the rendering of timestamps in JSON, this is actually a *good* test. But if the intent is to test that the response uses the correct timestamp—the postedAt time rather than the request time, for example—it's a little unnecessary to have to work out the exact format to use. Not only that, but if we later change the way timestamps are rendered in JSON, the test will break even if the timestamp is actually correct.

When writing this example, I initially had a feature method that failed 1 in 10 times because I'd used a subtly different DateTimeFormatter that dropped trailing zeros from the milliseconds value in the timestamp. You can avoid the kind of head-scratching that ensues with errors like that by using a typed response!

Using a typed response the feature method is a little simpler:

```
when:
def response = client.getForEntity("/api/messages/$messageId", Message)

then:
response.statusCode == OK
response.body.postedAt == timestamp
```

Directly comparing `Instant` instances is much less error prone.

Using `Map` or `List` as the response type is a good default when you just need to verify the size of an array or a simple property such as an error message. For anything more complex, a typed response is usually preferable.

Multiple HTTP Requests in a Feature Method

The examples we've seen so far have made a single request to the REST API in each feature method, but of course it's possible to make multiple requests. For example, it would be reasonable to ensure that a message appears in a user's timeline after being posted:

```
def "a message appears in a user's timeline after they post it"() {
  given:
  createUser(username)

  and:
  def request = post(url("/api/$username/messages"))
    .contentType(TEXT_PLAIN)
    .body(messageText)
  def response = client.exchange(request, Message) ❶

  expect:
  response.statusCode == CREATED ❷

  when:
  def request2 = get(url("/api/$username/timeline")).build()
  def response2 = client.exchange(request2, LIST_OF_MESSAGES) ❸

  then:
  with(response2.body.first()) { ❹
    text == messageText
    postedBy.username == username
  }

  where:
  username = "spock"
  messageText = "@kirk That is illogical, Captain!"
}
```

❶ The feature method makes an initial request to post a message as part of the given: block.

❷ We use a precondition expect: block to make sure the request was successful.

❸ The feature method makes a second request to a different URL as part of the when: block…

❹ …and verifies that the result corresponds to the data posted earlier.

You might be wondering what that weird response type is on the second request. Because Java generics uses type erasure, we cannot pass List<Message> to exchange and expect it to parse the response JSON correctly. At runtime, the <Message> part of the type is erased, so the Spring REST template code has no way to determine what class it should use as the element type of the list.

In the examples so far, we've just used a plain List with no specified element type. This has been adequate because the feature methods have made assertions only about the number of elements returned. Here, we want to actually inspect and verify one of the list elements. We *could* just leave the response type as List, which would mean we'd be dealing with Map elements. However, Spring provides an alternative way to specify the generic type.

Spring provides a class called ParameterizedTypeReference, and the exchange method will accept instances of that in place of Class to define the response type. Because ParameterizedTypeReference can retain generic type information at runtime, it's ideal for this kind of scenario.

The odd-looking response type in the feature method is defined like this:

```
protected final ParameterizedTypeReference<List<Message>> LIST_OF_MESSAGES =
    new ParameterizedTypeReference<List<Message>>() {}
```

Using a ParameterizedTypeReference like that means that when the feature method makes assertions about elements in the response, it's dealing with actual Message instances.

Backdoors or "Pure" API Testing?

In the previous example, the feature method inputs some data via the REST API and then reads it back via the API in order to verify that the data was created correctly. There are two conflicting schools of thought for scenarios like this, both of which have their merits:

Viewpoint 1: Data should not pass through the system-under-test in both directions

If you're testing how your system handles input of data, don't verify it by using its mechanism for outputting data.

Tests that pass data through the system in both directions are vulnerable to multiple points of failure in a single test.

End-to-end tests that insist on doing *everything* via the user interface can easily become brittle and long running. If the test has to perform a lot of preliminary steps in order to get the system into a state where the behavior it's interested in is exposed, those preliminary steps could break. Think of an online store; should end-to-end tests for the checkout process log in, visit product pages, add items to the cart, and so on, or should the test use a back-door that tweaks the system into a state where a user is logged in and has items in their cart? If the "__add to cart__" button is changed or broken by a regression, all the checkout-related tests will begin failing simply because they can't complete their "__given__" steps.

The cumulative time spent on preliminary steps in a medium-to-large test suite can seriously affect the speed of running that test suite, as well.

If we had followed this approach, we should have either set up the message *or* verified the message had been stored correctly by using the injected DAOs, *not* both. The way it's written now, if the message we expect doesn't appear in the timeline, we don't know if that is because the *POST* request failed to insert it to the database or because the *GET* request failed to read it back.

Viewpoint 2: An end-to-end test should not resort to backdoors

Although it makes sense for a unit test to only test the system in one direction, end-to-end tests are necessarily different. The aim of an end-to-end test is to verify the system by driving it as a user would—controlling it via its external interface. In the case of a REST API, that "user" is probably another application, but the principle holds.

Using a backdoor to insert or read back data, or to tweak the system into some state that enables testing of a particular feature is cheating. Users aren't able to do this, so the test might be missing some vital flaw in the end-to-end workflow by taking a shortcut.

Backdoors in the system are a security risk: it's easy to accidentally leave those backdoors enabled in released software.

Also, they tightly couple an interface-level test with the underlying details of how things like persistence and security are handled in the application. *Uncle Bob* Martin writes in *Clean Code* [cleancode] that a function should interact with the system only at one level of abstraction. Inappropriately leaking implementation details out into end-to-end tests can cause brittleness. Tests can begin failing because of minor changes in low-level implementation such as changes to the database schema.

Both of these viewpoints are worth bearing in mind. That's not to say either should be followed religiously. Be aware of the advantages and problems of each approach and make an informed decision about where and why you are going to make compromises when writing specifications.

Using "fixture methods" like the createUser and createMessage methods we've defined achieves a reasonable level of abstraction, and I think makes for a good compromise. I've seen extremely unwieldy end-to-end test suites that did everything via the user interface, and they *were* slow and brittle. Tests should always be as small, simple, and focused as possible. At the same time, I think reading data back for verification via the REST API in the previous example is probably straightforward enough that we can overlook the fact that it's introducing an additional point of failure into the test.

Handling Redirect Responses

Sometimes a REST API will issue an HTTP redirect response code. Many HTTP clients will by default follow a redirect and seamlessly return the response from the redirected URL.

Let's create an endpoint for Squawker that will redirect to the latest message posted by a user. If the client requests /spock/messages/latest, it will be redirected to /messages/__<id-of-latest-message>__. We can write a test for this easily enough:

```
def "can get a user's latest post"() {
  given:
  createUser(username)
  def messageId = createMessage(username, messageText) ❶

  when:
  def response = client.getForEntity("/api/$username/messages/latest", Message)

  then:
  response.statusCode == OK ❷
  response.body.id == messageId ❸

  where:
  username = "spock"
  messageText = "@kirk That is illogical, Captain!"
}
```

❶ We've added another data fixture method, which this time is returning a value—the *id* of the message it sets up.

❷ The HTTP client automatically follows the redirect, so the HTTP status code is the one returned by the *final* URL.

❸ We assert that the *id* of the message returned matches the one we set up at the beginning of the test.

The new fixture method is very simple:

```
protected Serializable createMessage(String username,
                                     String text,
                                     Instant postedAt = now()) {
  def user = userStore.find(username)
  messageStore.insert(user, text, postedAt).id
}
```

It just retrieves a User object from the database, uses the MessageStore.insert(Message) method to create a message, and then returns its *id*.

Remember that the value of the last statement in a Groovy method is returned even without a return keyword (unless the method is declared void).

Verifying Redirect Details

There are subtleties to redirects that are not being tested here. As soon as the user "@spock" posts another message, the /spock/messages/latest endpoint should begin redirecting to the new message URL. In other words, this is a temporary redirect. An HTTP *301* status code tells a client that it should not attempt to use the original URL again because the content has moved permanently. A *302* tells the client that the redirect is temporary and that the endpoint can begin redirecting to a different URL or stop redirecting at all at some time in the future.

The /spock/messages/latest URL should use a *302* status code and *not* a *301*. From the specification so far, we have no way to determine what type of redirect the client followed, so we're not testing for the correctness of this behavior. In fact, we're not even testing that a redirect is happening at all—the test would still pass if the endpoint responded with an HTTP *200* and returned the data directly.

Most of the time, you want an HTTP client to transparently follow redirects but when you're trying to test the specifics of the redirect like this, it gets in the way. Most HTTP clients have a way to disable automatic redirect following for exactly this reason. Let's do that in the feature method we just wrote. Instead of verifying the content of the response data, we'll verify the details of the redirect.

Spring's `TestRestTemplate` scans the classpath for various HTTP client libraries and will use whichever is available for the underlying HTTP transport. If the client it finds can disable following redirects, `TestRestTemplate` will do so. For example, just adding Apache HttpClient to the classpath will make `TestRestTemplate` not follow redirects.

If you find it *is* following redirects, just add the following to your *build.gradle*:

```
testRuntime "org.apache.httpcomponents:httpclient:4.5.2"
```

After the HTTP client is configured to not follow redirects, the feature method can change.

```
def "can get a user's latest post"() {
  given:
  createUser(username)
  def messageId = createMessage(username, messageText)

  when:
  def response = client.getForEntity("/api/$username/messages/latest", String)

  then:
  with(response) {
    statusCode == FOUND ❶
    headers.getFirst(LOCATION).toURI() == url("/api/messages/$messageId")
    ❷
  }

  where:
  username = "spock"
  messageText = "@kirk That is illogical, Captain!"
}
```

❶ Now, we can verify the specific redirect status code that the server returns.

❷ A redirect status should always be accompanied by a `Location` header instructing the client as to where to redirect. The `Location` header *must be* an absolute URL. Here, we're asserting that the server is redirecting us to the correct message.

REST API Security

So far, we've allowed data to be created with a simple, unauthenticated *POST* request. Obviously, this is not good enough for a production system, because we would be opening Squawker up to abuse by anyone able to send fake messages purported to be written by any user. We need to secure the REST API so that endpoints that create data require authentication.

Until now, the user posting the message has been determined by the username in the URL. In previous examples, when we post to /api/spock/messages our application works out that *@spock* is the user posting the message because the username is present in the URL. Although that URL scheme makes sense for retrieving data, which can be done by anonymous users, it's redundant after we begin using authentication.

With an authenticated request the application server can derive the user making the request from the credentials presented in the request headers, as you will see shortly. It would not make sense to allow posting if the credentials matched a different user than the one in the URL. In fact, because the authenticated user is determined by the security filter, there is no need to specify it in the URL at all. We'll change the application so that new messages are posted to just /api/messages and the posting user is determined by authentication.

Let's start with a simple test that ensures an unauthenticated request is rejected. In this example, we'll attempt to post a message exactly as we have to this point but using our new endpoint:

```
def "an anonymous user cannot post a message"() {
  given:
  createUser(username)

  when:
  def request = post(url("/api/messages"))
    .contentType(TEXT_PLAIN)
    .body(messageText) ❶
  def response = client.exchange(request, Map)

  then:
  response.statusCode == UNAUTHORIZED ❷

  where:
  username = "spock"
  messageText = "@kirk That is illogical, Captain!"
}
```

❶ The URL to which we're posting has changed, but the request is otherwise identical to those made in earlier examples.

❷ We should now get an HTTP *401* response code indicating that the action we tried to take requires authentication.

Now that we have shown authentication is required in order to post a message, it's time to update the earlier feature method that posts a message successfully. We'll need to generate credentials in the form of an API token and add it to the request in the *Authorization* header.

Token authentication is a typical scheme for REST APIs. An API token is associated with each user and provided to them. To make an authenticated request, the user adds an *Authorization* header that looks something like this:

```
Authorization: Token OGY2NTY3MTEtMjg3Zi00ZWY5LWJjYzAtZWJjNWNmMWY5MmZk
```

When the server receives the request, it identifies the requesting user by using the token provided in the header.

That's exactly what we'll implement in the example that follows. We'll use remote access to set up an API token in the database associated with the user and then use it in the request header:

```
def "a user can post a message"() {
  given:
  createUser(username)
  def authToken = generateToken(username) ❶

  when:
  def request = post(url("/api/messages")) ❷
    .header(AUTHORIZATION, authToken) ❸
    .contentType(TEXT_PLAIN)
    .body(messageText)
  def response = client.exchange(request, Message)

  then:
  response.statusCode == CREATED

  and:
  with(response.body) {
    postedBy.username == username ❹
    text == messageText
  }

  where:
  username = "spock"
  messageText = "@kirk That is illogical, Captain!"
}
```

❶ In addition to creating a user, we need to create an API token.

❷ The URL needs to change to the new authenticated endpoint.

❸ We attach an *Authorization* header to the request that contains the token.

❹ It's important to ensure that the message is posted by the correct user because that proves the authentication filter is identifying the user correctly.

Let's look at the fixture method that creates the API token:

```
@Autowired ApiTokenStore apiTokenStore ❶

protected String generateToken(String username) {
  def user = userStore.find(username)
  def token = apiTokenStore.generateTokenFor(user) ❷
  "Token $token" ❸
}

def cleanup() {
  dbi.open().withCloseable { Handle handle ->
    // ... existing code
    handle.execute("delete from api_token") ❹
  }
}
```

❶   We autowire a new DAO…

❷   … and then use that to generate an API key for a user.

❸   For convenience, the fixture method returns the token in the format used in an *Authorization* header.

❹   Of course, we don't want to leave any API tokens around for the next test.

Token Security

The sample code attached to this project uses a very naïve token scheme. This example is concerned with the details of how a generated token is attached to the request in a test, not how to properly secure a REST endpoint. In a real application, the API token should be salted and stored in an encrypted form. This book is not a security reference, so be sure to consult appropriate sources before implementing a security scheme in your own application.

Now we have a way to set up authenticated requests for REST API endpoints.

Authentication versus Authorization

In the context of a REST API like this, *authentication* means establishing who the requesting user is. We've done that when posting a message. Because that's an action open to *any* user, there's no need to perform any further checks beyond ensuring that the request is being made by a valid user.

Authorization, on the other hand, means establishing that the authenticated user is permitted to do whatever it is they're trying to do.

Authentication and authorization errors are represented in HTTP with two different status codes. There's a subtle difference between HTTP *401—Unauthorized* and

HTTP *403—Forbidden. 401—Unauthorized*, which we tested for when making an anonymous request to the `/api/messages` endpoint, means that either the request did not provide any credentials or the credentials provided are invalid. Examples of invalid credentials include an expired API token or an incorrect username and password combination.

403—Forbidden means that credentials were provided and they are valid but the authenticated user is not allowed to perform the action. For example, although the user *@spock* may delete messages he posted earlier, he may not delete a message posted by *@kirk*.

Let's put together a test to show the difference. First, we'll ensure that a user can delete a message he posted himself. In this example, we create a user, API token, and message, just as before, and then send a request to delete it:

```
def "a user can delete their own message"() {
  given:
  createUser(username)
  def authToken = generateToken(username)
  def messageId = createMessage(username, messageText)
  def messageUrl = url("/api/messages/$messageId")

  when:
  def request = delete(messageUrl) ❶
    .header(AUTHORIZATION, authToken)
    .build()
  def response = client.exchange(request, Map)

  then:
  response.statusCode == OK ❷

  and:
  client.getForEntity(messageUrl, Map).statusCode == NOT_FOUND ❸

  where:
  username = "spock"
  messageText = "@kirk That is illogical, Captain!"
}
```

❶ We're going to send an HTTP *DELETE* request to the URL for a specific message.

❷ The response should indicate the action was successful but does not contain any data.

❸ We then ensure that the message really was deleted by proving that we now receive a *404* when we try to make a *GET* request for it.

So far, so good. We've allowed a user to delete a message. However, we shouldn't allow just any user to do this. Users should be permitted to delete only messages they posted themselves; otherwise, our application is ripe for abuse.

To ensure this is the case, we'll add another test that sets up two users, posts a message as one, then tries to delete it as the other. The delete request should this time receive a *403* response code, indicating that even though the user provided valid credentials, she is not actually allowed to delete that particular message.

```
def "a user cannot delete another user's message"() {
  given:
  createUser(postingUser)
  def messageId = createMessage(postingUser, messageText) ❶
  def messageUrl = url("/api/messages/$messageId")

  and:
  createUser(requestingUser)
  def authToken = generateToken(requestingUser)

  when:
  def request = delete(messageUrl)
    .header(AUTHORIZATION, authToken) ❷
    .build()
  def response = client.exchange(request, Map)

  then:
  response.statusCode == FORBIDDEN ❸

  and:
  client.getForEntity(messageUrl, Map).statusCode == OK ❹

  where:
  postingUser = "spock"
  requestingUser = "kirk"
  messageText = "@kirk That is illogical, Captain!"
}
```

❶ Here a message is posted by postingUser.

❷ We then generate an API token for requestingUser and attach that to the request.

❸ The response code should be *403*, indicating that authentication succeeded but authorization failed.

❹ Of course, just getting a *403* doesn't prove we didn't do something silly in the implementation and just delete the message regardless, so it's prudent to also prove that the message is still accessible.

Now, we've shown that only the posting user can delete a message and we've responded appropriately to an unauthorized request.

Of course, we should also implement tests to ensure that anonymous users cannot delete messages and a *404* response code is returned when a user attempts to delete a message that does not exist or was deleted already.

Summary

In this chapter, we looked at testing a REST API via an HTTP client. You should now have a good idea how to do the following:

- Set data up using a backdoor into the server
- Access endpoints with different HTTP methods
- Send data along with a request
- Test for various error conditions
- Test for authentication and authorization

Although the examples have used the Spring Boot web application platform, the concepts are common to any kind of REST API testing. The specific way to attach an *Authorization* header might differ, but the content of the header and the general concept of token authentication are identical when using a different client or server platform.

CHAPTER 14

End-to-End Web Testing

One of the trickier types of automated testing is checking a web application via the browser. Differences in rendering in different browsers, frequent upgrades, and—more than anything—speed can be major issues when it comes to testing in a browser. Web UIs can change rapidly and break tests that are too tightly coupled to the fine-grained structure of the page. It's very important to develop a good abstraction so that the details of HTML structure, such as hierarchies of elements and particular classes and IDs, are not liberally spread throughout your test suite making it very difficult to change the structure without considerable rework repairing tests. If you're using a continuous integration server, it can be difficult to make browser-based tests work when the server probably does not have a display attached and typically might not even have a graphical environment at all.

In this chapter, we'll develop some in-browser tests using Spock and a library called *Geb*. We'll build and test a web frontend for the Squawker application. As we do this, we'll examine how to build a *page model* abstraction that decouples tests from the DOM structure of the web pages.

Geb

Geb (pronounced "jeb") is a browser automation API that wraps around Selenium. With Geb, Java code can issue commands to a browser and interact with pages. Although you can use it for scripting purposes, the primary use of Geb is to write functional or *end-to-end* tests for web applications.

Getting Started with Geb

Geb itself is a simple jar dependency. For example, if you're using Gradle to build your project, you can add the dependency for Geb like this:

```
testCompile "org.gebish:geb-spock:0.13.1"
```

In addition to Geb, you'll need a Selenium driver. Precisely which one depends on which browser you want to use. For example, assuming that we'll run the tests using Firefox, we need to add the following dependencies to our Gradle build:

```
testCompile "org.seleniumhq.selenium:selenium-firefox-driver:2.53.0"
```

Driving Chrome and Other Browsers

Chrome requires a special executable, called *chromedriver*, to be controlled by Selenium. You can avoid having to manage the executable by using WebDriverManager, a library that takes care of installing the executables required to drive Chrome and other browsers.

You can add the dependency to Gradle like this:

```
testCompile "io.github.bonigarcia:webdrivermanager:1.4.8"
```

Then, add the following to src/test/resources/GebConfig.groovy

```
import io.github.bonigarcia.wdm.ChromeDriverManager
import org.openqa.selenium.chrome.ChromeDriver
import org.openqa.selenium.firefox.FirefoxDriver


ChromeDriverManager.getInstance().setup()
driver = { new ChromeDriver() }
```

Running Tests with Different Browsers

You can run your test suite in different browsers by using the geb.env system property. First, specify the environment rules Geb will use, as follows:

```
// tag::chrome-imports[]
import io.github.bonigarcia.wdm.ChromeDriverManager
import org.openqa.selenium.chrome.ChromeDriver
import org.openqa.selenium.firefox.FirefoxDriver

// end::chrome-imports[]
environments {
  chrome {
    // tag::chromedriver[]
```

```
                ChromeDriverManager.getInstance().setup()
                driver = { new ChromeDriver() }
                // end::chromedriver[]
            }

            firefox {
                driver = { new FirefoxDriver() }
            }
        }
```

You can add branches for as many different browsers and system architectures as you like.

Next, ensure that Gradle will pass the geb.env property to the test task and provide a default.

```
        test {
            systemProperties "geb.env": System.properties."geb.env" ?: "chrome"
        }
```

You can now run tests with a different browser using gradle -Dgeb.env=firefox, for example. If you don't specify any geb.env value, the tests will run with the default (Chrome, in the preceding example).

Using this mechanism, it's easy to set up cross-browser test suites on continuous integration servers.

A First Frontend Test

We'll start by building a timeline page for a user. To begin with, we won't worry about logging in; let's assume that the user is authorized. We simply want to see a list of messages that include those from the user and anyone she follows but don't include messages from anyone else.

We want our page to be served up at 0. For example, using Spring Boot to run the application locally, we'd look at 1 to see our timeline. As we saw when looking at testing REST APIs, you'll need to be able to determine the address and port where your application is running.

The example in this chapter uses an Angular JS frontend to the same REST API we developed in previous chapters. We could serve up static pages from Spring Boot, but because single-page applications are so common these days and bring a handful of special considerations to the table when testing with Geb, it's useful to do the example that way.

```
        @SpringBootTest(webEnvironment = RANDOM_PORT, classes = [Main])
        class TimelineSpec extends GebSpec { ❶

            @LocalServerPort int port
```

```
@Autowired DBI dbi
@Autowired UserStore userStore
@Autowired MessageStore messageStore
@Autowired ApiTokenStore apiTokenStore

def cleanup() {
  dbi.open().withCloseable { Handle handle ->
    handle.execute("delete from message")
    handle.execute("delete from following")
    handle.execute("delete from api_token")
    handle.execute("delete from user")
  }
}

Serializable createUser(String username) {
  def user = userStore.insert(username)
  apiTokenStore.generateTokenFor(user)
  return user.id
}

Serializable createMessage(String username, String text) {
  def user = userStore.find(username)
  messageStore.insert(user, text, now()).id
}

void loginAs(String username) {
  // ...
}

def "a user can see their own messages in their timeline"() {
  given:
  createUser("spock")  ❷
  createMessage("spock", "Fascinating!")

  and:
  loginAs("spock")  ❸

  when:
  go("http://localhost:$port/#/timeline")  ❹

  then:
  waitFor {
    $(".page-header").text() == "Timeline"  ❺
  }
  $(".sq-message-text").text() == "Fascinating!"  ❻
  $(".sq-posted-by").text() == "@spock"
  }
}
```

❶ Specifications using Geb extend from geb.spock.GebSpec.

❷ First, we create some test data in a similar way as we did when testing REST APIs.

❸ A user must log in to see his timeline. We'll revisit the details of this shortly. For now, assume that it's a no-op or that we haven't actually implemented the authentication functionality yet.

❹ Then, we connect to the ❶ page in the application.

❺ We wait until Angular JS has composed and displayed the page.

❻ Finally, we assert that the test data we created is visible.

Data Fixtures for End-to-End Tests

Because we're building on top of the Spring Boot REST API, we can inject DAOs to set up our test data in exactly the way that we saw previously. If you're using a different platform, you might need to approach data setup differently. Some typical approaches are to use a special endpoint that accepts JSON data or that creates predefined named fixtures.

It is usually *not* a good idea to set up test data by having the test step through the application as a user would. Tests that do that are very brittle because a regression in parts of the system dealing with data setup can break a huge swathe of unrelated tests. For example, a test for an order checkout process that relies on adding items to the customer's cart by stepping through product pages and clicking *add to cart* will break if there's a regression in displaying product pages, adding items to the cart, user login, and so on.

Not only does setting up data in that way become brittle but it's usually too limiting. If you want to test that items expire from a user's cart after 30 minutes, you don't want to have your test wait around for 30 minutes after adding items to the cart! If you want to test that price changes that happen after a user adds items to her cart are reflected, do you really want to log in as a user, add items to the cart, log out, log in to the admin interface, tweak the prices, log out again, log in again as the user, view the cart, and assert that the prices have updated?

There are a couple of things here specific to Geb. The go method is provided by Geb and sends the browser to the specified URL. It's the equivalent of typing a full URL in the address bar of a browser and pressing *Enter*. The $ method finds elements in the page rendered by the browser. There are a handful of overloaded versions of the method, but the one shown in this example uses a CSS selector expression to locate the element or elements.

The return type of the $ method is a Geb `Navigator` object, which provides various further methods for interacting with the element or elements returned. The API deliberately emulates jQuery's, which many programmers will find familiar.

The $ method similarly locates elements on the page using a CSS selector expression and returns an object that wraps around those elements, allowing further interaction. The crucial aspect is that the `Navigator` value returned can represent zero, one, or many page elements. It provides the methods `isEmpty()` and `size()` to determine if the element set is empty or how many elements it contains, and an `iterator()` method for iterating over each element individually. The example uses the `text()` method of `Navigator`, which returns the text content of all elements in the set. This is typically useful only when there is a single element and that element is a leaf node. Otherwise, `text()` will return the text from all elements concatenated together.

Waiting for Pages to Be Ready

One of the trickiest things in browser-based end-to-end testing is knowing when it is safe to begin interacting with the page. With "traditional" web applications that reload the entire page when navigating, submitting forms, and so on, this is not an issue. There, the test can wait for the *load* event on the document or window and be sure that everything is ready at that time. When you begin adding JavaScript-powered components to the page that can take a few milliseconds to initialize, things become much less reliable.

Nowadays with the popularity of *single-page apps*, things are more difficult still. Single-page apps load a skeleton HTML file, trap navigation and form submission with JavaScript event handlers, and dynamically replace portions of the document rather than reloading the entire page. Unfortunately, it can be quite tricky to know when navigation has completed and the "new" page is ready.

If the test tries to interact with the page too soon, elements might not be present or data might not have been merged into the HTML template. Because JavaScript usually initializes pretty fast in modern browsers, the test might not fail every time. A typical tactic is to wait for some condition to be true before interacting with the page. In the previous example, the test waits until the page heading text is present, indicating that Angular JS has loaded the view template into the DOM.

Introducing Page Models

This feature method so far works okay, but it has a couple of issues that will affect its usefulness long term.

First, the address of the *timeline* page is hardcoded into the test. It's possible that might never change, but in a more complex suite of tests, it becomes less and less sus-

---

tainable to hardcode URLs. If a change to the application changes a URL scheme, there will suddenly be a spate of failing tests that need to be fixed individually.

Similarly, and worse still, the feature method has hardcoded details of the page structure. Whereas URLs might change infrequently and can probably be updated with a simple search-and-replace macro, hardcoding page structure can be catastrophically brittle. Classes and IDs in an HTML page can be a very low-impact change, and even switching around the relationship of elements to one another is simple. If browser-based tests like this have HTML classes hardcoded, they can break in ways that are very tedious to fix. If the structure changes, rather than use a simple search-and-replace macro, it will likely be necessary to tediously inspect and fix each test individually.

To combat this brittleness, browser-based tests frequently use an abstraction known as a *page model*. The idea is that instead of hardcoding the page structure directly into the test, that structure is encapsulated in a class or hierarchy of classes that represent the page and its various components in logical terms. The tests can then interact with the page model objects without making assumptions about the fine details of the page structure. If and when the HTML structure changes, the page model classes are updated in a single place. For simple changes such as a change in the name of an HTML class, the tests should immediately begin working again. For radical structural changes, the tests might still need to be changed as well as the page model classes, but at least when that's necessary, you can bring IDE refactoring tools to bear.

Geb has first-class support for page model classes. Let's restructure our feature method to use such a class:

```
def "a user can see their own messages in their timeline"() {
  given:
  createUser("spock")
  createMessage("spock", "Fascinating!")

  and:
  loginAs("spock")

  when:
  to(TimelinePage)

  then:
  page.messageText == "Fascinating!"
  page.postedBy == "@spock"
}
```

Now instead of using a hardcoded URL, we're telling the browser to go to a particular page using the to(Page) method. The page model class encapsulates the URL. Also, instead of directly referencing HTML classes in CSS expressions to find elements on the page, the feature method now just references properties on the page object. The page property is inherited from GebSpec.

Not only is the test less brittle now, but it actually reads better, too. It's simpler and deals with the logical structure of the page rather than any fine-grained detail.

So, what does the `TimelinePage` class look like?

Geb uses a template defined via static properties in the page class to construct the individual objects:

```
import geb.Page

class TimelinePage extends Page {

  static url = "#/timeline" ❶

  static atCheckWaiting = true
  static at = { ❷
    $(".page-header").text() == "Timeline"
  }

  static content = { ❸
    messageText {
      $(".sq-message-text").text()
    }
    postedBy {
      $(".sq-posted-by").text()
    }
  }
}
```

❶ First, the page's URL is declared as a static property named `url`.

❷ Then, the static property `at` defines a way to check that the page is indeed the correct one. In this case, we simply check that the header on the page is correct.

❸ Finally, a `content` property defines the structure of the page.

This probably looks quite unfamiliar—there are no instance properties or methods in this example, so where are the `messageText` and `postedBy` properties the feature method references coming from?

The static `content` property is a closure that allows us to use a DSL to define the page structure. Inside the `content` closure, you can see further named closures that contain the exact same CSS expressions that we earlier used directly in the test. Geb maps this content DSL against the actual page when it is loaded and can lazily evaluate the elements on the page when properties are referenced on the resulting page object.

Setting the Base URL

Notice that the url property in TimelinePage is a relative URL. In the very first test we wrote, we passed a fully qualified URL to go, but now that we're dealing with page objects, it wouldn't make sense to hardcode the entire URL into the pages themselves. Geb's browser has a baseUrl property that we can set once and then just use relative URLs everywhere, as shown here:

```
@LocalServerPort int port

def setup() {
  baseUrl = "http://localhost:$port"
}
```

Because we're using Spring Boot, we can inject the random server port by using the @LocalServerPort annotation. If you're using another platform, you'll need a way to determine the port or run on a known port.

Why a Content DSL?

Why define a content DSL rather than actual straightforward instance properties on a page class? You might reasonably think it's more straightforward to define content properties in the page class, like this:

```
String messageText = $(".sq-message-text").text()

String postedBy = $(".sq-posted-by").text()
```

However, this will attempt to initialize the properties before the page has actually been loaded in the browser and result in Geb throwing PageInstanceNotInitialize dException.

Instead, maybe we could define the content properties as methods by using the Java bean convention, which will ensure that the CSS expressions are not evaluated until the page is actually loaded.

```
String getMessageText() {
  $(".sq-message-text").text()
}

String getPostedBy() {
  $(".sq-posted-by").text()
}
```

This does actually work. However, there's a significant downside in that the CSS expressions are reevaluated every time the get methods are called. In more complex tests, that could be inefficient and slow down execution. Geb's content DSL will create lazily evaluated properties that cache the elements found on the page so that they can be reused at will throughout the test.

The key to the content DSL is Groovy's meta-programming model that allows references to nonexistent properties and methods to be intercepted. In our example, the `TimelinePage` class does not have a `messageText` property, but when the feature method tries to reference it, Geb intercepts the call and determines it can supply a value based on the model defined in the content DSL.

The `at` property is another closure that returns a Boolean value indicating whether the page loaded by the browser is the correct one. This check can be as simple or as complex as necessary. In our example, a simple check against the header text is performed. The `at` closure can reference properties from the content DSL if necessary.

We've also specified `static atCheckWaiting = true`. This is a convenience Geb provides for tests running against JavaScript applications running in the browser. By default, Geb will run the `at` check after it detects a "page loaded" event from the browser. However, in a JavaScript application, the page might appear to be loaded before any or all of the content appears because the content is created by the JavaScript application itself. By setting `atCheckWaiting` to `true`, Geb will wait until the `at` check passes rather than just evaluating it once.

Geb's Automatic Delegation

In the previous feature method, we referenced the `page` property defined by the `Geb Spec` superclass. In fact, this isn't necessary, because `GebSpec` automatically delegates to those objects. Using more idiomatic Geb style, we can write the test like this:

```
when:
to(TimelinePage)

then:
messageText == "Fascinating!"
postedBy == "@spock"
```

Authentication

At this point, we can look again at the `loginAs(String)` method introduced in the first example. Timelines are unique to users, so it's necessary to log in to access it. In the browser interface we're developing, this means having a typical username and password login form that drops a cookie with an authentication token when the login is successful.

The `GebSpec` base class automatically clears cookies at the end of each feature method, so we know that at the start of each we won't be logged in.

To handle the login process, we can build a page class similar to the `TimelinePage`:

```
class LoginPage extends Page {

  static url = "#/login"

  static atCheckWaiting = true
  static at = {
    $(".page-header").text() == "Log in"
  }

  static content = {
    usernameField {
      $(".sq-login #username")
    }
    passwordField {
      $(".sq-login #password")
    }
    submitButton {
      $(".sq-login [type=submit]")
    }
    authenticatedUser {
      $(".sq-authenticated-user").text()
    }
  }
}
```

The login page contains content properties for the *username* and *password* input fields, the submit button, and a text element that will display a message if a user is logged in successfully.

Encapsulating Interactions by Using Methods

Page model classes can define methods, and can be an effective way to encapsulate logical operations performed on the page. In our example, the logical operation is "logging in." It has a two inputs: the username and password. We can define an instance method login in the page class that encapsulates entering the username and password, submitting the form, and waiting for a confirmation message to appear showing that the login succeeded:

```
void login(String username, String password) {
  usernameField.value(username)
  passwordField.value(password)
  submitButton.click()
  waitFor {
    authenticatedUser == "Logged in as @$username"
  }
}
```

That's much neater than having to repeat each of those steps outside when interacting with the page object. It encapsulates the functionality of the page still further than just defining content properties.

If the login fails for whatever reason, the `waitFor` step will time out and the feature method will fail.

We can add a further method to a base specification class or trait so that we don't even need to explicitly go `to(LoginPage)` in the feature methods:

```
void loginAs(String username, String password = "password") {
  to(LoginPage)
    .login(username, password)
}
```

Default Parameter Values with Groovy

The `loginAs` method uses a default parameter value to save you from always having to specify a password when test users are always created with the same one by default. Groovy allows any or all parameters to have default values. The only restriction is that nondefaulted parameters must appear *before* defaulted ones. When called, the defaulted parameters can simply be omitted unless different values are needed.

To ensure that the login functionality is working as expected, we can create a test that logs in as two different users and verifies that different timelines are displayed:

```
def "different users see different timelines"() {
  given:
  createUser("kirk")
  createUser("spock")
  createMessage("kirk", "Report, Mr Spock.")
  createMessage("spock", "Fascinating!")

  when:
  loginAs("kirk")

  then:
  at(TimelinePage) ❶
  messageText == "Report, Mr Spock."
  postedBy == "@kirk"

  when: ❷
  loginAs("spock")

  then:
  at(TimelinePage)
  messageText == "Fascinating!"
  postedBy == "@spock"
}
```

❶ Geb's `at(Page)` method asserts that the browser is on the specified page by using the page class' *at* check. If successful, it also changes the current page object.

---

❷ This is an unusual feature method in that it has *multiple* when and then blocks. Although not frequently seen, this is valid.

Multiple when and then Blocks

As demonstrated in the preceding example, it's possible to have multiple pairs of when and then blocks. In the feature method here, there's a good reason to do so because we want to directly contrast the content seen when two different users log in.

It's not a good idea to abuse this capability to write very long feature methods that test multiple conditions or run through an entire workflow. Such tests "fail fast," meaning a problem early on must be fixed before later problems even become apparent.

Modules

Although we've seen the basics of how to define a page model, the model we have so far is a little naïve. Because we've created only a single message in the feature method, we can get away with a page model that defines a single messageText and postedBy property. But what happens when the page displays multiple messages? We need a way to reference the same messageText and postedBy property on each message so that the test can verify them. This is where breaking down the page model into subcomponents makes sense. The structure of the HTML block containing each message will be identical, so it makes sense to represent it in the page abstraction with a collection of smaller model objects that define the content for just that block.

The following is the structure of the relevant parts of the page:

```
<div class="container">            ❶
  <h1></h1>
  <ol class="sq-message-list">     ❷
    <li>                           ❸
      <figure class="sq-message">
        <figcaption class="sq-message-heading">
          <span class="sq-posted-by"><a></a></span>
          <time class="sq-posted-at"></time>
        </figcaption>
        <div class="sq-message-text"></div>
      </figure>
    </li>
    <li>
      <!-- ... -->                 ❹
    </li>
  </ol>
</div>
```

❶ The container `<div>` wraps around the main content of the page; only such things as a global header and footer will be outside it.

❷ The container for the list of messages is an ordered list element: `<ol>`.

❸ Each individual message is a list element (`<li>`) containing a `<figure>`.

❹ The same structure is repeated for each message.

We can represent that structure with a hierarchy of modules like this:

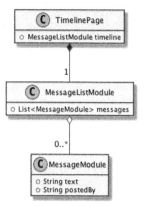

The `TimelinePage` is a page object like the one we have defined previously, but now instead of containing `messageText` and `postedBy` properties, it has a single `Message ListModule`. The `MessageListModule` itself contains any number of `MessageModule` objects and each of those will contain a `messageText` and `postedBy` property.

First, we'll change the `TimelinePage` class to contain a single content property `time line`. This uses Geb's `module` method to initialize a new module object using the selected node as the root:

```
static content = {
  timeline {
    $(".sq-message-list").module(MessageListModule)
  }
}
```

The `module` method is passed a class `MessageListModule`, so let's see how that looks next:

```
import geb.Module

class MessageListModule extends Module {
  static content = {
```

```
    messages {
      $("li").collect {
        it.module(MessageModule)
      }
    }
  }
}
```

Instead of extending Page module classes, extend Module. They do not have url or at properties, but their content is defined in exactly the same way as a page's. The vital thing is that the $ method works within the context of the module's root element, *not* the entire page. This means that here we can simply select all the li elements knowing we'll get those inside of the root element of the module and not any others that happen to appear somewhere in the page.

In MessageListModule we transform the node-set of li elements into a List<Messa geModule> using Groovy's collect method and a closure that simply applies the module class to every element.

Finally, the MessageModule class itself looks like this:

```
import geb.Module

class MessageModule extends Module {
  static content = {
    text { $(".sq-message-text").text() }
    postedBy { $(".sq-posted-by").text() }
  }
}
```

Now, we have our text and postedBy properties. This time they're defined in the context of a single message li element. We can have many such modules in the page.

Putting the new modules into use in a test is very easy. We can manipulate the module properties just like any other list:

```
def "a user can see their own messages in their timeline"() {
  given:
  createUser("spock")
  messages.each {
    createMessage("spock", it)
  }

  and:
  loginAs("spock")

  when:
  to(TimelinePage)

  then:
  timeline.messages.size() == messages.size() ❶
```

```
      timeline.messages[0].text == messages[1] ❷
      timeline.messages[1].text == messages[0]
      timeline.messages*.postedBy.every { it == "@spock" } ❸

    where:
    messages = [
      "Fascinating!",
      "I remind you that this is a silicon-based form of life."
    ]
}
```

❶ Assert that the number of modules matches the number of messages we expect to appear.

❷ Ensure that the text of each individual message is displayed correctly.

❸ Use Groovy's every method to assert that all of the messages display the same username as the postedBy value.

We can also reuse the module classes in other pages. If we want to build a *user* page that displays some details about a user along with a list of that user's recent messages, we can reuse the MessageListModule class:

```
class UserPage extends Page {

    static url = "#/user/spock"

    static atCheckWaiting = true
    static at = {
        $(".page-header").text() == "User @spock"
    }

    static content = {
        recent {
            $(".sq-message-list").module(MessageListModule)
        }
    }
}
```

Here, we have an identical content property to timeline from the timeline page, but in this instance, it's called recent. We can write a feature method to test the page in the same way we tested the content of the timeline:

```
def "a user can see their own messages on their user page"() {
    given:
    createUser("spock")
    createMessage("spock", "Fascinating!")

    when:
    to(UserPage)
```

```
then:
recent.messages.size() == 1
recent.messages[0].text == "Fascinating!"
}
```

Parameterized Pages

The UserPage class defined here has a pretty serious limitation: it works only for the user *@spock*! The username is hardcoded into the url property and the at check. What we really need is a page object that we can use to model *any* user page. Essentially, instead of just supplying the page class as a parameter to the to method, we need to be able to pass other parameters as well that will modify the state of the page object, including its url property.

To do this, we can simply remove the hardcoded /spock portion of the URL in the page class and instead pass it to the to method. Any extra parameters passed to the to method are appended to the URL automatically, like so:

```
static url = "#/user"

when:
to(UserPage, "spock")
```

Unfortunately, we had also hardcoded the username in the at check, so that also needs to be modified to make it work for any page. For example, it might be sufficient to check the page header by using a regular expression:

```
static at = {
  $(".page-header").text() ==~ /User @.+/
}
```

For situations in which the parameters to the page need to be used beyond just the URL, it's possible to simply define a property or properties in the page class.

When doing this, it's also necessary to override the method convertToPath, which is responsible for taking the parameters passed to the to method and converting them to a URL. The default implementation just chains parameters together separated by 0 and appends them to the url property. For example, with a url property of "foo" and a call to FooPage, "bar", "baz", the resulting URL will be /foo/bar/baz:

```
private final String username

UserPage(String username) {
  this.username = username
}

@Override
String convertToPath(Object... args) {
  super.convertToPath(username, *args) ❶
}
```

```
static url = "#/user" ❷
```

❶ Here we prepend the username property before any other parameters in convert
ToPath. There might not *be* any other parameters when the page is loaded.

❷ The url is just 0 because we know that we'll be adding the username in convert
ToPath.

The nice thing is we can now use the username property to make the at check simpler
again.

Spreading varargs with Groovy

You might be wondering what 0 means in the previous example. The 1 prepended
before an array or collection reference is Groovy's "spread" operator. It *spreads* the
values from the array or collection to fill varargs.

Here's the signature of the superclass method we're calling:

```
String convertToPath(Object... args)
```

We want to pass it a single known value, plus any others that might or might not be
present in the args parameter. In Java, that would require us to create a new array one
element larger than the args parameter, add in username, and then use System.array
copy to copy over the remaining values from args. Finally, we could pass the new
array to the superclass method, as shown here:

```
Object[] newArgs = new Object[args.length + 1];
newArgs[0] = username;
System.arraycopy(args, 0, newArgs, 1, args.length);
super.convertToPath(newArgs);
```

In Groovy, the spread operator makes this *much* easier.

```
static at = {
  $(".page-header").text() == "User @$username"
}
```

We now have a flexible UserPage class that we can use in a variety of scenarios rather
than being restricted to a particular test user.

Interacting with Forms

The page model is not used only to read and verify data on the page—it can also be
used interactively.

We're going to add a page that allows the user to post a message. To do that, we'll need to have the user type into a text area and click a submit button. Figure 14-1 shows what the page will look like.

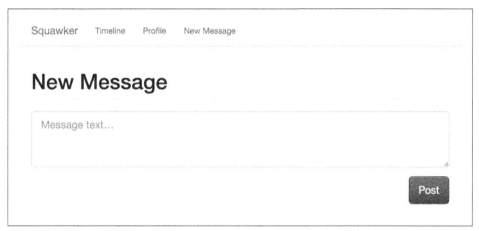

Figure 14-1. The new message page

The HTML for the form section of the page looks approximately like this (I've removed some irrelevant classes and other attributes):

```
<form class="sq-new-message">
  <div class="form-group">
    <label>
      Message
      <textarea name="text" ng-model="message.text"></textarea>
    </label>
  </div>
  <div class="btn-group">
    <button name="submit" type="submit" ng-click="post()">Post</button>
  </div>
</form>
```

The page model is easy enough to define. We'll need a content property for the tex tarea and another for the submit button:

```
class NewMessagePage extends Page {

  static url = "#/new-message"

  static atCheckWaiting = true
  static at = {
    $(".page-header").text() == "New Message"
  }

  static content = {
    textarea {
```

```
      $(".sq-new-message textarea") ❶
  }
  postButton {
    $(".sq-new-message button[type=submit]") ❷
  }
}
}
}
```

We can then write a test fairly easily:

```
def "a user can post a message"() {
  given:
  createUser("spock")

  and:
  to(NewMessagePage)

  when:
  textarea.value(text) ❶
  postButton.click()   ❷

  then:
  // ...

  where:
  text = "Fascinating!"
}
```

❶ The value(String) method enters the form value.

❷ The click() method is self-explanatory. In this case, it will also submit the form because the button has type="submit".

So far, so good. But how do we verify that the message was created successfully?

It would make sense to have a page that displays a single message. Not only would this be useful for deep links into the site, but it's a sensible place to which to redirect to after successfully submitting a new message.

Because we've already defined a MessageModule class, we can simply wrap that in a very simple page and begin to see some reuse from our page model.

```
class MessagePage extends Page {

  static url = "#/message" ❶

  static atCheckWaiting = true
  static at = {
    $(".page-header").empty && $(".sq-message") ❷
  }

  static content = {
```

```
        message {
            $(".sq-message").module(MessageModule) ❸
        }
    }
}
```

❶ The URL for the page is 0, where :id is the unique ID of the message. The ID value will come from the convertToPath method as in the UserPage class.

❷ The at check is a little more complex because the message page has no header but should have a message block.

❸ We can reuse the MessageModule class we developed for the timeline page model earlier. Note that there is no MessageListModule, because this page displays a single message.

With that page model in place we can complete the feature method like this:

```
at(MessagePage)        ❶
message.text == text ❷
```

❶ Geb's at method confirms that the browser is now *at* a new page. It runs the specified page's at check and, if successful, updates the current page so that subsequent delegated calls go to the new page type.

❷ We can then refer to content properties of the new page. In this case, we just want to verify the message text.

Accessing Form Elements by Name

The textarea is defined as a unique content property of NewMessagePage, but on larger forms, this might become unwieldy. Geb has special support for forms, allowing data to be read and updated on named form elements. This is particularly useful for larger forms, but we can reimplement NewMessagePage to take advantage of it:

```
static content = {
    form {
        $("form.sq-new-message") ❶
    }
}
```

Instead of defining separate properties for the textarea and submit button we just define a single property for the entire form.

Any field in the form can then be automatically accessed by name on the Navigator object represented by the content property. If referenced as a property, a field name is used to get or set the value of a form field. If referenced as a method, a field name provides access to the element as a Navigator object.

Let's update the feature method to use this technique:

```
def "a user can post a message"() {
  given:
  createUser("spock")

  and:
  to(NewMessagePage)

  when:
  form.text = text         ❶
  form.submit().click()    ❷

  then:
  at(MessagePage)
  message.text == text

  where:
  text = "Fascinating!"
}
```

❶ The textarea's value is set by just assigning a string to a property on the form whose name matches the form element's name attribute.

❷ The button is accessed by using the button's name attribute like a method name. This returns a Navigator object that we can click.

This is neat and convenient, but we're back to exposing page structure in the test rather than in the page model. If the form structure changes, we might need to revisit a number of tests in order to update element names. We've also rather artificially added a name property on the submit button when it doesn't really need one, just so that we can access it conveniently.

Encapsulating Interactions with Methods

As we saw with page model classes earlier, modules can define methods, and doing so can be an effective way to encapsulate logical operations performed on the page. In our example, the logical operation is "posting a message." It has a single direct input: the message text. We can easily define a method on the page class, as follows:

```
void postMessage(String text) {
  form.text = text
  form.find("[type=submit]").click()
}
```

Instead of accessing the submit button by name, we define a content property that accesses it by its type attribute. This means that we can remove the redundant name property from the button itself.

At this point, we've completely encapsulated any detail of the page structure in the page model, and the feature method deals only with high-level behavior:

```
def "a user can post a message"() {
  given:
  createUser("spock")

  and:
  to(NewMessagePage)

  when:
  postMessage(text)

  then:
  at(MessagePage)
  message.text == text

  where:
  text = "Fascinating!"
}
```

Form Validation

It's typically important to test not only that users can submit forms successfully, but also that errors are detected and displayed.

In the case of Squawker's message form, the user should not be allowed to post a message that is too long and an error should display if that happens, as depicted in Figure 14-2.

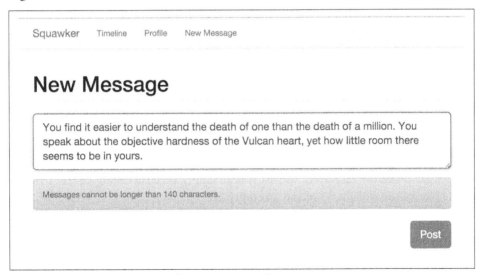

Figure 14-2. Error messages in the new message form

The feature method to test that behavior could look like this:

```
def "a user cannot post a message with too much text"() {
  given:
  createUser("spock")

  and:
  to(NewMessagePage)

  when:
  postMessage(text)

  then:
  at(NewMessagePage)
  errors == ["Messages cannot be longer than 140 characters."]

  where:
  text = "You find it easier to understand the death of one than the death " +
    "of a million. You speak about the objective hardness of the Vulcan " +
    "heart, yet how little room there seems to be in yours."
}
```

After attempting to submit the form as before, the feature method asserts that the browser has remained on the NewMessagePage using the at method. Then we look for some validation error text to ensure an appropriate message is visible that explains what is wrong.

The errors property is a fairly simple example of mixing Geb's Navigator class with Groovy's functional iterator style. The content property extracts a list of error message strings from an HTML <ul> element:

```
static content = {
  form {
    $("form.sq-new-message")
  }
  submitButton {
    form.find("[type=submit]")
  }
  errors {
    $(".alert li").collect { it.text() }
  }
}
```

If there are no errors displayed, the list will be empty because calling collect on an empty Navigator will always return an empty list.

We can go on to ensure that particular fields in the form are highlighted, the submit button is disabled when errors are present, and so on.

CHAPTER 15

Testing JavaScript Using Spock

So far, we've used Spock exclusively to test Java code. One of the reasons all of the examples in the book use Java is that I want to stress that Spock is able to test more than just Groovy. However, Java is not the only other language that we can test using Spock.

In this chapter, we take a brief look at testing JavaScript using Spock. We'll use the Nashorn script engine (introduced in Java 8) to evaluate JavaScript and invoke it from Spock.

Nashorn

The Java Virtual Machine (JVM) has long had a JavaScript interpreter—Rhino—shipped along with it, and it has been possible to run simple scripts in the JVM. However, Rhino had some limitations with respect to performance and the interoperability of objects created in Java and JavaScript. Typically, it's necessary to convert Java objects to a JavaScript representation before passing them to a script running in Rhino and then convert any response value back again.

Nashorn (from the German for "rhino"), introduced alongside Java 8, has fewer such limitations. It is very fast and can in many cases handle regular Java objects passed as arguments to functions. It *is* necessary to translate lists and arrays to a JavaScript version, but many other structured object types work seamlessly.

Nashorn can also compile JavaScript code for more efficient repeated execution.

Why Test JavaScript from the JVM?

Why would we want to test JavaScript code from the JVM when JavaScript has its own rich suite of testing tools? One possibility might be that you want to test some small JavaScript components alongside a much larger Java codebase. Setting up the infrastructure required to execute Jasmine tests as part of your build might seem like unnecessary effort. Another is that in the production application, you'll be invoking JavaScript from Java and it would be beneficial to test that there aren't any interoperability issues; for example, if you're developing web page templates that are rendered both on the server and in the browser. In fact, we'll take a look at doing just that later in this chapter.

Setting Up Nashorn for Tests

JavaScript is executed by a `javax.script.ScriptEngine` instance. In a Spock specification, we'll probably want to create the engine once and reuse it across all our tests. Here's how we can do that:

```
@Shared ScriptEngine engine

def setupSpec() {
  def manager = new ScriptEngineManager()
  engine = manager.getEngineByName("nashorn")
}
```

Calling JavaScript Functions

After we have a script engine, we can use it to evaluate and execute bits of JavaScript code. The `javax.script` package includes an interface, `Invocable`, that Nashorn's script engine implements. With the `Invocable` interface, we can call functions or methods on objects inside the context of the script engine.

In the following simple example, we declare a JavaScript function in Nashorn and then call it from a Spock specification:

```
def "can call a named function"() {
  given:
  engine.eval """ ❶
    function up(s) {
      return s.toUpperCase();
    }
  """

  expect:
  (engine as Invocable).invokeFunction("up", "Fascinating") == "FASCINATING" ❷
}
```

❶ The `engine.eval` call parses a chunk of JavaScript code in the context of the script engine. Here we're declaring a simple function.

❷ After it is cast to `Invocable`, we can call the `invokeFunction` method on the script engine, passing the name of the function and a vararg array of parameters. The return value is whatever the JavaScript function returns.

Why Do We Need to Cast ScriptEngine to Invocable?

Unfortunately, the declared return type of `ScriptEngineMan ager.getEngineByName` is just `javax.script.ScriptEngine`, and instances of that interface do not necessarily implement `Invocable`.

This means that we either need to cast our script engine instance to `Invocable` or let Groovy dynamically call the method. A dynamic call will succeed but obviously runs the risk of a typo and doesn't allow the IDE to help find and complete the `invokeFunction` call.

`Invocable` does not extend `ScriptEngine`, so if we declared `engine` as `Invocable`, we'd have the exact same problem with the `eval` method.

Because Groovy does not have intersection types like Ceylon— where we could declare `ScriptEngine & Invocable engine` and avoid any casting—we're stuck with a couple of different imperfect solutions.

JavaScript Functions as Objects

Instead of using `invokeFunction`, it's also possible to use a JavaScript function as an object that we can pass around and call in the same way we would a Groovy closure or a Java functional interface.

Using the previous example, we can actually use the return value from `engine.eval`, which in this case is the function declared in the script.

```
def "can call a function"() {
  given:
  def fn = engine.eval("""
    function up(s) {
      return s.toUpperCase();
    }
  """) as JSObject

  expect:
  fn.call(null, "Fascinating") == "FASCINATING"
}
```

Because `eval` can return almost anything, it's return type is declared as `Object`. For cases like this in which `eval` returns a JavaScript function, the actual type will be `jdk.nashorn.api.scripting.JSObject`.

The method of `JSObject` we need in order to call the function it represents is `call(Object this, Object... arguments)`. You can dynamically bind JavaScript functions to a `this` context, so the first parameter of the `call` method provides a way of supplying such a context. We do not need to bind our up function to any context, so we can just supply `null`. The remaining parameters are whatever arguments the JavaScript function expects; in this case, it's a single string.

Because `call` is a special method name in Groovy that can be represented with the brace operator, we can even use the JavaScript function almost as though it were a Groovy closure:

```
expect:
fn(null, "Fascinating") == "FASCINATING"
```

Specifying this in a JavaScript Function

As I mentioned just a moment ago, that first parameter to which we're passing `null` is the function's `this`.

If we change our simple function so that it operates on `this` instead of a parameter, we can invoke it like this:

```
def "can bind tho 'this'"() {
  given:
  def fn = engine.eval("""
    function up() {
      return this.toUpperCase();   ❶
    }
  """) as JSObject

  expect:
  fn("Fascinating") == "FASCINATING"   ❷
}
```

❶ The JavaScript function itself no longer declares a parameter and now assumes its `this` value is a string.

❷ To invoke the function, we just pass the `this` value as the first parameter.

What we've done is roughly equivalent to the JavaScript, as illustrated here:

```
var up = function() {
  return this.toUpperCase();
}
```

```
var boundUp = up.bind('Fascinating');
return boundUp();
```

Testing an Isomorphic View Component

Let's look at a slightly more involved example. When a message is rendered in Squawker, we'll include a timestamp displayed in a "friendly" way with text such as *"a few minutes ago"* or *"last month"* instead of an absolute date and time.

Because we want Squawker to be a dynamic JavaScript application, we're using client-side rendering of the various pages, so we'll need a little view component that translates the absolute timestamp in a JSON representation of a message into the friendly format we'll show to the user. However, because we're concerned about the time it takes a user to begin interacting with the page and we also want search engines to index Squawker, we want to be able to render the pages on the server, as well.

Isomorphic Web Applications

An isomorphic web application is one that can render its views on either the server or client browser. Typically, a first load of a page will be rendered on the server and delivered to the user's browser as HTML. Subsequent interactions make API calls to endpoints on the server, which returns JSON, and the page in the browser is modified in place by using JavaScript.

Search engines can "spider" an isomorphic application. In addition, users do not need to wait for multiple HTTP round-trips before they see the initial page. It retains the stateful flexibility of a rich client web application, though.

It would be crazy to duplicate the logic for rendering the views in JavaScript on the client and Java on the server, so using Nashorn to execute the same JavaScript on the server side as the browser uses on the client side seems like a good idea.

Our simple JavaScript function will accept a timestamp in the form of a number of milliseconds and return a string.

This time, instead of inlining the JavaScript in the specification itself, we'll load the actual file that is deployed as part of the web application. Because Nashorn's script engine can accept a `java.io.Reader`, that's easy enough to do:

```
@Shared ScriptEngine engine
@Shared CompiledScript script

def setupSpec() {
  def manager = new ScriptEngineManager()
  engine = manager.getEngineByName("nashorn")
  getClass().getResource("relative-time.js").withReader { reader -> ❶
```

```
            script = ((Compilable) engine).compile(reader) ❷
        }
    script.eval() ❸
}
```

❶ We can load the JavaScript file just like any other classpath resource.

❷ Notice we're also compiling the script. Nashorn is able to compile JavaScript for
    more efficient repeated execution. The `Compilable` interface is another optional
    interface like `Invocable` that script engines can implement.

❸ After compiling the script, we still need to call `eval` to load it into the running
    script engine.

After we have loaded, compiled, and evaluated the script, we can write the following
feature method that exercises it, just as we would for a Java or Groovy function:

```
@Unroll
def "can render relative timestamp"() {
  expect:
  (engine as Invocable)
    .invokeFunction("relativeTime", timestamp.toEpochMilli()) == expected

  where:
  timestamp                | expected
  now()                    | "just now"
  now().minus(1, MINUTES)  | "a minute ago"
  now().minus(5, MINUTES)  | "a few minutes ago"
  now().minus(1, HOURS)    | "an hour ago"
  now().minus(2, HOURS)    | "earlier today"
  now().minus(1, DAYS)     | "yesterday"
}
```

The JavaScript function itself is simple. It's easy to see how we could extend it to cover
further cases, test driving by adding rows to the `where:` table:

```
function relativeTime(timestamp) {
  var now = new Date();
  var difference = now.getTime() - timestamp;
  if (difference >= 86400000) {
    return 'yesterday';
  } else if (difference >= 7200000) {
    return 'earlier today';
  } else if (difference >= 3600000) {
    return 'an hour ago';
  } else if (difference >= 120000) {
    return 'a few minutes ago';
  } else if (difference >= 60000) {
    return 'a minute ago';
  } else {
    return 'just now';
```

```
    }
}
```

An Invocable Script Engine as a Delegate

That ugly cast to Invocable is annoying, so it would make sense to provide a helper method to hide it. One thing we could also do is use a @Delegate-annotated field with type Invocable, allowing us to just call invokeFunction as though it were a method of the specification class itself:

```
@Delegate Invocable invocableScriptEngine = engine as Invocable

@Unroll
def "can render relative timestamp"() {
  expect:
  invokeFunction("relativeTime", timestamp.toEpochMilli()) == expected

  where:
  timestamp                 | expected
  now()                     | "just now"
  now().minus(1, MINUTES)   | "a minute ago"
  now().minus(5, MINUTES)   | "a few minutes ago"
  now().minus(1, HOURS)     | "an hour ago"
  now().minus(2, HOURS)     | "earlier today"
  now().minus(1, DAYS)      | "yesterday"
}
```

This seems much neater and will certainly be clearer to read and easier to write as we add more feature methods to the specification.

> You cannot use @Shared fields as delegates, so the Invocable is reinitialized for every feature method.

Passing Mocks to JavaScript

For the moment, our friendly timestamp function returns a string, but another common pattern in JavaScript is to use a callback function, which is passed the result.

Unlike Java methods, JavaScript functions can be called with fewer (or more) parameters than they declare in their signature. Any missing parameters are undefined in the body of the function.

This means that our function could accept a second argument: a callback. If the callback parameter is present, the result value is passed to the callback instead of being returned.

But how do we test such a thing? Our existing feature method is still valid for the case in which we don't supply a callback and the function should return its result. What can we pass as the callback parameter, though? If we were testing the same kind of callback in Java or Groovy, we'd probably use a mock; luckily, Spock's mocks are totally compatible with Nashorn:

```
@Unroll
def "can pass result to a callback"() {
  given:
  def callback = Mock(Consumer) ❶

  when:
  invokeFunction("relativeTime", timestamp.toEpochMilli(), callback)

  then:
  1 * callback.accept(expected) ❷

  where:
  timestamp                 | expected
  now()                     | "just now"
  now().minus(1, MINUTES)   | "a minute ago"
  now().minus(5, MINUTES)   | "a few minutes ago"
  now().minus(1, HOURS)     | "an hour ago"
  now().minus(2, HOURS)     | "earlier today"
  now().minus(1, DAYS)      | "yesterday"
}
```

❶ The Nashorn script engine can use any Java type annotated with @FunctionalIn terface as if it were a JavaScript function. Consumer seems a logical choice for the mock because it simply accepts a single value.

❷ The mock verification is done just as it would be when testing Java or Groovy code.

The updated JavaScript function with the optional callback looks like this:

```
function relativeTime(timestamp, callback) {
  var now = new Date();
  var difference = now.getTime() - timestamp;
  var result;
  if (difference >= 86400000) {
    result = 'yesterday';
  } else if (difference >= 7200000) {
    result = 'earlier today';
  } else if (difference >= 3600000) {
    result = 'an hour ago';
  } else if (difference >= 120000) {
    result = 'a few minutes ago';
  } else if (difference >= 60000) {
    result = 'a minute ago';
  } else {
```

```
      result = 'just now';
    }

    if (callback === undefined) {
      return result;
    } else {
      callback(result);
    }
  }
}
```

Using stubs can also be very useful for simulating other JavaScript components with which the function that's being tested interacts.

Rendering a View with the Handlebars Library

If we're really going to attempt to build an isomorphic application, we'll want to do more than just run simple script functions on the server. JavaScript has numerous solutions for templating HTML, and we will probably want to use one to construct the pages and components for the Squawker website.

In the following examples, we'll use the *Handlebars* template library, but most of the techniques we'll look at for loading libraries and template files and using them to construct HTML would be equally applicable to Mustache, Jade, Underscore, Dust.js, or whatever template library you end up using.

Handlebars

Handlebars is one of the most popular JavaScript template libraries. Although primarily used for rendering HTML, you can use it for any kind of text template.

Handlebars' tags are delimited by double curly braces (that look like handlebar mustaches, hence the name). Expressions within the braces can refer to properties on the current context object, helper methods, and their parameters or "partial" templates used to render modular parts of the document.

Handlebars is "logicless" in that you cannot embed logical operations within the template itself. What you can do is define helper methods that can either return a value to be rendered or selectively render the content between their opening and closing tags.

Handlebars includes built-in helpers such as if and each that allow for conditional and loop constructs. The if helper renders or skips the content between its opening and closing tags, depending on the *truthiness* of the value passed as a parameter. The each helper renders the content between its opening and closing tags once for each element in the array value passed as a parameter.

Because we'll want to render a Squawker message in various contexts—individual message pages, timelines, search results, user profiles, and so on—we'll definitely need a template to render a message that we can reuse in various contexts.

Let's start with a simple form of the template and add some more detail later:

```
<article class="message">
  <div class="text">{{text}}</div>
  <footer>
    Posted by
    <a href="/users/{{postedBy.username}}">@{{postedBy.username}}</a>
  </footer>
</article>
```

When rendered, the template will produce HTML something like this:

```
<article class="message">
  <div class="text">Fascinating!</div>
  <footer>
    Posted by <a href="/users/spock">@spock</a>
  </footer>
</article>
```

The Template Context

Handlebars templates have the concept of a "context," which can be thought of as the object the template is rendering. In this case, the template is referring to the properties of a message, so the message object is the template's context.

You use the keyword this if a template needs to refer to the context object itself rather than one of its properties.

Some helper functions in Handlebars can affect the context within their tag body. For example, the context within the body of an {{#each}}...{{/each}} helper block is the individual element of the current iteration.

Compiling Handlebars Templates

Handlebars has a compile function that turns a template string into a JavaScript function. We don't want to embed the template as a string in the specification class, so the first thing we'll need to do is load the template from a file and have Handlebars compile it.

Because this is something we'll need to do repeatedly with different templates it makes sense to create some helper methods that encapsulate some of the necessary steps:

```
@Shared ScriptEngine engine
@Shared JSObject handlebars

def setupSpec() {
  def manager = new ScriptEngineManager()
  engine = manager.getEngineByName("nashorn")  ❶
  loadResource("/handlebars.js") { reader ->
    (engine as Compilable).compile(reader).eval()  ❷
  }
  handlebars = engine.eval("Handlebars") as JSObject  ❸
}

@Delegate Invocable invocableEngine

def setup() {
  // end::jackson[]
  invocableEngine = engine as Invocable
}
// end::jackson[]

protected JSObject compile(String path) {
  loadResource(path) { reader ->
    invokeMethod(handlebars, "compile", reader.text) as JSObject  ❹
  }
}

protected <T> T loadResource(
  String path,
  @ClosureParams(value = SimpleType, options = "java.io.Reader")
    Closure<T> callback) {
  getClass().getResource(path).withReader(callback)  ❺
}
```

❶ We set up the Nashorn script engine just as before.

❷ We need to load and evaluate the Handlebars library itself.

❸ Then, we get a reference to the Handlebars object in the script engine.

❹ To compile a template, we call the compile method on that Handlebars object. invokeMethod is a method on the Invocable script engine delegate. It's similar to invokeFunction except that it requires a target object as the first parameter and a method name as the second.

❺ Our loadResource helper method is used to read any JavaScript or template file from src/main/resources and pass a reader to a callback.

Testing Template Rendering

INow that we have Handlebars itself loaded into the script engine and have set up a mechanism for compiling templates, we can move on to the following simple test for our message template:

```
def "can render a message"() {
  given:
  def template = compile("message.hbs") ❶

  expect:
  with(render(template, message)) { ❷
    find(".text").text() == message.text
    find("footer a").attr("href") == "/users/$user.username"
    find("footer a").text() == user.toString()
  }

  where:
  user = new User("spock")
  message = new Message(user, "Fascinating", now())
}

Jerry render(JSObject template, Object... parameters) {
  $(template(null, *parameters) as String)
}
```

❶ We begin by compiling the message template using the helper method we defined earlier.

❷ To make assertions against individual elements of the rendered HTML, we parse the template result into a DOM tree–like structure.

There are a couple of things worth discussing here. First, note that the feature method passes an actual Message instance to the template function. We're passing a POJO to a JavaScript function that is able to access the object's properties by name. Remember that the message.hbs template referred to the text and postedBy.username properties.

Second, to turn the string result of the template function into something we can make sensible assertions about, we're using the *Jerry* library again. (You saw this library earlier in Chapter 8.) To recap quickly, Jerry parses an HTML string into a JQuery-like structure that can be navigated and queried by using CSS selectors. It's extremely useful for this kind of scenario in which trying to use regular expressions or other text-parsing techniques to verify the rendered content would result in an extremely brittle test.

To make Jerry seem very JQuery-like, we can import its factory method like this:

```
import static jodd.jerry.Jerry.jerry as $
```

Handling Properties That Don't Convert to JavaScript

So far, we've used a regular `Message` as the context parameter for our template function. That's been fine because we accessed only plain string properties of the message.

But `Message` also has a `postedAt` property that is a `java.time.Instant`. Although there's nothing preventing a template from accessing properties or calling methods on an `Instant`, if this was the case we'd then be tying our template to the server-side representation of the message.

It makes sense to include information about when a message was posted in our template. Let's extend what we currently have to include that:

```
<article class="message">
  <div class="text">{{text}}</div>
  <footer>
    Posted by
    <a href="/users/{{postedBy.username}}">@{{postedBy.username}}</a>
    at
    <time>{{postedAt}}</time>
  </footer>
</article>
```

If we really want to use this template for both server- and client-side rendering, we need to remember that the client-side rendering will use a JSON representation of the message that looks something like this:

```
{
  "id":"852abf98-e519-4e99-abe2-51ace53498e5",
  "postedBy":{
    "id":"384e7e80-ba14-4325-b3f4-843602ab237c",
    "username":"spock",
    "registered":1485958195153
  },
  "text":"Fascinating",
  "postedAt":1485958195153
}
```

The `postedAt` timestamp is expressed as milliseconds since epoch. We can't reference that millisecond value in the same way we'd reference a `java.time.Instant` and expect the same rendered output.

We'll need to convert the `Message` instance into a JSON-like form. One way to do that is to just produce a `java.util.Map`:

```
def "can render a message"() {
  given:
  def template = compile("message.hbs")

  and:
  def messageObj = [
```

```
      text    : message.text,
      postedBy: message.postedBy,
      postedAt: message.postedAt.toEpochMilli() ❶
    ]

    expect:
    with(render(template, messageObj)) {
      find(".text").text() == message.text
      find("footer a").attr("href") == "/users/$user.username"
      find("footer a").text() == user.toString()
      find("footer time").text() == message.postedAt.toEpochMilli() as String
    }

    where:
    user = new User("spock")
    message = new Message(user, "Fascinating", now())
}
```

❶ As part of the map declaration, the `Instant` value is converted to a millisecond value.

This works but is a little clunky. We're dealing with only a couple of properties here, but this will get tedious when we're dealing with more complex objects.

The REST API is presumably already converting `Message` instances back and forth to JSON. It makes sense to simply reuse that conversion here, so that we know we're dealing with values formatted in the same way.

We can configure a Jackson `ObjectMapper` instance and use it to convert the `Message` instance to a `Map`. This is essentially the same conversion we were previously doing manually, but now it's a far less cumbersome process. We also have some confidence that the resulting structure will be the same as the JSON emitted by the API that we'll be dealing with when rendering templates client-side:

```
def mapper = new ObjectMapper()
// tag::compile-templates[]

def setup() {
  mapper.registerModule(new JavaTimeModule()) ❶
  mapper.disable(WRITE_DATE_TIMESTAMPS_AS_NANOSECONDS) ❷
  // tag::compile-templates[]
}

def "can render a message"() {
  given:
  def template = compile("message.hbs")

  and:
  def messageObj = mapper.convertValue(message, Map) ❸

  expect:
```

```
    with(render(template, messageObj)) {
      find(".text").text() == message.text
      find("footer a").attr("href") == "/users/$user.username"
      find("footer a").text() == user.toString()
      find("footer time").text() == message.postedAt.toEpochMilli() as String
    }

    where:
    user = new User("spock")
    message = new Message(user, "Fascinating", now())
  }
  // tag::jackson-convert[]
}
```

❶ We register a `JavaTimeModule` with Jackson that has converters for serializing and deserializing various `java.time` types.

❷ By default, `Instant` instances are converted to values with nanosecond precision, but we don't need that.

❸ We can then convert our `Message` to a `Map` using the object mapper.

The conversion done by Jackson has arbitrary depth, so this technique will scale to more complex objects.

Jackson Dependencies

The `JavaTimeModule` class comes from an optional Jackson package that provides support for the `java.time` API. The minimum set of dependencies we need to add to run this specification is:

```
dependencies {
  testCompile
    "com.fasterxml.jackson.core:jackson-databind:2.8.6"
  testCompile
    "com.fasterxml.jackson.datatype:jackson-datatype-
    jsr310:2.8.6"
}
```

Registering Handlebars Helper Functions

We're now dealing with a consistent model in both server- and client-side template rendering. However, rendering a millisecond timestamp to HTML is not exactly user-friendly! It would be nice to reuse our `relativeTime` JavaScript function to display something more human readable.

Handlebars allows registration of helper functions for exactly this kind of use case. We can register our `relativeTime` function as a Handlebars helper, which makes it available to templates:

```
def setupSpec() {

  // ...

  // end::java-from[]
  loadResource("relative-time.js") { reader ->
    (engine as Compilable).compile(reader).eval()
  }
  engine.eval """
    Handlebars.registerHelper("relativeTime", relativeTime);
  """

}
```

Now that the helper function is registered, we can reference it from our templates:

```
<article class="message">
  <div class="text">{{text}}</div>
  <footer>
    Posted by
    <a href="/users/{{postedBy.username}}">@{{postedBy.username}}</a>
    <time>{{relativeTime postedAt}}</time>
  </footer>
</article>
```

To ensure everything works, let's update the feature method:

```
def "can render a message"() {
  given:
  def template = compile("message.hbs")

  and:
  def messageObj = mapper.convertValue(message, Map)

  expect:
  with(render(template, messageObj)) {
    find(".text").text() == message.text
    find("footer a").attr("href") == "/users/$user.username"
    find("footer a").text() == user.toString()
    find("footer time").text() == "just now" ❶
  }

  where:
  user = new User("spock")
  message = new Message(user, "Fascinating", now())
}
```

❶   We can now check for a friendly relative value for the postedAt property.

Composing Templates with Handlebars Partials

So far we've used a single template, `message.hbs`, which renders one `Message` instance. One place we'll want to use that rendered format is in a list of messages such as in a user's timeline or on his profile page. Obviously, we don't want to have to copy and paste the HTML code for our message template, so we need to be able to delegate to that template from other contexts.

To do so, we can register the template with Handlebars as a "partial." Partial templates can be referenced from other templates.

Let's look at an example in which we render a list of messages. We'll start with a new template for the message list that delegates to our existing message template for each individual message:

```
<div class="message-list">
  {{#each this}}
    {{> message}}
```

```
    {{/each}}
  </div>
```

The context of the template is an array of messages that is iterated over with Handlebars' built-in `each` helper. That `{{> message}}` line is a reference to a partial template called "message" that needs to be registered with Handlebars.

We can create a new helper method in our specification that wraps the `Handlebars.registerPartial` method in the same way we already wrap the `Handlebars.compile` method. Here's how:

```
protected void registerPartial(String name, String path) {
  loadResource(path) { reader ->
    invokeMethod(handlebars, "registerPartial", name, reader.text)
  }
}
```

Passing Iterable Values to JavaScript

One limitation of the interoperability of Java objects in Nashorn is that Java's lists and arrays don't work seamlessly as though they were JavaScript arrays. You need to explicitly convert them to JavaScript before you can use them. The Nashorn script engine provides a built-in function, `Java.from`, that can do the conversion (and an equivalent, `Java.to`, that is used for the reverse conversion). We just need to call that, passing our list of messages.

Of course, it doesn't make much sense to call `Java.from` in a Handlebars helper or reference it directly from a template, because the function *won't* be either available or necessary when rendering templates in the browser.

Instead, we can make the `Java.from` method accessible to Spock and convert the list parameter before we pass it to the template.

First, we'll declare a `@Shared` field, much like the one we use to hold a reference to the Handlebars JavaScript object:

```
@Shared JSObject java

// tag::register-helper[]
def setupSpec() {

  // ...

  java = engine.eval("Java") as JSObject
  // tag::register-helper[]
}
// end::register-helper[]
```

Then we can write a Spock helper method that converts a Java vararg into a JavaScript array using the `Java.from` method:

```
Object array(Object... elements) {
  invokeMethod(java, "from", elements.toList())
}
```

Okay, now we can convert a Java list or array to a JavaScript form. We also need to translate the elements in the list—Message instances—to a JSON-like form as we did for each individual message in the earlier example. It makes sense to define a helper that will do both of those things in a single step:

```
Object array(List<?> list) {
  def targetType = new TypeReference<List<Map>>() {} ❶
  def json = mapper.convertValue(list, targetType) ❷
  invokeMethod(java, "from", json) ❸
}
```

❶ Because we're converting our list to a type with generic type information, we need to use a TypeReference rather than just a raw class. It's important that Jackson converts the *elements of* the list.

❷ Applying the conversion transforms each individual Message instance in the list into a JSON-like map, just as before.

❸ Now we can call the Java.from method to convert everything to a JavaScript array.

With our partial template and the helper function that converts a list to a JavaScript array, we're finally ready to put together a feature method to test the rendering of an entire list of messages:

```
def "can render a list of messages"() {
  given:
  registerPartial("message", "message.hbs") ❶
  def template = compile("messages.hbs") ❷

  and:
  def messagesArray = array(messages) ❸

  expect:
  with(render(template, messagesArray)) { ❹
    def elements = find(".message-list article")
    elements.size() == messages.size()
    elements.first().find(".text").text() == messages[0].text
    elements.first().find("time").text() == "just now"
    elements.last().find(".text").text() == messages[1].text
    elements.last().find("time").text() == "a few minutes ago"
  }

  where:
  user = new User("spock")
  messages = [
```

```
        new Message(user, "Fascinating", now()),
        new Message(user, "Live long and prosper", now().minus(10, MINUTES))
    ]
}
```

❶ First, we register our original `message.hbs` template as a partial.

❷ Then we compile the `messages.hbs` template that calls `message.hbs`.

❸ The list of messages to render is converted to a JavaScript array.

❹ Finally, we render the template and make assertions about the resulting HTML structure.

Summary

We've looked at testing JavaScript in Spock from very basic examples—calling a simple function—to fairly complex ones.

Hopefully, it's clear that the combination of Nashorn and Spock can be powerful. The ability to directly pass (most) Java types to Nashorn greatly simplifies interaction with scripts. Where conversion *is* necessary—either because of limitations in the script engine's automatic conversion, as with array types, or because we need the data in a different format as with our conversion of `Message` instances to a JSON-like structure —there are ways to accomplish what we need.

Being able to pass Spock's mocks and stubs to JavaScript functions means that we can test interactions occurring within the script engine seamlessly.

None of this is to suggest testing JavaScript code with Spock is preferable to testing with native JavaScript tools such as Jasmine. It's not. However, when your application is using JavaScript in the JVM, whether for the server-side component of an isomorphic web app, nested script functionality, or whatever other reason, it might make sense to test from the JVM, too, and Spock is certainly up to the task.

CHAPTER 16

Test Driving an RxJava Application

In this chapter, we work through an example of test driving an implementation. We're going to implement a class that polls for new messages on a user's Squawker timeline and then hands them off to another component for processing. We could use this as the core of a simple command-line client, a desktop GUI application, or a websocket-based browser application.

For the implementation we'll use *RxJava (https://github.com/ReactiveX/RxJava)*.

RxJava

RxJava is an implementation of the reactive streams pattern for the JVM. It was first developed as an open source project by Netflix.

If you've looked at some of the API extensions added in Java 8, stream processing will be familiar to you. If not, don't worry too much. The point of this chapter is to provide an example of test driving a solution with the implementation following a failing test. We won't be using any particularly complex RxJava code and won't be getting into advanced reactive streams topics such as *backpressure*.

It will be helpful for you to be familiar with the Java 8 concept of a *function type* and the syntax for lambdas and method references.

Before starting, let's consider what we mean by "test-driven development" and what a test-driven development (TDD) workflow looks like.

Rather than trying to implement the entire solution at once, either before or after its tests, we'll work iteratively. Each iteration involves deciding on a feature or behavior to implement next, writing a failing test, implementing the behavior in the test subject so the test passes, and then refactoring until we're happy with the code we've written.

I find it useful to break down the behavior required of a unit into bullet points. Each bullet point is represented by one (or occasionally more) feature methods. Any compound behaviors—*it should x and y*—are broken out into separate points. Doing so helps keep each feature method focused and frequently simplifies the required setup code.

Often the behaviors will have some reasonably logical order or at least an initial behavior without which none of the others will be possible. That will become the first feature method. From there we can decide what feature makes sense to implement next after we've finished with the previous one. Generally it's just a case of picking the lowest hanging fruit—the easiest next step.

When developing using this method, it's important to resist the urge to rush ahead when the next step of the implementation seems obvious. The code required to make each successive test pass might be obviously wrong given what we know of the other required behaviors, but in this way, we can ensure behavior is not implemented without being tested and the tests will guide the solution.

Tests, Behaviors, and Properties

We can think about the behaviors we expect our unit of code to exhibit and the properties it should have. Each of those will become one or more feature methods in a specification class. As we progress, we'll refactor the tests to remove duplication in setup.

Before we begin, we should think about the "surface" of the unit of code—the interface with which our test will interact. This can evolve over time as further tests refine our understanding of what we're trying to achieve, but it's good to have some kind of starting point.

The Skeleton Implementation

We'll need an interface to the Squawker REST service. The interface looks like this:

```
public interface SquawkerApi {
  List<Message> getTimeline(String username, Serializable sinceId); ❶
}
```

❶ The getTimeline method accepts a username and a message ID and returns a list of messages on the user's timeline, starting with the one after the specified ID. If sinceId is null, the method returns all messages.

We've seen the implementation of this REST endpoint in Chapter 13. When we run the Squawker client for real, we will use a library like Retrofit to bind this interface to the REST endpoint. For the purposes of this chapter, it just needs to be an interface because we'll be using a test double in our specification.

Next, we'll define our subject class TimelineStream, which we'll flesh out over the course of the chapter. TimelineStream will poll Squawker at a regular interval and pass any messages to a subscriber. At this stage, we have only a skeleton:

```java
public class TimelineStream {

  private final String username;      ❶
  private final int interval;         ❷
  private final TimeUnit intervalUnit;
  private final SquawkerApi squawker; ❸

  public TimelineStream(String username,
                        int interval,
                        TimeUnit intervalUnit,
                        SquawkerApi squawker) {
    this.username = username;
    this.interval = interval;
    this.intervalUnit = intervalUnit;
    this.squawker = squawker;
  }

  public void start() {
    ❹
  }
}
```

❶ We'll need the *username* to fetch the timeline.

❷ We'll poll the API at a regular interval.

❸ Obviously, we'll need the API interface itself.

❹ The start method should connect to the API and begin streaming messages.

Test Driving the Implementation

With the skeleton implementation in place, we can begin defining the behavior we expect. From there, we can move on to writing tests.

Defining the Behavior

The TimelineStream class should do the following:

- Poll the user's timeline once every minute

- Ask for messages since the last one received

- Pass received messages to a subscriber one at a time

- Continue in the event of a REST service outage

- Continue if the subscriber experiences an error

A First Test

Given that skeleton, where do we start? The first thing we know we want to do is to poll the Squawker API at a regular interval, so let's write a test to ensure that happens.

Naïvely, we could implement a test by calling `start` and then waiting until a multiple of the polling interval is expired and asserting that some calls were made to the API, as demonstrated here:

```
@Shared interval = 1 ❶
def squawker = Mock(SquawkerApi) ❷
@Subject timeline = new TimelineStream("spock", interval, SECONDS, squawker)
❸

@Unroll
def "polls Squawker #ticks times in #delay seconds"() {
  when:
  timeline.start() ❹
  sleep SECONDS.toMillis(delay) ❺

  then:
  ticks * squawker.getTimeline(*_) ❻

  where:
  ticks << [2, 3] ❼
  delay = ticks * interval ❽
}
```

❶ We'll use a shared property for the interval so we can refer to it in a `where:` block.

❷ We want to assert that calls are made to the `SquawkerApi` interface, so we'll use a mock to represent it.

❸ The subject of the test is an instance of `TimelineStream`.

❹ First, the test calls the `start` method to being polling the Squawker API.

❺ The test waits for the expected interval.

---

❻ After that time the API interface should have received a number of calls. Because we're not concerned with validating the parameters passed in this particular test, we'll use Spock's wildcard parameter matcher.

❼ We can try a couple of different variations of ticks.

❽ The time we need to wait is simply the number of ticks multiplied by the interval between them.

Running the test results in an assertion failure because `SquawkerApi` is never called. We're off to a good start. Now we can implement the first bit of behavior.

Polling at Regular Intervals

To poll regularly in RxJava, we can use the `Observable.interval` method. It returns an `Observable<Long>` that emits an incrementing value at the specified interval. We don't care about the value emitted; we simply want to do something at each interval. At each *tick*, we want to call `SquawkerApi.getTimeline` and do something with each `Message` returned. In RxJava terms, we can think of this as a transformation from an `Observable<Long>` to an `Observable<Message>`.

RxJava uses various *map* operations to transform streams. We'll start by simply calling `SquawkerApi.getTimeline` in a *map* operation.

```
public void start() {
  Observable
    .interval(interval, intervalUnit) ❶
    .map(tick -> squawker.getTimeline(username, null)) ❷
    .subscribe(System.out::println); ❸
}
```

❶ `Observable.interval` accepts parameters that define the regularity with which it will emit ticks.

❷ We use `map` to transform the stream of ticks. At each tick we call `Squawker Api.getTimeline`.

❸ Without some kind of subscription, the stream will not emit any values. We haven't defined the downstream behavior in the test yet, so for now, we'll simply dump the message to standard output.

No Sleep `Til the Test Goes Green

Running our test shows an annoying inconsistency: the test sometimes passes and sometimes fails. We're using `Thread.sleep` to wait until we *think* the API should have been called. Of course, the instructions to call into `TimelineStream.start`, create an RxJava stream, and so on do not take *zero* time, so waiting for exactly the polling interval might not be enough. We can wait a little longer—say another 100 ms—but how can we ensure that this is long enough? Just as important, how can we ensure that it's not *too long*?

One of the key goals of TDD is to give *fast* feedback. To this end, tests should run in the absolute minimum time possible. We might think a one-second sleep in a test is acceptable, but we're going to be writing an entire suite of tests for `TimelineStream`. All of them are going to need to wait until *at least* one polling cycle happens. Those one-second waits are going to start adding up very soon.

As we've already seen, sleeping is unreliable. We can never really be sure we're waiting long enough that we won't occasionally get a test failure. The only solution is to sleep longer, making the test run slower still.

Hopefully, you're getting the idea here. Tests should never, ever sleep!

What can we do, though, in a situation like this in which the subject of the test is using a timer to do things at regular intervals? Let's think about *how* it's doing that. Underlying that behavior is a reliance on a piece of global state: the system clock. The system clock sends timing events that `Observable.interval` waits for. After a certain number, it responds by emitting a value to the stream. If we can isolate the test subject from that dependency, substituting a fake clock that emits timing events without any time actually having passed, we can make our test work without sleeping. If the emission of the timing events is directly controlled by the test, we can also eliminate the unreliability we've experienced when we don't know how long we need to wait for something to happen.

In TDD, we talk about introducing a "seam" to the system under test. A seam is defined as a place that allows the behavior to be modified without modifying the code. What we're considering here is using a seam to separate the generation of ticks by `Observable.interval` from the system clock. We want to substitute our own source of timing events that *look like* they come from the system clock but happen when we instruct them to rather than after some period of time has passed.

 "Seam" might be an unfamiliar term to you, but we've already used one in our test. We're using a test double of the `SquawkerApi` interface to separate the subject from its dependency on a real REST API. A mock is really just a particular type of seam that allows us to verify that an interaction happened without having it happen for real.

Luckily, the RxJava library exposes a seam that allows to replace the `rx.Scheduler` used by `Observable.interval`. The library also includes a test implementation that gives us the fake clock behavior we need. Let's add that to the `TimelineStream` class and its specification:

```
private final Scheduler scheduler; ❶
private final int interval;
private final TimeUnit intervalUnit;
private final SquawkerApi squawker;
private final String username;

public TimelineStream(Scheduler scheduler,
                      String username,
                      int interval,
                      TimeUnit intervalUnit, SquawkerApi squawker) {
  this.scheduler = scheduler;
  this.username = username;
  this.interval = interval;
  this.intervalUnit = intervalUnit;
  this.squawker = squawker;
}

public void start() {
  Observable
    .interval(interval, intervalUnit, scheduler) ❷
    .map(tick -> squawker.getTimeline(username, null))
    .subscribe(System.out::println);
}
```

❶ We now inject a `Scheduler` into the `SquawkerApi` class.

❷ The `Scheduler` is passed directly to the `Observable.interval` method.

```
def scheduler = Schedulers.test() ❶
@Subject timeline = new TimelineStream(
  scheduler, "spock", interval, SECONDS, squawker
)

@Unroll
def "polls Squawker #ticks times in #delay seconds"() {
  when:
  timeline.start()
  scheduler.advanceTimeBy(delay, SECONDS) ❷

  then:
  ticks * squawker.getTimeline(*_)

  where:
  ticks << [2, 3]
  delay = ticks * interval
}
```

❶ We can use RxJava's test `Scheduler` implementation in our specification.

❷ To simulate system clock timing events, we use the `advanceTimeBy` method.

Now, we can test long-running processes without introducing wait times into the specification itself.

Because we're going to be calling `scheduler.advanceTimeBy` a lot, it makes sense to introduce a helper method that clarifies what we're doing and lets us simply wait for a number of interval ticks rather than having to use seconds. Here's how we can do that:

```
@Unroll
def "polls Squawker #ticks times in #delay seconds"() {
  when:
  timeline.start()
  waitForTicks(ticks) ❶

  then:
  ticks * squawker.getTimeline(*_)

  where:
  ticks << [2, 3]
  delay = ticks * interval
}

private void waitForTicks(int ticks) {
  scheduler.advanceTimeBy(ticks * interval, SECONDS)
}
```

❶ Our test is now a little easier to read because the intent of waiting for a certain number of ticks is clearer and we've removed the multiplication used to convert ticks into seconds.

Testing Subscription to the Stream

The next piece of behavior we need to implement is one that lets us subscribe to the message stream. To do this, we'll inject a *function type* into `TimelineStream` that receives each `Message` emitted by the `Observable` stream. The actual functionality of the subscriber is not the concern of the `TimelineStream` class. The subscriber could log the messages, display them in a GUI window, stream them over a web-socket to a browser client, etc.—there are all kinds of possibilities.

This means there's another seam between the generation of the message stream and the handling of that stream. Because what our test is interested in is whether the subscriber is sent the right messages, we can introduce another mock, as follows:

```
def subscriber = Mock(Action1) ❶
@Subject timeline = new TimelineStream(
  scheduler, "spock", interval, SECONDS, squawker, subscriber
)
```

```
@Shared user = new User("spock")

def "passes each message to the subscriber"() {
  given:
  squawker.getTimeline(*_) >> [message1] >> [message2] ❷

  when:
  timeline.start()
  waitForTicks(ticks)

  then: ❸
  1 * subscriber.call([message1])
  1 * subscriber.call([message2])

  where:
  ticks = 2
  message1 = new Message(1L, user, "fascinating", now())
  message2 = new Message(
    2L, user, "The complexities of human pranks escape me", now()
  )
}
```

❶ We'll define a mock subscriber. The class `rx.functions.Action1` is a functional interface with a method that accepts a single argument.

❷ The new feature method will use the `SquawkerApi` as a *stub* rather than a *mock*. On successive calls it will return a different group of messages.

❸ We can then assert that the subscriber receives each group of messages once.

To implement the behavior required by the specification, we just need to inject a subscriber into the `TimelineStream` class and use it when we subscribe to the `Observable` stream:

```
private final Action1<List<Message>> subscriber;

public void start() {
  Observable
    .interval(interval, intervalUnit, scheduler)
    .map(tick -> squawker.getTimeline(username, null))
    .subscribe(subscriber);
}
```

Unchunking the Message Stream

We're now subscribing to the stream successfully, but we're processing it in "chunks." Each call to `getTimeline` produces a `List<Message>`, which is passed to the subscriber.

There are a couple of problems with this. First, on a practical level it's quite possible that an individual iteration of the polling loop will find *no* new messages on the timeline. If that's the case, it seems unnecessary to call the subscriber with an empty list.

Let's implement a feature method that asserts that should not happen:

```
def "if no new messages are received the subscriber is not called"() {
    given:
    squawker.getTimeline(*_) >> []   ❶

    when:
    timeline.start()
    waitForTicks(1)

    then:
    0 * subscriber.call(_)   ❷
}
```

❶ We stub the getTimeline call to return an empty list as it would if no new messages were on the timeline.

❷ We assert that the subscriber is not called.

When we run this new feature method, it fails because we're passing each chunk of messages to the subscriber:

```
rx.exceptions.OnErrorNotImplementedException: Too many invocations for:

0 * subscriber.call(_)    (1 invocation)

Matching invocations (ordered by last occurrence):

1 * subscriber.call([])    <-- this triggered the error
```

We could fix this by filtering the stream to ignore empty lists. That's easy enough, but there's really a second problem with dealing with the messages in chunks.

By producing a chunked stream of messages, we're tying the downstream operations to the mechanism used to produce the stream of messages. If the subscriber is an Action<List<Message>>, it makes it more difficult to later refactor the Timeline Stream implementation to produce the message stream in a different way, such as subscribing to a socket that sends each message individually.

It's much more natural in this scenario to have the downstream operations deal with each individual message. This means that we'll need to change the actual *map* operation used to transform the interval stream.

First, we'll write the following new feature method to specify the behavior we want:

```
def "transforms chunked messages into a continuous stream"() {
  given:
  squawker.getTimeline(*_) >> [message1] >> [] >> [message2, message3] ❶

  when:
  timeline.start()
  waitForTicks(chunks)

  then: ❷
  1 * subscriber.call(message1)
  1 * subscriber.call(message2)
  1 * subscriber.call(message3)

  and:
  0 * subscriber.call(_) ❸

  where:
  chunks = 3
  message1 = new Message(
    1L, user, "fascinating", now()
  )
  message2 = new Message(
    2L, user, "The complexities of human pranks escape me", now()
  )
  message3 = new Message(
    3L, user,
    "the statistical likelihood that our plan will succeed is less than 4.3%",
    now()
  )
}
```

❶ We stub getTimeline to produce a chunked stream of messages. One message on the first call, none on the second, and two on the third.

❷ We assert that the subscriber receives each individual message once.

❸ Additionally we ensure no further calls are made to the subscriber to ensure that we're not doing something like passing null when the empty chunk is processed.

To implement the behavior we want, we simply need to change the RxJava *map* operation:

```
private final Action1<Message> subscriber; ❶

public void start() {
  Observable
    .interval(interval, intervalUnit, scheduler)
    .flatMapIterable(tick -> squawker.getTimeline(username, null)) ❷
    .subscribe(subscriber);
}
```

❶ The type of the subscriber changes from `Action1<List<Message>>` to `Action1<Message>`.

❷ Using `flatMapIterable` rather than `map` produces an `Observable<Message>` by iterating over each list returned by `getTimeline` and coalescing the results into a single stream.

After making that change, we'll also need to update our previous feature method to expect single messages rather than lists.

Requesting Messages Since the Last Received

Recall that when `TimelineStream` calls `SquawkerApi.getTimeline`, it should pass the ID of the last message seen so that the next call only returns new messages. So far, we haven't made any assertions about the parameters we pass to `getTimeline`. In fact, our implementation thus far has just been passing `null` in place of a message ID. Hooked up to the real REST API, that would mean each call gets an ever-increasing number of duplicate messages.

To specify this behavior correctly, we'll introduce a new feature method in which we assert that on subsequent calls the ID of the most recent message is passed to `getTimeline`:

```
def "passes the id of the last message seen on each poll"() {
  when:
  timeline.start()
  waitForTicks(ticks)

  then:
  1 * squawker.getTimeline(_, null) >> [message1] ❶
  1 * squawker.getTimeline(_, message1.id) >> [message2, message3] ❷
  1 * squawker.getTimeline(_, message3.id) ❸

  where:
  ticks = 3
  message1 = new Message(1L, user, "fascinating", now())
  message2 = new Message(
    2L, user, "The complexities of human pranks escape me", now()
  )
  message3 = new Message(
    3L,
    user,
    "the likelihood that our plan will succeed is less than 4.3%",
    now()
  )
}
```

❶ The first call should pass null because we have no previous messages. We're specifying that the call should return a single message.

❷ The second call should pass the ID of the message seen previously. This time we'll return multiple messages.

❸ Finally, we'll test that the last message's ID is passsed. Here we're not specifying a return value, because we're not going to go round the loop again.

This is a fairly complex feature method. We're using a mock that is both asserting that a call is made and returning a value that will drive the next iteration of the polling loop. Recall that in "When Should I Use a Mock and When Should I Use a Stub?" on page 64, I said that a test double that both asserted a call was made and specified a return value was often an indication that you should really just be using a stub. This is a good example of a situation in which it actually *is* valid to do both.

We're primarily concerned with asserting that on successive iterations of the polling loop we pass the correct parameter to the getTimeline method. However, it's also necessary that the same interaction returns the value used on the next iteration of the loop.

To implement the behavior, we can simply store each message ID in a field in Timeli neStream, as shown here:

```
private Serializable lastMessageId = null; ❶

public void start() {
  Observable
    .interval(interval, intervalUnit, scheduler)
    .flatMapIterable(tick -> squawker.getTimeline(username, lastMessageId)) ❷
    .doOnNext(message -> lastMessageId = message.getId()) ❸
    .subscribe(subscriber);
}
```

❶ The field lastMessageId starts out null.

❷ We pass lastMessageId to the getTimeline method.

❸ The doOnNext operation allows us to define a side effect on processing each item in the stream. Here we're simply recording the ID of the message.

Recovering from Polling Errors

What would happen if the Squawker REST API experienced a temporary outage? Our call to getTimeline would throw an exception. At that point, we'd really want to just ignore (and possibly log) the error and try again at the next polling interval.

If we write a test to enforce that resilience, we see that it currently fails:

```
def "continues polling if the API experiences an error"() {
  given:
  squawker.getTimeline(*_) >> { throw unavailable() } >> [message] ❶

  when:
  timeline.start()
  waitForTicks(2)

  then:
  1 * subscriber.call(message) ❷

  where:
  message = new Message(1L, user, "fascinating", now())
}

Throwable unavailable() { ❸
  throw new RuntimeException("HTTP 503: Service Unavailable")
}
```

❶ We *stub* getTimeline to throw an exception the first time it is called and return a single message on subsequent calls.

❷ The subscriber should receive the message despite the error on the first attempt at polling.

❸ The exception class is quite general here because we really just want to retry in the event of any error.

Running this test, we find that the exception actually halts the RxJava stream:

```
rx.exceptions.OnErrorNotImplementedException: HTTP 503: Service Unavailable
```

To fix this, we simply need to tell RxJava to retry upstream operations in the event of an error:

```
public void start() {
  Observable
    .interval(interval, intervalUnit, scheduler)
    .flatMapIterable(tick -> squawker.getTimeline(username, lastMessageId))
    .doOnError(this::onApiError) ❶
    .retry() ❷
    .doOnNext(message -> lastMessageId = message.getId())
    .subscribe(subscriber);
}

private void onApiError(Throwable throwable) {
  System.out.println(throwable);
}
```

① We can use doOnError to log or notify the user of an error.

② The retry operation just directs RxJava to ignore the error and continue with the next item in the stream, in our case the next interval tick.

Recovering from Downstream Errors

We're now resilient to errors when polling the API, but what happens if the subscriber fails to handle a message and instead throws an exception?

The behavior we want here depends very much on what we're trying to do with the subscriber. It might be appropriate to halt processing on an error. Effectively, this means that the subscriber is responsible for handling its own errors, and any it allows to propagate will halt the stream. Alternatively, we might want to retry later, do so conditionally depending on the type of error, or implement a more complex policy such as retrying a certain number of times before failing.

Let's assume that we want to retry if the subscriber throws a certain type of exception and allow the program to halt otherwise.

In this case, it's very important that we do not store the ID of the message that was passed to the subscriber because we want to retry the same message again.

We'll start by implementing a pair of feature methods that describe the behavior we want:

```
def "stops processing if the subscriber throws an unrecoverable error"() {
  given:
  subscriber.call(_) >> { throw new RuntimeException("unrecoverable") } ①

  when:
  timeline.start()
  waitForTicks(2)

  then:
  1 * squawker.getTimeline(*_) >> [message] ②

  where:
  message = new Message(1L, user, "fascinating", now())
}

def "re-tries the chunk if the subscriber throws an recoverable error"() {
  given:
  subscriber.call(_) >> { throw new RecoverableSubscriberException() }

  and:
  def messageIds = [] ③
  squawker.getTimeline(*_) >> { username, messageId ->
    messageIds << messageId
    [message]
```

```
        }
        when:
        timeline.start()
        waitForTicks(2)

        then:
        messageIds[0] == messageIds[1] ❹

        where:
        message = new Message(1L, user, "fascinating", now())
    }
```

❶ The first feature method is very simple. It *stubs* subscriber.call to throw an exception...

❷ ...and then it ensures that getTimeline is called only once because the exception will stop the subscription.

❸ The second feature method capture the second parameter of the *stub* getTime line call...

❹ ...and then asserts that both calls to getTimeline are sent the same message ID.

To implement this behavior, we'll introduce an error handler when we subscribe to the stream:

```
public void start() {
  Observable
    .interval(interval, intervalUnit, scheduler)
    .flatMapIterable(tick -> squawker.getTimeline(username, lastMessageId))
    .doOnError(this::onApiError)
    .retry()
    .subscribe(this::onMessage, this::onSubscriberError); ❶
}

private void onMessage(Message message) {
  subscriber.call(message);
  lastMessageId = message.getId(); ❷
}

private void onSubscriberError(Throwable throwable) {
  if (throwable instanceof RecoverableSubscriberException) {
    System.err.println("Caught recoverable error");
  } else {
    throw new OnErrorFailedException(throwable); ❸
  }
}
```

❶ The doOnNext operation has been removed given that we don't want to store every message ID, only those that are successfully processed. We now define our own success and error handling functions for subscribing to the stream.

❷ We store the message ID after the subscriber is called. If the subscriber throws an exception, this statement will never be reached.

❸ The error handler reraises an unhandled exception.

Final Implementation

Now that we have all our tests in place, we can tidy up the implementation while keeping the tests passing. For reference, here is the final implementation that passes all the tests:

```java
public class TimelineStream {

  private final Scheduler scheduler;
  private final int interval;
  private final TimeUnit intervalUnit;
  private final SquawkerApi squawker;
  private final String username;
  private final Action1<Message> subscriber;

  private Serializable lastMessageId = null;

  public TimelineStream(Scheduler scheduler,
                        String username,
                        int interval,
                        TimeUnit intervalUnit,
                        SquawkerApi squawker,
                        Action1<Message> subscriber) {
    this.scheduler = scheduler;
    this.username = username;
    this.interval = interval;
    this.intervalUnit = intervalUnit;
    this.squawker = squawker;
    this.subscriber = subscriber;
  }

  public void start() {
    Observable
      .interval(interval, intervalUnit, scheduler)
      .flatMapIterable(this::onPollingInterval)
      .doOnError(this::onApiError)
      .retry()
      .subscribe(this::onMessage, this::onSubscriberError);
  }
```

```
    private List<Message> onPollingInterval(long tick) {
      return squawker.getTimeline(username, lastMessageId);
    }

    private void onMessage(Message message) {
      subscriber.call(message);
      lastMessageId = message.getId();
    }

    private void onSubscriberError(Throwable throwable) {
      if (throwable instanceof RecoverableSubscriberException) {
        System.err.println("Caught recoverable error");
      } else {
        throw new OnErrorFailedException(throwable);
      }
    }

    private void onApiError(Throwable throwable) {
      System.err.println(throwable);
    }
  }
```

Exercise: Message Ordering

We've assumed that the API returns messages in oldest-first order. That way we can just use the ID of the last message we processed to request the next chunk.

See if you can test drive an implementation in which the messages in a chunk returned by the API might be out of sequence.

Hint: the Message class has a postedAt timestamp property.

Exercise: Greater Resilience

See if you can test drive a change in the subscriber error handling such that if the subscriber throws a recoverable error the chunk is retried. If the subscriber throws any other kind of error, we should log and continue polling at the *next* chunk.

Exercise: Backpressure

Implement a test to ensure that if the API call responds slowly or the subscriber processes messages slowly, the polling intervals do not "stack up."

Groovy Primer

This appendix is a crash course in the features of the Groovy programming language that you need to know in order to write Spock specifications effectively. It is not meant to be an exhaustive language reference. Partly because there are some language features—metaprogramming, for example—that are very complex but of limited use in understanding the examples in this book, but mostly because there is already a plethora of books on Groovy written by much smarter people than me.

History

Groovy was started in 2003 by James Strachan. Version 1.0 was released on 2007, and version 2.0 in 2012. In 2015, Groovy became a project of the Apache foundation. As of this writing, the current version is 2.4.8.

The language is syntactically derived from Java. In fact most pre–Java 8 Java code is also valid Groovy code. However, Groovy also takes a lot of inspiration from Ruby and Smalltalk.

From its inception, Groovy was a dynamic language. Method calls and property references are dispatched at runtime and can be intercepted by a type's "metaclass" in order to extend the functionality of a class.

Groovy 2.0 added optional compile-time type checking and static compilation.

Syntactic and Semantic Differences to Java

There are some obvious syntactic differences that are noticeable the first time you look at Groovy code.

Semicolons

Groovy does not require a semicolon at the end of each statement. In fact, it is considered nonidiomatic to use semicolons. The only time semicolons are necessary is to separate multiple statements on a single line; however, that's a fairly rare use.

Import Statements

Groovy automatically imports 0, 1, and 2.

Class Literals

When referring to a class literal, it is not necessary to use `.class`.

Visibility

By default, Groovy methods are `public`. The `protected` and `private` scopes are the same as in Java. Java's default scope can be emulated by using the `@PackageScope` annotation.

Exceptions

Groovy does not have checked exceptions. Although you *may* declare a `throws` clause on a method you are not required to, and all exceptions are effectively treated like `RuntimeException`.

Implicit Return

Groovy methods return the value of the last statement by default unless defined `void`. This means that the `return` keyword is unnecessary, although you are free to use it and it sometimes enhances the clarity of the code.

Implicit returns mean functional code in Groovy can be very concise because closures can contain simple expressions without the `return` keyword.

Default Parameters

Groovy allows methods to define default parameter values. Any parameter or parameters can have default values, the only restriction being that no parameters without defaults can appear after those with defaults.

For example, if we define a method with a default parameter value like this:

```
String crewTitle(String name, String title = "Mr") {
  title + " " + name
}
```

we can then call the method with or without the second parameter:

```
assert crewTitle("Kirk", "Captain") == "Captain Kirk"
assert crewTitle("McCoy", "Doctor") == "Doctor McCoy"
assert crewTitle("Spock") == "Mr Spock"
```

To achieve the same thing in Java, we would need to create two overloaded methods:

```
String crewTitle(String name, String title) {
  return title + " " + name;
}

String crewTitle(String name) {
  return crewTitle(name, "Mr");
}
```

Method Dispatch

Java dispatches calls by using compile-time type information. For example, given these method declarations:

```
void method(String s) {
}

void method(Object o) {
}
```

the following call will invoke the overload that accepts `Object`:

```
Object o = "Spock";
method(o);
```

Groovy uses runtime type information for dispatch, so it would invoke the method that accepts `String`.

Valid Java Code That Is Not Valid Groovy Code

There are a handful of things in Java that are *not* valid syntax in Groovy.

Array initialization

Array literals are not valid in Groovy. For example:

```
int[] array1 = {1, 2, 3};
int[] array2 = new int[] {1, 2, 3};
```

Instead of array literals, Groovy allows for list literals (that can be converted to arrays):

```
int[] array = [1, 2, 3] as int[]
```

This also affects annotation parameters, which are written with square braces rather than curly braces in Groovy (square braces being Groovy's syntax for list literals).

Multiple for loop variables or increments

Groovy's for loop cannot have multiple variables or increments; thus, an accumulator like this would not compile:

```
StringBuilder seq = new StringBuilder();
for (int i = 0, j = 0; i < 5; i++, j += i) {
  seq.append(j).append(" ");
}
assert "0 1 3 6 10".equals(seq.toString().trim());
```

The do…while loop

The rarely used do…while loop is not available in Groovy:

```
do {
  text.append(" ");
} while (text.length() < 80);
```

Instead, you can almost always use a regular while loop or some other construct.

Try with resource (Java 7+)

Groovy does not support the try-with resource construct introduced in Java 7.

```
try (Writer writer = new FileWriter(file)) {
  writer.append("Fascinating!");
}
```

Instead, Groovy decorates the Closeable interface with a withCloseable(Closure) method that does the same thing:

```
new FileWriter(file).withCloseable { writer ->
  writer.append("Fascinating!")
}
```

In fact, there's an even shorter form when dealing with things like InputStream, Out putStream, Reader, and Writer:

```
file.withWriter { writer ->
  writer.append("Fascinating!")
}
```

Lambdas (Java 8+)

The lambda syntax in Java 8 is not compatible with Groovy. Groovy's closures predate lambdas and use a slightly different syntax. However, the good news is that Groovy closures are compatible with the functional interfaces lambda support relies on, so you can use a closure in Groovy anywhere you can use a lambda in Java.

Method references (Java 8+)

Along with the lambda syntax, Groovy does not support the Java 8 `::` operator for getting a callable reference to a method. Groovy's own `.&` operator does the same thing.

Dynamic-Typed Variables

Variables, method return types, parameters, and fields can be declared by using `def` in place of a specific type.

A `def` variable or field may be assigned a value of any type. A method returning `def` may return any type, as shown here:

```
def x = "hi"
assert x instanceof String

x = 1
assert x instanceof Number

x++
assert x == 2

x += "0"
assert x == "20"

x = { -> x instanceof String }
assert x instanceof Closure

assert !x()
```

However, it's actually fairly unusual to reassign variables different types like that. One of the primary benefits of `def` is that it can reduce the clutter of redundant type information seen in Java code. Groovy's compiler—and developer tools such as IDEs—can usually infer the type of a variable declared with `def` based on the way it is initialized or the value subsequently assigned to it.

Many developers new to Groovy from Java are often wary of using `def`. Shortly after that they often start overusing `def` in places where a definitive type would actually be helpful!

When to Use def and When to Use a Type

My own rule of thumb is to use def whenever additional type information does not enhance the readability of the code or is redundant.

I almost always use def for local variables because their type can be inferred from their initialization. I find the type on the left of the expression totally redundant here:

```
Person p = new Person(firstName: "James", lastName: "Kirk")
```

I will always declare a type for a method return because it's more difficult to infer from context (although the compiler can probably do it in many cases). A strongly typed method return also has documentation value and helps an IDE keep track of the type of a reference initialized with a call to the method.

Similarly, method parameters are better with specified types. It can be terribly confusing and frustrating to have to dig in to a method's implementation to figure out what type of value you are expected to pass to each of its parameters.

List and Map literals

Although Groovy does not have array literals, it does have List and Map literals. These are a huge improvement on the way lists and maps need to be created in Java.

Lists

A List is defined by using comma-separated values surrounded by square braces. Thus,

```
def crew = ["Kirk", "Spock", "Bones"]
```

defines a three-element ArrayList. It is equivalent to the following Java code:

```
List<String> crew = new ArrayList<>();
crew.add("Kirk");
crew.add("Spock");
crew.add("Bones");
```

Indexing lists

List elements can be accessed by using square braces with a numeric index or range value:

```
assert crew[0] == "Kirk"   ❶
def i = 1
assert crew[i] == "Spock"   ❷
assert crew[0..1] == ["Kirk", "Spock"]   ❸
assert crew[1..-1] == ["Spock", "Bones"]   ❹
```

```
assert crew[1..0] == ["Spock", "Kirk"] ❺

crew[2] = "McCoy" ❻
assert crew == ["Kirk", "Spock", "McCoy"]

crew[3] = "Sulu" ❼
assert crew == ["Kirk", "Spock", "McCoy", "Sulu"]

crew[5] = "Chekov" ❽
assert crew == ["Kirk", "Spock", "McCoy", "Sulu", null, "Chekov"]
```

❶ Accessing a literal index

❷ Accessing an index by using an `int` variable

❸ Slicing the list by using an inclusive range literal

❹ Slicing the list by using the -1 range bound to indicate the end of the list

❺ Slicing the list by using a reverse range

❻ Replacing a list element

❼ Assigning to a new list index

❽ Any missing indexes are initialized with `null`

Maps

A `Map` is defined by using comma-separated key-value pairs, each separated by a colon.

```
def crew = [captain: "Kirk", science: "Spock", medical: "Bones"]
```

The keys in a map literal are treated as literal strings. There is no need to quote the keys. The preceding listing is identical to this:

```
def crew = ["captain": "Kirk", "science": "Spock", "medical": "Bones"]
```

Map literals create instances of `LinkedHashMap`. That map implementation preserves the insertion order of its entries so that it's possible to make assumptions about the order of keys, values, and entries in the map. For example:

```
assert crew.values().asList() == ["Kirk", "Spock", "Bones"]
```

In many map implementations, we could not assume that `values()` would return the values in any particular order.

Programmatically assigning map keys

Map keys can reference variables or nonstring literals if they are bracketed, as shown here:

```
def posts = ["captain", "science officer", "chief medical officer"]
def crew = [(posts[0]): "Kirk", (posts[1]): "Spock", (posts[2]): "Bones"]
```

Accessing map values

Like lists, map elements can be accessed by using square braces. If the keys are strings, they can also be accessed by using property notation.

```
def post = "captain"
assert crew[post] == "Kirk"  ❶
assert crew.captain == "Kirk"  ❷

crew.medical = "McCoy"  ❸
assert crew == [captain: "Kirk", science: "Spock", medical: "McCoy"]

crew["engineer"] = "Scotty"  ❹
assert crew.size() == 4
assert crew.engineer == "Scotty"
```

❶ Accessing a map value by using square braces

❷ Accessing a map value by using property notation

❸ Assigning a map value by using property notation

❹ Assigning a map value by using square braces

Ranges

Ranges are a special form of iterable that encapsulate a range of values between low and high values. Simple ranges such as integer ranges are implemented in Groovy as lists. More complex ranges (e.g., floating-point ranges) would not be.

Ranges are defined by using two values separated by .. for an inclusive range or ..< for a range that's exclusive at the upper bound:

```
def ints = 1..5
assert ints == [1, 2, 3, 4, 5]

def ints = 1..<5
assert ints == [1, 2, 3, 4]
```

Ranges are frequently used for slicing strings and lists, such as the following:

```
def name = "James T Kirk"
assert name[0..4] == "James"
assert name[0..<5] == "James"
assert name[8..-1] == "Kirk"
```

Immutability

To create an immutable form of a list or map you can call `.asImmutable()` on it. The Groovy declaration

```
def crew = ["Kirk", "Spock", "Bones"].asImmutable()
```

is equivalent to this Java code:

```
List<String> crew = new ArrayList<>();
crew.add("Kirk");
crew.add("Spock");
crew.add("Bones");
crew = Collections.unmodifiableList(crew);
```

Maps as Named Arguments

When passing a map literal to a method that takes a single map parameter, the square braces can be omitted.

In addition, a Groovy class with no explicitly defined constructor is given a default constructor accepting a `Map<String, ?>` that will assign any properties to the values found in the map:

```
def person = new Person(firstName: "James", lastName: "Kirk")
assert person.firstName == "James"
assert person.lastName == "Kirk"
```

Set and Array Literals

sGroovy does not have Set or array literals, but you can convert a list to a set or an array by using Groovy's safe cast:

```
def crew = ["Kirk", "Spock", "Bones"] as Set
assert crew instanceof HashSet
```

```
def crew = ["Kirk", "Spock", "Bones"] as String[]
assert crew instanceof String[]
```

Truthiness

Any value in Groovy can be coerced to a Boolean. This often results in slightly more terse conditional expressions than in Java. For example, it's common to check for `null` like this:

```
def person = ship.getScienceOfficer()
if (!person) {
  throw new NoScienceOfficerAboardException(ship)
}
```

This is valid because the value of person will coerce to false if it is null, and to true otherwise.

null, a numeric zero (but not the string "0"), an empty string, an empty collection, an empty map, and a nonmatching java.util.regex.Matcher all coerce automatically to false.

It's possible to customize the "truthiness" of your own classes by implementing asBoolean(). Hopefully, I don't need to emphasize that it's wise to be careful that the resulting behavior is intuitive.

Properties

Whereas methods are public by default, fields are not, although it might look like they are:

```
class Person {
  String firstName
  String lastName
}
```

In this example, firstName and lastName might look like fields but are in fact *properties*. The important difference is that in the bytecode produced by the Groovy compiler there is a private field, a *getter*, and a *setter*, just as there would be in a typical Java POJO or bean class.

The following example shows that the declaration is identical in Java:

```
public class Person {
  private String firstName;
  private String lastName;

  public String getFirstName() {
    return firstName;
  }

  public String getLastName() {
    return lastName;
  }

  public void setFirstName(String firstName) {
    this.firstName = firstName;
  }

  public void setLastName(String lastName) {
    this.lastName = lastName;
```

```
    }
  }
```

If you want to define your own *getter* or *setter* you can do so just as you would in Java. Explicitly declared *getters* and *setters* take precedence over the default ones.

If a property is declared `final`, it has no *setter*, only a *getter*.

Accessing Properties

You access properties in Groovy by name. For example, if we define an instance of our `Person` class, we can refer to its `firstName` and `lastName` properties directly:

```
def person = new Person(firstName: "Leonard", lastName: "Nimoy")
assert person.lastName == "Nimoy"
```

In this example, `person.lastName` is equivalent to `person.getLastName()` in Java.

To set a property value, you assign to it as though it were a variable:

```
def person = new Person(firstName: "James", lastName: "Kirk")
person.firstName = "Jim"
assert person.firstName == "Jim"
```

Note the = assignment operator. The statement `person.lastName = "Spock"` is equivalent to the Java `person.setLastName("Spock")`.

It's also possible to access property *getters* and *setters* the more verbose Java way, of course.

Properties of Java Classes

The property syntax does not only apply to types defined in Groovy. When accessing an instance of a Java class from Groovy, the same property syntax can be used. A Java method with no arguments that takes the form `getName()` or `isValid()` can be accessed from Groovy by using simply `.name` or `.valid`, respectively.

Strings in Groovy

Strings in Groovy can use several different delimiters. The double-quote delimiter of Java is valid. In addition, single quotes are acceptable as are forward slashes and the less frequently seen $/ opening and /$ closing delimiter.

Why all the different delimiter types?

Templated Strings

A single-quoted string is a literal; all other types of strings can contain templated expressions delimited with ${...}.

```
def name = "Spock"
def str = "Report, Mr ${name}"
assert str == 'Report, Mr Spock'
```

Simple expressions that are just variable or property references can omit the curly braces:

```
def str = "Report, Mr $name"
assert str == 'Report, Mr Spock'
```

You can access property paths by using the . operator, without needing curly braces:

```
def person = new Person(firstName: "Mr", lastName: "Spock")
def str = "Report, $person.name"
assert str == 'Report, Mr Spock'
```

Expressions can contain any valid Groovy code including method calls:

```
def str = "Report, ${person.toString()}"
assert str == 'Report, Mr Spock'
```

Or even complex expressions:

```
def str = "Report, ${person.firstName + ' ' + person.lastName}"
assert str == 'Report, Mr Spock'
```

You must escape literal $ characters in all string types (except single-quoted strings):

```
def str = "Report, Mr \$name"
assert str == 'Report, Mr $name'
```

Regular Expression Literals

The / string delimiter is primarily intended for regular expression literals.

You use the \ character in Java strings to escape special characters or reference non-printable characters such as line breaks (\n) or tabs (\t). Unfortunately, in regular expressions, \ also has a special meaning. For example, \d matches a decimal numeric character, \1 is a "back-reference" to an earlier match, and so on.

The two uses of \ collide, so when writing regular expression strings in Java, it's necessary to "double escape" the \ character. This can be extremely confusing in complex regular expressions.

Groovy's / delimited strings do not require double escaping of the \ character, so they are ideal for writing regular expressions.

```
assert "Fascinating!" ==~ /\w+!/
assert "Report, Mr Spock!" ==~ /(\w+[,!]?\s*)+/
```

Yes, that ==~ symbol is a regular expression match operator! We'll discuss it further when looking at Groovy's operators later in this appendix.

The "Dollar-Slashy" String

The "dollar slashy" string delimiter is also commonly used for regular expressions. In particular, it's useful when the expression contains a / character that would otherwise be interpreted as the end of the string.

The most common reason I've found to use this is when using regular expressions to match URLs or filepaths. For example:

```
def url = "http://shop.oreilly.com/product/0636920038597.do"
assert url ==~ $/https?://(\w+\.)+com(/\w+)*(\.\w+)?/$
```

Multiline Strings

A string enclosed in triple-single or double quotes can span multiple lines. That is, the string literal can contain literal line breaks, as shown here:

```
def str = """
$name: Fascinating!
Kirk: Report, Mr $name!
"""
assert str == '\nSpock: Fascinating!\nKirk: Report, Mr Spock!\n'
```

To assist in indenting code neatly, it's possible to exclude a line-break from a multiline string by escaping it with \:

```
def s = """\
Fascinating!"""
assert s == "Fascinating!"
```

Groovy also provides a method stripIndent() on strings that will remove common leading whitespace from each line of a string. This is very useful in allowing multiline strings to be indented more readably, as demonstrated here:

```
def s = """\
  Kirk: Report, Mr Spock!
  Spock: The lifeform is most unusual, Captain.
       I have never encountered anything like it.\
""".stripIndent()
assert s.startsWith("Kirk:")
assert s.contains("\nSpock")
```

Single Quotes or Double Quotes?

When writing noninterpolated strings, some Groovy developers prefer to use single-quoted strings.

In the distant past there was a small performance penalty when using potentially interpolated double-quoted strings, but that has long since been eliminated.

I prefer to default to double-quoted strings and the examples throughout this book are written that way. This way if I need to add interpolation to a string later, I can do so without changing the delimiters.

Use whichever convention you prefer.

Operator Overloading

Unlike Java, Groovy supports operator overloading. Each operator has a matching named method. Implementing `equals` in a class overrides the == and != operators, implementing `compareTo` overrides the >, <, >=, 0 and 1 operators, and so on.

Because of operator overloading, it is *not* incorrect to use the == operator to compare two objects in Groovy.

In Java, == is a pointer comparison; it returns `true` only if both operands are pointers to the same object instance. To check logical equality, a developer should use the `equals(Object)` method. This is not the case in Groovy where the == operator is actually an alias for `equals` (well, it's slightly more complicated than that; see the related sidebar). In fact, it is considered nonidiomatic to spell out a call to the `equals` method in Groovy. The preferred way to express logical equality is by using the == operator.

What Is == Really Doing?

Although it's typical (and usually safe) to consider == an alias for the Java-style `equals` method, that's something of an oversimplification.

Even though we can think of

```
assert a == b
```

as the Groovy equivalent to the Java

```
assert a.equals(b);
```

in fact, if the class of a implements `Comparable`, Groovy will use:

```
a.compareTo(b) == 0;
```

The primary reason this is done is so that the == operator can be reflexive between java.lang.String and groovy.lang.GString (the class that backs Groovy's interpolated strings). Because java.lang.String is final, Groovy cannot extend it. Subsequent versions of Java have introduced the CharSequence class to work around this kind of problem in alternative JVM languages, but Groovy's implementation predates this.

Unary Math Operators

The unary sign prefix operators + and - are aliases for positive() and negative(), respectively. I'm not sure that I've ever seen these overridden on anything other than numeric types, but the option is there.

Comparison Operators

In addition to the == and != operators, the standard Java comparison operators are aliases for compareTo. Implementing Comparable and the compareTo method means instances of a class can be compared by using the >, <, >=, and 0 operators.

Mathematical Operators

You can override standard mathematical operators by using plus(?), minus(?), multiply(?), and div(?).

In addition, the modulo operator % aliases to mod(?) and the power operator ** to power(?).

All those mathematical operators also have assignment forms; for example, += and **= that are also aliased to the same methods. Thus, if you implement plus(?) you can use the + and += operators with instances of your class.

Bitwise Operators

The bitwise logical operators &, |, and ^ alias to and(?), or(?), and xor(?), respectively.

Like the mathematical operators, bitwise operators also have assignment forms: &=, |=, and ^=.

Also, the unary bitwise negation operator ~ is an alias for bitwiseNegate().

In Groovy, `String` implements the `bitwiseNegate()` method to return a `java.util.regex.Pattern`:

```
def pattern = ~/\w+/
assert pattern instanceof Pattern
```

The `bitwiseNegate()` on a string is equivalent to the following Java code:

```
Pattern.compile("\\w+");
```

Shift Operators

Java-like bit-shift operators `<<`, `>>`, and `>>>` are implemented in Groovy as aliases for `leftShift(?)`, `rightShift(?)`, and `rightShiftUnsigned(?)`, respectively.

As well as the original bit-shifting intent, Groovy typically uses `<<` for chainable append operations.

For example, on collections:

```
def list = []
list << "a"
list << "b" << "c"
assert list == ["a", "b", "c"]
```

Or Appendable types such as `OutputStream`, `Writer`, or `String Builder`:

```
def buffer = new StringBuilder()
buffer << "a" << "," << "b" << "," << "c"
assert buffer.toString() == "a,b,c"
```

Operators Not Present in Java

Groovy also has some operators that Java does not. We've already seen the regular expression match operator `==~` (also known as the "firecracker operator") and briefly mentioned the comparison operator `0` (also known as the "spaceship operator"). There are several more.

Safe Dereference Operator

As every Java developer has no doubt found out the hard way, the Java-style dereference operator—`.`—will throw `NullPointerException` if the object on the left side of the operator is `null`.

When an object could be `null`, it's necessary to check whether that is actually the case before calling methods on it. Groovy has an operator that simplifies this check. If the object on the left of the `?.` operator is `null`, the expression will yield `null`. Any method call or property access is short-circuited, so no `NullPointerException` is thrown.

Call Operator

The standard braces used to indicate a method call are in fact an operator in Groovy. If a class implements `call()` with any number of parameters (including zero), it can be treated as a callable function.

For example, given a class

```
class Greeter {
  def call() {
    "Ahoy!"
  }
}
```

we can treat instances of the class as first-class functions, as follows:

```
def greeter = new Greeter()
assert greeter.call() == "Ahoy!"
assert greeter() == "Ahoy!"
```

Any number of parameters can appear on the `call` method. Varargs also work, of course:

```
class Greeter2 {
  def call(String... names) {
    names.collect { "Ahoy $it!" } join("\n")
  }
}

def greeter = new Greeter2()
assert greeter("Spock", "Kirk", "Bones") == """\
Ahoy Spock!
Ahoy Kirk!
Ahoy Bones!"""
```

Subscript Operators

The subscript operators are square braces and are aliases for `getAt(?)` and `putAt(?)`. They are most commonly encountered when dealing with `List` and `Map` instances, but you can implement them on any class:

```
def list = ["a", "b", "c"]

assert list[0] == "a" ❶

list[1] = "d" ❷
assert list.join("") == "adc"
```

❶ An example of the subscript operator aliasing `getAt`

❷   When followed by an assignment, the operator is an alias for `putAt(?)`

Of course, with list instances, the argument to the subscript is an integer, but this does not need to be the case. With a `Map`, the subscript can accept an argument of any type.

Elvis Operator

Java programmers will be familiar with the ternary operator: `x ? a : b`. There is a very common use case for this operator in which a value is tested for `null` and either used as is if it is not `null`, or replaced with a default if it is—`x != null ? x : y`.

In fact, this use is *so* common that Groovy allows a shortened form of the ternary operator known as the "Elvis operator"—`x ?: y`. The operator will yield the lefthand value if it is "truthy," or the righthand value otherwise:

```
def a = "a"
def b = "default"

assert a != null ? a : b == "a"
assert a ?: b == "a"

a = null
assert a != null ? a : b == "default"
assert a ?: b == "default"
```

Remember, the lefthand value is evaluated for truthiness, not just `null`, so the operator is useful in a variety of situations.

Spaceship Operator

We briefly saw the 0 or "spaceship operator" earlier. It is simply an alias for `compareTo`.

For example, we can use it to delegate a `compareTo` implementation to the properties of a class, as follows:

```
class Person implements Comparable<Person> {
  String firstName
  String lastName

  @Override
  int compareTo(Person o) {
    lastName <=> o.lastName ?: firstName <=> o.firstName
  }
}
```

This is considerably simpler than the equivalent Java implementation. As we've discussed already, implementing `compareTo` enables us to use the entire range of standard comparison operators:

```
def kirk = new Person(firstName: "James", lastName: "Kirk")
def scotty = new Person(firstName: "Montgomery", lastName: "Scott")

assert kirk < scotty

def beverley = new Person(firstName: "Beverley", lastName: "Crusher")
def wesley = new Person(firstName: "Wesley", lastName: "Crusher")

assert wesley > beverley
```

Spread Operators

You use the spread operator `*.` to apply the same method call to each element in an iterable and collect the results:

```
def crew = ["Kirk", "McCoy", "Spock"]
crew*.toUpperCase() == ["KIRK", "MCCOY", "SPOCK"]
```

Spreading parameters

You can use a variant of the spread operator to apply the elements of list or other iterable value to the parameters of a method, as shown here:

```
def crew = ["Kirk", "McCoy", "Spock"]
def params = [0, "Picard"]
crew.set(*params)
assert crew == ["Picard", "McCoy", "Spock"]
```

In this example, the values in the list `params` are spread over the parameters of `List.set(int, Object)`.

This form of spread operator is also commonly used to pass the elements of a list to a vararg parameter. For example, if we have a method that counts the number of items passed to its vararg parameter, such as

```
int countParams(Object... params) {
  params.size()
}
```

calling it with a list will pass the entire list to a single parameter, whereas spreading the list with * will assign each list element to a separate vararg element:

```
def crew = ["Kirk", "McCoy", "Spock"]
assert countParams(crew) == 1
assert countParams(*crew) == 3
```

Regular Expression Operators

You use the =~ operator to create a Matcher, which is equivalent to the following Java code:

```
Pattern.compile("\\w+!").matcher("Fascinating!");
```

Because of Groovy's concept of "truthiness", a Matcher has a truth value that corresponds to the result of its find() method. This means that you also can use the =~ operator to assert a partial regular expression match.

For example, this assertion will succeed:

```
assert "Fascinating!" =~ /\w/
```

but this one will fail:

```
assert "Fascinating!" =~ /\d/
```

You use the ==~ operator to assert a complete match. Thus the following two assertions are equivalent:

```
assert "Fascinating!" ==~ /\w+!/
assert "Fascinating!" =~ /^\w+!$/
```

Field Access Operator

You can use the .@ operator to bypass Groovy's usual property access conventions and access the underlying field.

For example, let's add an optional "middle name" property to our Person class. The backing field itself can be null, but we'll specify a *getter* that returns an Optional<String>:

```
String middleName

Optional<String> getMiddleName() {
  Optional.ofNullable(middleName)
}
```

Referring to the property .middleName on an instance will use the *getter*. *Assigning to* the property will use the implied *setter*. If, for whatever reason, we need to access the String backing field rather than the Optional<String> value of the *getter*, we can use the .@ operator:

```
def person = new Person(firstName: "James", lastName: "Kirk")
assert person.middleName == Optional.empty()
assert person.@middleName == null

person.middleName = "Tiberius"
assert person.middleName == Optional.of("Tiberius")
assert person.@middleName == "Tiberius"
```

It's rare to see the .@ operator in use.

Method Pointer Operator

It's possible to get a callable reference to a method as a standalone variable by using .&:

```
def ref = "Spock".&contains
assert ref instanceof Closure
assert ref("k")
assert !ref("x")
assert ["S", "p", "o"].every(ref)
```

Method References in Java 8

Groovy's .& operator predates the :: operator in Java 8 but is very similar.

Here's the same example implemented with the method reference operator in Java 8:

```
Predicate<String> ref = "Spock"::contains;
assert ref.test("k");
assert !ref.test("x");
assert Stream.of("S", "p", "o").allMatch(ref);
```

Operator-Like Keywords

Groovy has a handful of keywords that behave like operators. Let's take a look at them:

in

The in keyword is an alias for the isCase(?) method.

is

The is method is used to determine strict, Java-style referential equality.

as

The as operator is used to perform a type cast in a controlled manner. Although Java-style casts work in Groovy, they are less flexible. Casting with as will look for an implementation of asType(T) on the class and use that to perform a coercion.

Closures

Groovy's closures are first-class functions. They are similar to Java 8 lambdas, although the syntax is slightly different and they have some additional capabilities such as the ability to delegate method calls and property references to an object.

You can pass closures as parameters like objects, and you can call them like methods.

Defining Closures

A closure is simply some code surrounded by curly braces with an optional parameter definition:

```
def closure = { String s ->
  s.toUpperCase()
}
assert closure("Spock") == "SPOCK"
```

The closure here has a single parameter s that is a String. It also returns a String using the Groovy implicit return convention. The type of the closure variable is groovy.lang.Closure<String>. The generic type on the Closure class specifies the return type.

Optional parameter types

The type information on the closure parameter is optional and is often omitted in places where it can be inferred from context:

```
def closure = { s ->
  s.toUpperCase()
}
assert closure("Spock") == "SPOCK"
```

The implicit closure parameter

Closures that take a single parameter can omit the parameter declaration altogether and refer to the parameter by using it:

```
def closure = {
  it.toUpperCase()
}
assert closure("Spock") == "SPOCK"
```

Methods That Accept Closures

When passing a literal closure to a method as the last parameter, the closure can sit outside the braces of the method call, which frequently looks neater.

For example, if we have a method that applies an arbitrary transformation to a string

```
String transform(String s, Closure<String> transformer) {
  transformer(s)
}
```

it can be called with a closure appearing after the closing method call brace.

```
def result = transform("Spock") {
  it.toUpperCase()
}
```

If the closure is the *only* parameter, you can omit the braces altogether.

Closure Delegates

Closures can delegate to an object, which means method and property references will be resolved against the delegate.

For example, we could change our string transformer method as follows:

```
String transform(String s, Closure<String> transformer) {
  transformer.delegate = s
  transformer()
}
```

The closure can then be parameterless, as is the case here:

```
def result = transform("Spock") {
  toUpperCase()
}
```

Parameter and Delegate Type Information

The Closure class has a single generic type indicating the return type. When using static type checking or static compilation, it is necessary to specify the parameter and/or delegate types the closure expects; otherwise, the type checker will not be able to validate the code inside the closure.

For parameters, it's sufficient to declare specific types on the closure's parameters. There is also an annotation that can supply the same information to the compiler (or other tools such as IDEs). If type information is supplied by the annotation, the parameter types can be inferred in the actual closures.

For example, if we want to specify parameter type information on our earlier method, we can do it like this:

```
String transform(String s,
                 @ClosureParams(
                   value = SimpleType,
                   options = "java.lang.String"
                 ) Closure<String> transformer) {
  transformer(s)
}
```

Now, statically compiled code can make calls to the method and use type inference to determine the type of the parameters passed to the closure itself.

We can go further and make the method completely generic and have the closure expect to receive a parameter type based on the type passed to the method itself:

```
<T> T transform(T s, @ClosureParams(FirstParam) Closure<T> transformer) {
  transformer(s)
}
```

There are a number of different options for specifying parameter types. For example, if we want to make a version of the same method that transforms all elements in an iterable, we can determine the closure parameter type from the generic type signature of the method argument, as shown here:

```
<T> Iterable<T> transform(Iterable<T> s,
                    @ClosureParams(
                      FirstParam.FirstGenericType
                    ) Closure<T> transformer) {
  s.collect {
    transformer(it)
  }
}
```

Similarly, when using a closure delegate, there is an annotation that can supply missing type information to the type checker:

```
String transform(String s, @DelegatesTo(String) Closure<String> transformer) {
  transformer.delegate = s
  transformer()
}
```

The @ClosureParams and @DelegatesTo annotations are very useful when developing DSLs that use closures extensively because they make IDEs much more helpful. Developers working with the DSL don't need to specify parameter types on closures, because they can be inferred from the information provided by the annotation.

Closures and Java 8 Functional Interfaces

Closures will coerce to Java 8 functional interfaces just as lambdas will. This means that when writing Groovy code, you can use Java APIs designed for lambdas:

```
def result = ["Kirk", "Spock", "Bones"]
  .stream()
  .map({ it.toUpperCase() })
  .collect(toList())
assert result == ["KIRK", "SPOCK", "BONES"]
```

Here, a closure stands in for the Function<? super T, ? extends R> parameter passed to java.util.stream.Stream.map.

The Groovy Development Kit

The Groovy Development Kit (GDK) is Groovy's extension to the standard Java Development Kit (JDK). Groovy augments many of the standard Java types with additional methods and capabilities.

This appendix is not the place for an exhaustive list of the capabilities added to classes with the GDK. A Javadoc-like reference is available at *http://groovy-lang.org/gdk.html*.

Let's look at a few of the more common capabilities, though.

Functional Iterator Methods

Some of the most frequently used methods in the GDK are functional iterators.

These methods are present on *all* classes. On most types (including Object), they will "iterate" over a single instance. On collection types, they will iterate over each element. On maps, they will iterate over the entry set. On strings, they will iterate over characters.

Let's look at some of the most common iterator methods you might encounter in the examples in this book. These are operations typically useful in writing Spock specifications.

each(Closure)

Calls the closure once for every element. The each method is often used in preference to a for loop in Groovy for iterating through elements of a collection:

```
def result = new StringBuilder()
["Kirk", "Spock", "McCoy"].each {
  result << it << ", "
}
assert result.toString() == "Kirk, Spock, McCoy, "
```

eachWithIndex(Closure)

Like each, but passes an index as well as the element to the closure:

```
def result = new StringBuilder()
["Kirk", "Spock", "McCoy"].eachWithIndex { name, i ->
  if (i > 0) {
    result << ", "
  }
  result << i + 1 << ": " << name
}
assert result.toString() == "1: Kirk, 2: Spock, 3: McCoy"
```

find(Closure)

Returns the first element for which the closure returns `true`, or `null` if none do:

```
def result = ["Kirk", "Spock", "McCoy"].find {
  it.contains("o")
}
assert result == "Spock"
```

findAll(Closure)

Returns a list of all elements for which the closure returns `true`:

```
def result = ["Kirk", "Spock", "McCoy"].findAll {
  it.contains("o")
}
assert result == ["Spock", "McCoy"]
```

collect(Closure)

Groovy's version of the functional programming *map* operation. Returns a collection of the values returned by the closure:

```
def crew = [
  [firstName: "James", lastName: "Kirk"],
  [firstName: "Montgomery", lastName: "Scott"],
  [firstName: "Hikari", lastName: "Sulu"]
]
assert crew.collect { it.lastName } == ["Kirk", "Scott", "Sulu"]
```

 Implicit collect

Groovy has a shorthand for `collect` when collecting properties. Instead of using the `collect` method explicitly, you can just refer to the property name as though it were a property of the collection:

```
assert crew.lastName == ["Kirk", "Scott", "Sulu"]
```

It's also possible to use the `*.` operator to apply a method call to every element of a collection and collect the results:

```
assert crew.lastName*.toUpperCase() ==
  ["KIRK", "SCOTT", "SULU"]
```

any(Closure)

Returns `true` if the closure returns `true` for at least one element.

```
assert ["Kirk", "Spock", "McCoy"].any {
  it.contains("o")
}
```

every(Closure)

Returns `true` if the closure returns `true` for all elements.

```
assert ["Kirk", "Spock", "McCoy"].every {
  it.contains("c") || it.contains("k")
}
```

Chained Functional Style

It's very common to chain functional methods, and Groovy allows the `.` to be omitted in some circumstances:

```
def crew = [
    [name: "Crusher", active: true, dateOfBirth: "2348-01-01"],
    [name: "Kirk", active: false, dateOfBirth: "2233-03-22"],
    [name: "McCoy", active: false, dateOfBirth: "2227-01-01"],
    [name: "Picard", active: true, dateOfBirth: "2305-07-13"],
    [name: "Spock", active: false, dateOfBirth: "2230-01-06"],
    [name: "Worf", active: true, dateOfBirth: "2340-01-01"]
]

def result = crew.findAll {
  it.active
} sort { a, b ->
  a.dateOfBirth <=> b.dateOfBirth
} collect {
  it.name
} join(", ")

assert result == "Picard, Worf, Crusher"
```

AST Transformations

Groovy has a number of annotations that are processed by the compiler. These are used to apply common patterns, doing away with the boilerplate code that might otherwise be necessary.

AST transformations are a big topic, but briefly, here is an overview of some you're likely to encounter:

`@Memoized`
> Causes the result of the annotated method to be cached so that subsequent calls are faster. The cache is keyed on the method's parameters. This is extremely useful for long-running idempotent methods.

`@TupleConstructor, @EqualsAndHashCode, @ToString`
> Generate a Java-like constructor with a parameter for each property in the annotated class, a standard `equals` and `hashCode` implementation, or a standard

`toString` implementation, respectively. Parameters to the annotation can specify which properties to include or exclude.

`@Canonical`
Combines `@TupleConstructor`, `@EqualsAndHashCode`, and `@ToString`.

`@Immutable`
Similar to `@Canonical` but also makes all properties and the class itself `final`.

`@Sortable`
Generates a `compareTo` method based on the properties of the annotated class.

`@TypeChecked`, `@CompileStatic`
Cause the compiler to perform compile-time type checks or statically compile the annotated method or class. Metaprogramming is not available in statically compiled Groovy code, but more rigorous type checking and inference becomes possible.

`@Lazy`
Causes the annotated property to be lazily initialized.

`@Singleton`
Transforms the annotated class into a singleton with a static `instance` property containing the single instance of the class.

There are many more annotations, and of course, it's also possible to write your own annotation-driven AST transformations.

Summary

In this appendix, we took a quick tour of the Groovy language, which should be enough to enable you to follow the examples throughout this book and get you writing effective, idiomatic Spock specifications. There is much more to the language including metaprogramming, scripting support, multiple inheritance via traits, DSL builders, and so on.

You can find more information online:

- The Groovy language website (*http://www.groovy-lang.org*)
- Javadocs for Groovy's enhancements to the Java standard library (*http://groovy-lang.org/gdk.html*)
- Groovy's own standard library (*http://docs.groovy-lang.org/latest/html/gapi*)

Bibliography

[goos] Steve Freeman & Nat Pryce. *Growing Object-Oriented Software Guided by Tests*. Addison-Wesley. 2009.

[osherove] Roy Osherove. *The Art of Unit Testing*. Manning. 2009.

[pood] Robert C. Martin. *Principles of Object-Oriented Design*. *http://www.butuncle bob.com/ArticleS.UncleBob.PrinciplesOfOod*.

[cleancode] Robert C. Martin. *Clean Code: A Handbook of Agile Software Craftsmanship*. Prentice Hall. 2008.

Index

About the Author

Rob Fletcher is a senior software engineer at Netflix, where he focuses on using automated testing as a design tool. He has more than 15 years of experience in the software industry and has contributed to several open source projects, including Groovy, Geb, Ratpack, and Grails.

Colophon

The animal on the cover of *Spock: Up and Running* is a large treeshrew (*Tupaia tana*), a mammal found in Borneo, Sumatra, and other small islands in Indonesia and Malaysia. *Tupaia* is derived from *tupai*, the Malaysian word for squirrel. Despite their common name, they are not true shrews, and this particular species spends more time on the ground than any other treeshrew.

Large treeshrews have reddish-brown fur that becomes darker toward the tail. They are 7 to 13 inches long on average, and weigh between 5.5 to 11 pounds. Though they don't see well in daylight, their night vision is very good, and they also have an acute sense of smell and hearing. The animal lives in a forest habitat (primarily tropical), and does spend part of its time in trees. Most of their foraging is done on the forest floor, however, as they feed on fruit, earthworms, insect larvae, and arthropods like centipedes.

Treeshrews have the highest brain-to-body-mass ratio among mammals, including humans. Such a high ratio is common in smaller animals such as mice and bats, but is only a rough indicator of intelligence.

Many of the animals on O'Reilly covers are endangered; all of them are important to the world. To learn more about how you can help, go to *animals.oreilly.com*.

The cover image is from *Meyers Kleines Lexicon*. The cover fonts are URW Typewriter and Guardian Sans. The text font is Adobe Minion Pro; the heading font is Adobe Myriad Condensed; and the code font is Dalton Maag's Ubuntu Mono.

Learn from experts.
Find the answers you need.

Sign up for a **10-day free trial** to get **unlimited access** to all of the content on Safari, including Learning Paths, interactive tutorials, and curated playlists that draw from thousands of ebooks and training videos on a wide range of topics, including data, design, DevOps, management, business—and much more.

Start your free trial at:

oreilly.com/safari

(No credit card required.)

Lightning Source UK Ltd.
Milton Keynes UK
UKOW07f2259110517
300942UK00003B/5/P